PRIMER ON FLSA & OTHER WAGE & HOUR LAWS

Third Edition

PRIMER ON FLSA & OTHER WAGE & HOUR LAWS

Third Edition

Joseph E. Kalet
Assistant Legal Counsel
Metropolitan Washington Airports Authority

The Bureau of National Affairs, Inc., Washington, D.C.

Copyright © 1987, 1990, 1994
The Bureau of National Affairs, Inc.

Library of Congress Cataloging-in-Publication Data

Kalet, Joseph E., 1951-
    Primer on FLSA & other wage & hour laws / Joseph E. Kalet.—3rd ed.
      p. cm.
    Rev. ed. of: Primer on wage & hour laws. 2nd ed. 1990.
    Includes index.
    ISBN 0-87179-833-6
    1. Wages—Law and legislation—United States. 2. Hours of labor—Law and legislation—United States. I. Kalet, Joseph E., 1951- Primer on wage & hour laws. II. Title. III. Title: Primer on FLSA and other wage and hour laws.
KF3489.K35 1994
344.73'0121—dc20
[347.304121]
                                                                                                                 90-18155
                                                                                                                  CIP

Authorization to photocopy items for internal or personal use, or the internal or personal use of specific clients, is granted by BNA Books for libraries and other users registered with the Copyright Clearance Center (CCC) Transactional Reporting Service, provided that $1.00 per page is paid directly to CCC, 27 Congress St., Salem, MA 01970. 0-87179-883-6/94/$0 + 1.00.

Published by BNA Books
1250 23rd St., N.W., Washington, D.C. 20037

PREFACE

Legal developments in the field of wages and hours have accelerated in the past few years, making this area of the law turbulent where it once was quiescent. The change was abrupt rather than gradual: Early in 1985, the U.S. Supreme Court in *Garcia v. San Antonio Metropolitan Transit Authority* decided that there was no constitutional bar to applying the Fair Labor Standards Act (FLSA) to state and local governments. This decision had the explosive impact of another Supreme Court decision from 1946, *Anderson v. Mt. Clemens Pottery Co.*, wherein the Court held that employers must compensate their employees for time spent in pre- and postshift activities, if these activities are a "necessary prerequisite" to their principal work activity. The intricate network of federal laws and regulations governing wages and hours of work has grown increasingly complex in recent years. This book represents a broad canvas on which the outlines of each of the major statutes have been drawn, with a general idea of the individual profiles of each law and how each law interacts with other laws within the network.

Other wage-hour laws existed prior to the FLSA, but Congress intended the FLSA to be the most comprehensive and pervasive federal statute in this area. The Act has been amended several times, most recently in the FLSA Amendments of 1989, which raised the minimum wage (for the first time in a decade), introduced a subminimum training wage for teenage workers, increased the amount of "tip" credit that may be applied toward a tipped employee's minimum wage, and set a new "annual dollar sales" volume threshold for determining which businesses meet the minimum for FLSA enterprise coverage. In addition, the 1985 and 1989 amendments to the FLSA, and more recent amendments to the FLSA regulations, have created confusion concerning coverage, retaliation, compensatory time eligibility, and exemptions. After promulgating regulations implementing the "civil money penalties" amendment to the FLSA, the Wage and Hour Division of the Labor Department has embarked on an aggressive campaign to apply these penalties. Finally, Congress is engaged in its perennial attempt to "improve" the FLSA by refining definitions, adjusting the minimum wage provisions, and reviewing the scope and propriety of FLSA exemptions, including continued viability of the "salary basis" test, as applied to the "white collar" exemptions, both in the private and public sectors. The constant legislative, judicial, and regulatory developments under the FLSA ensure that this "New Deal" legislation will continue to play a vibrant role in our society.

Regulations interpreting and applying the wage-hour laws are the responsibility of the U.S. Department of Labor. The Wage-Hour Division and the Equal Employment Opportunity Commission (EEOC) are the two main enforcement agencies within the Labor Department's wage-hour mandate. The Division historically has had responsibility for ensuring compliance with these statutes and has been designated as the agency responsible for administering and enforcing the multifaceted and complex wage-hour legislation entitled the "Family and Medical Leave Act of 1993." The EEOC was delegated authority to enforce the Equal Pay Act under the 1977 Reorganization Act. Together, these agencies constitute a comprehensive adjudicatory process that will enable the wage and hour laws to develop along consistent and predictable lines.

Employees are granted the right to bring a private lawsuit under several, but not all, wage-hour laws. Congress has determined that, in many instances, allowing employees to operate as "private attorneys-general" would enhance the policies underlying a particular statute, and to that end have granted employees the right to sue. Generally, where an act grants such a right, it also subordinates that right to the federal government's right to sue, on the theory of the greater good. That is, a lawsuit by the Secretary of Labor will create a greater benefit to the public as a whole than will an action by a private individual. Different remedies are available to the party instituting the action, depending on whether it is a private individual or a government official.

The Fair Labor Standards Act, the Walsh-Healey Act, the Davis-Bacon Act, and the McNamara-O'Hara Service Contract Act comprise the bulk of the wage-hour statutes discussed in this *Primer*. They are the primary statutes that govern wages and hours in the United States today. These laws were created during specific historic periods, with specific goals. They have withstood the test of time and continue to play a very important part in the federal statutory apparatus, despite amendments and putative changes. Conflicts in the area of wages and hours appear to be proliferating beyond traditional battlegrounds and into new arenas of combat. For this reason, these laws must be clearly understood to ensure faithful compliance and fair enforcement.

Throughout the *Primer*, abbreviations have been used to designate various sources. In addition to abbreviations in the text, several abbreviations appear without explanation. These abbreviations include references to such publications of The Bureau of National Affairs, Inc. (BNA) as: "LRX" (Labor Relations Expediter); "WH Cases" (Wage and Hour Cases); "LRRM" (Labor Relations Reference Manual); and "FEP Cases" (Fair Employment Practice Cases). BNA is the exclusive publisher of the source material that is cited in the *Primer*, unless otherwise noted. Where no source for a particular document or decision is provided, none was available.

Although much of the wage-hour statutory scheme was passed in a different era, the continued vitality of this area of the law is evidenced by the ever-increasing breadth of this *Primer*, and the daily onslaught of new decisions involving these statutes. To paraphrase Lewis Carroll, "it takes all one's energy, running as fast as one can, just to keep from falling behind." This edition of the *Primer* could not have been achieved without the support and assistance of several people. I must express my special gratitude to the members of the Fair Labor Standards Act Subcommittee of the Federal Labor Standards Legislation Committee, Labor and Employment Section of the American Bar Association, and in particular, Donna S. Galchus of McGlinchey, Stafford, Cellini & Lang, Little Rock, Ark. Last, but not least, I wish to thank Anne Scott, BNA Books Senior Editor, for her invaluable assistance on this *Primer*, and the four prior books on which we have worked together. Her professionalism and dedication to detail are evident on every page of this book.

Joseph E. Kalet

Washington, D.C.
February 1994

Contents

Preface v

1: THE FEDERAL SCHEME OF WAGE AND HOUR LEGISLATION 1
Fair Labor Standards Act 2
Portal-to-Portal Pay Act 6
Equal Pay Act 7
Walsh-Healey Act 8
McNamara-O'Hara Service Contract Act 9
Davis-Bacon Act 10
Contract Work Hours and Safety Standards Act 10
Consumer Credit Protection Act 11
Child Support Enforcement Act 12
Family and Medical Leave Act 15

2: FAIR LABOR STANDARDS ACT 15
Amendments 16
Interstate Commerce Requirement 19
Employer Coverage 20
"Enterprise Coverage" 22
Employer Exemptions 24
Employee Coverage 26
Employee Exemptions 30
Salary Basis Test 32
Hours of Work 41

Minimum Wages 43
  Overtime 47
  State and Local Government Employees 51
  Recordkeeping 58
  Child Labor 59
  Enforcement 60
  Civil Money Penalties 60
  Statute of Limitations 62
  Liquidated Damages 63

3: PORTAL-TO-PORTAL PAY ACT 65
  Preliminary and Postliminary Activities 66
  Basic Purpose 67
  Willful Violations 69
  Other Provisions 71
  Good-Faith Defense 72
  OPM Regulations 75

4: EQUAL PAY ACT 77
  Major Provisions 78
  Enforcement 80
  Coverage 81
  Exceptions to Coverage 84
  Penalties 87
  Remedies 88

5: WALSH-HEALEY PUBLIC CONTRACTS ACT 89
  Requirements 90
  Covered Contracts 92
  Covered Contractors 93
  Personal Liability 95
  Exemptions 96
  Recordkeeping 99
  Enforcement 100
  Safety and Health Standards 101

6: McNAMARA-O'HARA SERVICE CONTRACT ACT 103
  Coverage 104

Prevailing Wage Standard   108
Successors   109
Variance Proceedings   110
Wage Payments and Deductions   111
Fringe Benefits   112
Fringe Offsets and Payments   114
Enforcement   115
Limitations Period   117
Blacklist Penalty   118
Attorneys' Fees   119

7: **DAVIS-BACON ACT**   123
Coverage   123
Conflict With Other Laws   128
Prevailing Wages   129
Fringe Benefits   134
Enforcement   135
Debarment   140

8: **CONTRACT WORK HOURS AND SAFETY STANDARDS ACT**   143
Coverage   144
Health and Safety Standards   145
Enforcement   146
Liquidated Damages   147
Debarment Penalty   149
Other Laws   151

9: **OTHER FEDERAL LAWS**   153
Anti-Kickback Law (Copeland Act)   153
Title III, Consumer Credit Protection Act   153
Child Support Enforcement Act   155
Occupational Safety and Health Act   156
Family and Medical Leave Act   157
Miscellaneous Statutes   159

APPENDICES
    A.   Directory of U.S. Department of Labor Administrative and Regional Offices   163

B.	Chart of FLSA White-Collar Exemption Tests	169
C.	Chart of FLSA Exemptions From Minimum Wage and Overtime	173
D.	Directory of U.S. Department of Labor Employment Standards Administration, Administrative and Regional Offices	179
E.	Chart of State Minimum Wages	189
F.	Coefficient Table for Computing Overtime	193
G.	Chart of State Maximum Hours-Overtime	197
H.	Chart of Overtime Compensation Rules for State and Local Government Employees (Part 553, 29 C.F.R.)	231
I.	Directory of U.S. Equal Employment Opportunity Commission Administrative and District Area Offices	235
J.	Directory of U.S. Department of Defense, Defense Contract Management Command, Regional Offices	245
K.	Salary Basis Test for Public Sector Exempt Employees	249
L.	Civil Money Penalties Regulations	253
M.	Family and Medical Leave Act WH Poster	257

TABLE OF CASES   261

INDEX   269

1
THE FEDERAL SCHEME OF WAGE AND HOUR LEGISLATION

The federal law governing the payment of wages and the regulation of hours worked had its roots in the Hours of Work Laws enacted between 1892 and 1913. The most important piece of legislation enacted, however, is the Fair Labor Standards Act of 1938 (FLSA), because of its broad sweep. Currently, the federal statutory scheme for regulating wages and hours in the United States consists of the FLSA, the Portal-to-Portal Pay Act (Portal Act), five narrower statutes (Equal Pay Act, Walsh-Healey Public Contracts Act, McNamara-O'Hara Service Contract Act, Davis-Bacon Act, and Contract Work Hours and Safety Standards Act), and three laws directed at protecting specific classes of individuals (Consumer Credit Protection Act, Child Support Enforcement Act, and Family and Medical Leave Act).

These laws can be categorized under three classes of federal wage-hour statutes: the first class consists of the FLSA, the Portal Act, and the Equal Pay Act. These statutes are designed to reach most employees in the nation and to ensure fair compensation in terms of minimum wages, overtime pay, and equal pay for equal work.

The second class of federal laws consists of the Walsh-Healey Public Contracts Act (WHA), the McNamara-O'Hara

Service Contract Act (SCA), the Davis-Bacon Act (DBA), and the Contract Work Hours and Safety Standards Act (CWHSSA). These statutes establish "prevailing" wage rates for certain classes of employees performing work for a contractor that has a contract to provide material or services to the federal government.

The third class of statutes consists of, among others, the Consumer Credit Protection Act (CCPA), the Child Support Enforcement Act (CSEA), and the Family and Medical Leave Act (FMLA). These laws are designed to protect specific classes of individuals. The CCPA limits the amount of wages that can be garnished from an employee's paycheck and establishes the conditions under which an employee may be discharged for having his wages garnisheed excessively. The CSEA requires employers to withhold from employees' wages any amounts determined to be due under support orders issued by a court or an administrative body. This law also protects employees from employer retaliation as a result of having wages withheld pursuant to the CSEA. The FMLA requires employers to provide "family leave" or "medical leave" and to observe certain pay and leave practices.

This *Primer* discusses the federal statutory scheme governing wages and hours according to the three classes previously mentioned, and in that sequence.

In addition to the federal laws, it should be pointed out that most states have adopted their own versions of some of the federal laws. Under principles established in the U.S. Constitution, states may pass laws that are stricter, but not less stringent, than the federal apparatus. As a consequence, many states have enacted "little" Davis-Bacon laws, and "little" Walsh-Healey acts, and so on. These state statutes coexist with the federal apparatus, and employers and contractors may be liable for wage violations under either or both statutes simultaneously. For further information, contact the U.S. Department of Labor (see Appendix A), or the appropriate state agency.

FAIR LABOR STANDARDS ACT

Prior to passing the Fair Labor Standards Act (FLSA) in 1938, Congress attempted to establish fair minimum and overtime wage standards with limited success. These efforts to regulate wages and hours had been limited to workers employed either by the federal government or by specific industries in the private sector. Between 1892 and 1913, for example, Congress passed a series of statutes governing public works employees that became known collectively as the Eight-Hour Law, since the legislative purpose of these enactments was to establish a standard eight-hour work day for these workers. Once this limit had been exceeded, overtime pay was mandatory, to be calculated at the rate of one-and-one-half times (or time-and-one-half) the employee's basic rate of pay. This overtime rate was payable for all overtime hours worked.

When the onset of the Great Depression led to widespread unemployment, the scarcity of jobs was perceived as an invitation to wage abuses by employers who knew that it was a "buyer's market" for labor, particularly since many industries were not covered by either state or federal wage-hour laws. In 1937, for example, the employer in *West Coast Hotel v. Parrish*, contended that the state's Minimum Wage Law violated the Due Process Clause of the Fifth Amendment to the U.S. Constitution. But the Supreme Court affirmed the validity of a Washington State law setting minimum wages for women, reasoning that the statute was a legitimate and reasonable exercise of the state's police power to protect the health of women, to guard them against unscrupulous employers, and to correct the abuse of casting a direct burden upon the community for the support of women who are denied a living wage. This decision created the impetus for the federal government to establish wage and hours of work standards for industries not covered by state law.

The FLSA regulates employment practices in the areas of minimum wage, overtime pay, equal pay, recordkeeping, and child labor. The Act specifically requires employers to maintain adequate records reflecting employees' hours of work and pay for all hours worked. It covers employees who are "engaged in interstate commerce," or in the "production" of goods for travel in interstate commerce, or employed in "an enterprise engaged in commerce or the production of goods for commerce."

Coverage was extended to certain federal government employees and to state and local hospitals and educational institutions by the 1966 amendments to the Act. The 1974 amendments extended coverage to household domestic service workers and to most federal employees and to employees of any "state, political subdivision of a state" and interstate government agencies. However, this latter aspect of the 1974 amendments was overturned by the Supreme Court in 1976 when it decided in *National League of Cities v. Usery* that the amendments "operated to directly displace the States' freedom to structure integral operations in areas of traditional governmental functions."

In February 1985, however, the Supreme Court decided that the FLSA applies to state and local government employees, notwithstanding the principle of state sovereignty under the Tenth Amendment to the U.S. Constitution. (*Garcia v. San Antonio Metropolitan Transit Auth.* overruling *National League of Cities v. Usery*) The extention of the FLSA to cover these governmental entities created a chaotic situation, and soon Congress was forced to act. In November 1985, Congress passed and President Ronald Reagan signed into law the Fair Labor Standards Amendments of 1985, effective April 15, 1986.

The 1985 amendments govern the wage and hour practices of state and local government employers. They provide for the payment of compensatory (comp) time in lieu of cash payments for overtime work; the comp time is calculated at the rate of time-and-one-half of the employee's regular rate of pay for each hour of overtime worked. The amendments provide limits on the amount of comp time that may be accrued, a higher ceiling being allowed for safety, emergency, and seasonal personnel than is allowed for other public employees. They also provide special rules for firefighters and police personnel concerning tour-of-duty practices. (The FLSA is discussed in greater detail in Chapter 2.)

In 1989, Congress finally addressed several important issues that had surfaced years earlier. For example, the most recent increase in the federal minimum wage had been implemented in 1980. There was strong support for, and substantial opposition to, increasing the minimum wage. In addition, there was a perception that an increased minimum wage would create serious financial burdens on employers while overcompensating young, unskilled employees. Finally, a consensus developed that FLSA coverage of businesses should not depend on the type of business, but on the amount of business done. Therefore, after much wrangling, Congress passed the FLSA Amendments of 1989, which:

- Raised the minimum wage in increments, from $3.35 per hour to $4.25 per hour;
- Introduced a subminimum training wage for teenage workers, aged 16–19;
- Increased the amount of "tip" credit that may be applied toward a tipped employee's minimum wage; and
- Set a new, uniform "annual dollar sales" volume threshold for determining which businesses meet the minimum for FLSA enterprise coverage. (See Chapter 2 for more detailed information on these changes.)

Employers are covered under the Act if they meet a minimum threshold dollar-volume-of-business test of $500,000 per annum. If the employer takes in this much money per year, then the next step is to determine whether the employer is an "employer" within the meaning of the Act. For this determination, the courts apply the "economic realities" test to the employer's relationship with the employee: Do the *economic realities* of the relationship indicate that the employer in fact controls the employee in the payment of wages and performance of work? The test is complex and is addressed in greater detail in Chapter 2. An employer may also be covered under the Act by virtue of the "enterprise" concept, which means that the employer's total business operations, taken as a single enterprise, may bring the employer within the Act's coverage under the dollar-volume test. FLSA case law also indicates that an employer may be covered if it is a "joint employer" with another entity; in such situations all individual businesses that make up the "joint employer" can be liable for wage violations.

The Act provides numerous exemptions from coverage for certain classes of employees, along with "tests" to determine whether individuals fall within these classes. Executive, administrative, and professional employees fall within the so-called "white-collar" exemptions. An individual may qualify for more than one exemption, but the effect is not cumulative. In addition, state and local government employees are treated differently, and the FMLA also provides exceptions to these exemptions. Finally, the Act provides a list of employees involved in certain industries who are exempt from FLSA coverage.

The Act states that an employer who *willfully* violates the minimum wage or overtime requirements is liable for liquidated damages in an amount equal to the back pay due the employee. A two-year statute of limitations is established for filing a timely action under the Act. (The FLSA is discussed in greater detail in Chapter 2.)

PORTAL-TO-PORTAL PAY ACT

The 1947 Portal-to-Portal Pay Act (Portal Act) was enacted to rectify a situation that arose after the U.S. Supreme Court decided in *Anderson v. Mt. Clemens Pottery Co.* that employees were entitled to compensation for time spent in preliminary and postliminary activities ("from portal to portal"). The Portal Act also amends the Davis-Bacon and Walsh-Healey Public Contracts acts, which govern the construction of public buildings for the federal government and the manufacture or supply of goods for the government, in the same way it affects the FLSA.

The Portal Act, which is discussed in Chapter 3, provides a "good-faith" defense to the otherwise mandatory provision of the FLSA, which imposes liquidated damages liability on employers who *willfully* violate the wage provisions of the FLSA. If an employer can demonstrate that it acted in good faith with a reasonable belief that its actions did not violate the Act, then the Portal Act gives the court discretion to reduce or deny any liquidated damages award. The U.S. Department of Labor's Wage-Hour Division has participated in the development of regulations applying this difficult aspect of the Portal Act; a more detailed discussion of this area of the law is provided in Chapter 3.

The Portal Act also provides a two-year limitations period for actions brought under the FLSA and the Walsh-Healey and Davis Bacon acts; this period will be extended to three years upon a finding that the employer's violations were willful. Since Congress did not define "willfulness," the courts were left to give meaning to this very important phrase. For almost two decades, the courts applied a standard known as "in the picture," which meant that if the employer knew or had reason to know that the FLSA was "in the picture," then the employer was presumed to have acted willfully. (*Coleman v. Jiffy June Farms*)

In 1988, the Supreme Court rejected the "in the picture" standard, and determined that, for purposes of the three-year statute of limitations, a "willful" violation requires a showing that the employer either "knew or had reckless disregard" for whether its conduct was prohibited. (*McLaughlin v. Richland Shoe Co.*) (See Chapter 3 for a more detailed discussion of this area.)

The Portal Act also banned actions brought by unions or other representatives of employees, but allowed employees to sue on behalf of themselves and similarly situated employees. In these actions, each participant is required to give his or her consent in writing, that is, affirmatively to "opt in" to the action.

EQUAL PAY ACT

In June 1963, President John F. Kennedy signed into law the Equal Pay Act of 1963 (EPA). The EPA requires employers to pay equal pay to men and women performing work requiring equal skill, effort, and responsibility and performed under similar working conditions. The Act amended the FLSA and was incorporated into Title VII of the Civil Rights Act of 1964; it may be enforced in an action initiated under either amended statute.

Congress specified that the EPA would cover employers who are covered under the FLSA. However, Congress removed the "enterprise" concept from EPA coverage, thus restricting the number of employers (and hence, employees) who were covered under the EPA. Although the FLSA provides for enterprise coverage, any EPA action is limited to the employer's individual "establishment" and may not extend to the employer's enterprise.

While the EPA requires equal pay for work of equal skill, effort, and responsibility, it provides an exception where such payment is made pursuant to a seniority system, a merit system, a system that measures earnings by quantity or quality of production, or a differential based on any factor other than sex. (The EPA was inadvertently drafted with the phrase "any *other* factor other than sex.") The EPA, perhaps anticipating employer intransigence in complying, precludes employers from reducing the wage rate of any employee to comply with the requirement to pay equal wages for equal work.

The EPA is essentially enforced, as is the FLSA, by private actions, class actions, or actions by the Secretary of Labor. However, the EPA also provides an administrative route to enforcement under Title VII through the Equal Employment Opportunity Commission, which is specifically authorized to enforce the EPA. Any amounts owing under the EPA are treated as if they were owed under the FLSA, including the imposition of liquidated damages and attorney's fees liability, where appropriate. (The EPA is discussed in greater detail in Chapter 4.)

WALSH-HEALEY ACT

The Walsh-Healey Public Contracts Act (WHA) was enacted in June 1936 to regulate employment conditions under government contracts. In addition to regulating hours of work and wages, the Act deals with the problems of child labor, convict labor, and hazardous working conditions. It covers all government contracts for the manufacture or furnishing of materials, supplies, articles, and equipment in any amount exceeding $10,000. Any contract covered by the WHA must provide that all workers will be paid not less than the prevailing minimum wage rate determined by the Secretary of Labor for similar work in the locality. Employees are entitled to overtime pay for any work in excess of 40 hours per week. Prior to the passage of the Department of Defense Authorization Act of 1986 (DOD

Act), which amended the WHA, employees who worked on a contract that was covered by the WHA were entitled to overtime for any work in excess of 8 hours per day, but the DOD Act removed the 8-hour limit, while maintaining the 40-hour per week overtime limit. As with most other wage-hour laws, overtime under the WHA is calculated on the basis of time-and-one-half the employee's regular rate of pay.

The Secretary of Labor is authorized to investigate and decide cases involving alleged violations of the WHA. Liquidated damages found due in such proceedings may be obtained by the government through a lawsuit, or may be deducted by the government from amounts due the contractor under another contract.

The most significant sanction for violating the WHA is the rarely used debarment ("blacklist") penalty, under which contractors who are serious and willful violators of the Act are barred from receipt of government contracts for a period of three years. (The WHA is discussed in greater detail in Chapter 5.)

McNAMARA-O'HARA SERVICE CONTRACT ACT

The McNamara-O'Hara Service Contract Act (SCA; WHM 90:225), commonly known as the Service Contract Act, was enacted in 1965 to complement the WHA in regulating labor standards for employees who work under contracts let by the federal government.

Whereas the WHA covers the manufacture or furnishing of materials and supplies which exceed $10,000, the SCA covers contracts for the performance of services for the federal government which exceed $2,500. (Attempts were made in 1986 to raise the minimum dollar amount, but they were unsuccessful. In light of government efforts to reduce federal spending, additional attempts to raise the threshold may be expected.)

The SCA requires the payment of wages and fringe benefits found to be prevailing locally or as found in a previous existing contract, but in no event less than the federal minimum wages under the FLSA. The same enforcement provisions as apply in the WHA—the withholding of payments to a contractor to correct underpayments to its employees—applies in the SCA, including the three-year debarment penalty. (The SCA is discussed in greater detail in Chapter 6.)

DAVIS-BACON ACT

The Davis-Bacon Act of 1931 (DBA; WHM 90:251) regulates the rate of wages for laborers and mechanics employed in the construction of public buildings for the federal government by contractors and subcontractors, where the contract calls for an expenditure of more than $2,000. (Attempts were made to raise the minimum amount in Congress in 1986, but they were unsuccessful.) The Act also applies to work performed under certain other laws, such as the Federal Aid Highway Act and the Area Redevelopment Act of 1961. Under the DBA, the Secretary of Labor is required to establish prevailing minimum wage rates to be incorporated into contracts covered by the Act. The Comptroller General, however, is the official authorized to withhold payments to the contractor if necessary to make good any underpayments to employees; employees may sue the contractor for back pay owing to them if the amount withheld by the Comptroller General is insufficient to reimburse them.

The DBA provides a three-year debarment of blacklist penalty which bars *willful* violators of the Act from obtaining a contract under the DBA. (The DBA is discussed in greater detail in Chapter 7.)

CONTRACT WORK HOURS AND SAFETY STANDARDS ACT

The Contract Work Hours and Safety Standards Act (CWHSSA) was enacted in 1962 to regulate employer practices in the area of contracts calling for the performance of services for the federal government. The Work Hours Act, as it is commonly called, covers mechanics and laborers employed on any public work for the federal government and employees performing services similar to those of mechanics and laborers in connection with dredging or rock excavation in any river or harbor of the United States or the District of Columbia. The CWHSSA also requires the payment of overtime at the rate of time-and-one-half the employee's regular rate of pay for all hours worked in excess of 40 per week. Prior to the enactment of the Department of Defense Authorization Act of 1986 (DOD Act), the Work Hours Act required overtime pay when an employee exceeded 8 hours per day or 40 hours per week. The DOD Act eliminated the 8-hour day limit for overtime so that only the 40-hour per week limit now applies.

The enforcement mechanism for the CWHSSA is different from most of the federal labor standards acts in that inspectors must report to the contracting officer any violations of the Act they find. The officer may then withhold from the contractor any amounts due the employees, including penalties, as a result of such violation. Decisions made by the contracting officer can be appealed to the head of the contracting agency and then to the U.S. Court of Claims. Willful violations of the Act are punishable by a fine of up to $1,000 and/or imprisonment of up to six months. (The CWHSSA is discussed in greater detail in Chapter 8.)

CONSUMER CREDIT PROTECTION ACT

The Consumer Credit Protection Act (CCPA), enacted in 1968, limits the amount of an employee's wages that can be subjected to garnishment to not more than 25 percent of the employee's "disposable earnings" for any work week; or to the amount by which his disposable earnings are greater than 30 times the federal minimum hourly wage, whichever is greater. It covers all employees, regardless of the size of the employer's business. Under the Act, the Secretary of Labor is authorized to bring enforcement proceedings; however, proceedings are carried out by the Wage-Hour Division which is the Department of Labor's enforcement arm. The Act's restrictions on the amount of an employee's wages that are subject to garnishment do not apply in cases of wage deductions based on a court order for the payment of support, or on an order from a bankruptcy court, or to a wage deduction for any debt due on any state or federal tax.

Under the Act, employers are precluded from discharging employees solely because of a single wage garnishment. This relatively straightforward language had led to much litigation over whether the issuance of consecutive, but not concurrent, garnishment orders constitutes a "single" order for purposes of the protection afforded the employee under the Act. Employers who violate this prohibition are subject to criminal penalties of a $1,000 fine and/or one year imprisonment.

One important aspect of the Act concerns state sovereignty under the Tenth Amendment to the U.S. Constitution. The CCPA purports to set standards in areas that have traditionally been controlled by the states. In view of the constitutional protections retained by the states, the Act does not prohibit states from applying their own garnishment laws where they prescribe stricter garnishment restrictions than federal law. The Act also does not affect or alter state laws which prohibit an employer from discharging an employee because the employee had more than one wage garnishment. Any state may have garnishments that are issued under its own laws exempted from the Act, where the state laws provide for restrictions that are substantially similar to the Act. The state must apply to the Secretary of Labor for this exemption. (The CCPA is discussed in greater detail in Chapter 9.)

CHILD SUPPORT ENFORCEMENT ACT

The Child Support Enforcement Act of 1984 (CSEA) requires employers to withhold from employees' wages any amounts determined to be due under support orders issued by a court or administrative body.

Employers are prohibited from disciplining, discharging, or refusing to hire an individual because of a withholding order for support. Employees are entitled to advance notice and a hearing before the order becomes effective. Employers who fail to comply with the Act may be subject to penalties. (The CSEA is discussed in greater detail in Chapter 9.)

FAMILY AND MEDICAL LEAVE ACT

The Family and Medical Leave Act of 1993 provides for "family leave" and "medical leave" under certain conditions. These provisions address employer coverage; employee eligibility for the Act's benefits; entitlement to leave, maintenance of health benefits during leave, and job restoration after leave; notice and certification of the need for FMLA leave; and protections for employees who request or take FMLA leave. The Act also requires employers to keep certain records of FMLA leave.

Unlike most federal laws, the FMLA does *not* preempt state laws that regulate in this same area. As between the FMLA and differing state law leave provisions, the FMLA provides that employers are to observe the more generous leave provisions and to follow the least burdensome procedural provisions for allowing the leave. The FMLA and its regulations are complex and require careful scrutiny. The Act is enforced by the Wage and Hour Division of the Employment Standards Administration, U.S. Labor Department. (The FMLA is discussed in greater detail in Chapter 9.)

2
FAIR LABOR STANDARDS ACT

The Fair Labor Standards Act of 1938 (FLSA) was enacted to meet the economic and social problems existing during the Great Depression. Low wages, long working hours, and high unemployment were rampant during this time, and Congress sought a way to establish minimum wage standards while encouraging the spread of employment. The policy of the FLSA was to correct and, as rapidly as practicable, to eliminate labor conditions detrimental to the Act's goals of establishing minimum wage standards.

The Act, as amended, sets general standards for minimum wages, overtime compensation, equal pay, and child labor for all employees who are not specifically exempted under the Act. All covered employees include those who are:

- Engaged in interstate commerce. "Commerce," under the Act and case law developed under it, includes both incoming and outgoing foreign transportation of goods, as well as such trade between the states; or
- Engaged in the production of goods for commerce. This production of goods includes not only the actual production operations but also "any closely related process or occupation directly essential" to the production; or
- Employed in an "enterprise engaged in commerce or in the production of goods for commerce." This standard relates directly to the "enterprise" coverage for employers, all of whose employees in a particular

business unit may be covered, regardless of how their individual duties relate to commerce or the production of goods for commerce. In 1966, the Act was amended to bring state and local hospitals and educational institutions within the definition of an "enterprise engaged in commerce."

AMENDMENTS

In 1963, Congress passed the Equal Pay Act (EPA), which amended the FLSA in several important respects. The EPA requires that male and female workers receive equal pay for work requiring equal skill, effort, and responsibility, where the work is performed under similar working conditions. Since EPA coverage is the same as that for the minimum wage provisions of the FLSA, an employer covered by the minimum wage provisions of the FLSA is therefore also covered by the EPA.

The EPA does not exempt from coverage those categories of executive, administrative, and professional employees and outside salesmen who are exempt from FLSA minimum wage and overtime provisions. The EPA provides specific exemptions from liability when wage differentials are:

- Based on any factor other than sex;
- Paid pursuant to a bona fide seniority system;
- Paid pursuant to a bona fide merit system; and
- Paid pursuant to a system that measures earnings by quantity or quality of production.

In equalizing past wage disparity based on sex, an employer may not lower the wages of the higher-paid worker to those of the lower-paid worker.

As with the FLSA, unpaid wages may expose an employer to liquidated damages liability for willful violations, and to attorneys' fees and costs. The EPA is enforced by private actions and by the Equal Employment Opportunity Commission for agency actions, unlike the FLSA, which is enforced by private actions and by the Secretary of Labor through the U.S. Department of Labor's Wage-Hour Division. (For further information on the EPA, see Chapter 4.)

In 1966, the Act was amended to bring state and local hospitals and educational institutions within the definition of enterprises engaged in commerce, the third prong of the coverage test discussed earlier in this chapter. At that time, Congress also extended coverage of the FLSA to certain federal employees, without regard to the three prongs of the coverage test.

In 1974, Congress amended the Act to cover most federal employees; to employees of states, political subdivisions of states, and interstate agencies; and to private household domestic service workers.

In 1976, the U.S. Supreme Court ruled in *National League of Cities v. Usery* that the 1974 FLSA amendments extending the Act's coverage to state and local government employees were unconstitutional, insofar as the amendments operate "directly to displace the States' freedom to structure integral operations in areas of traditional governmental functions." The Court said that the Commerce Clause of the U.S. Constitution, which authorizes Congress to regulate in areas involving interstate commerce, did not provide a sufficient basis for Congress to interfere with states' relationship with their employees in such areas as fire prevention, police protection, sanitation, and public health.

In 1985, the Supreme Court overruled the *National League of Cities* decision, stating that the extension of the FLSA to state and local government employees did not violate any affirmative limit placed on Congress under the Commerce Clause. (*Garcia v. San Antonio Metropolitan Transit Auth.*) The effect of this decision was to impose FLSA overtime requirements and the Act's general ban against using compensatory time to most state and local government employees.

Following a storm of criticism from public sector employers, who said the decision would wreak havoc on state and local budgets and services, Congress passed the Fair Labor Standards Amendments of 1985, which became effective on April 15, 1986.

The 1985 amendments allow for the payment of compensatory (comp) time in lieu of cash payments to certain employees, establish limits on how much comp time an employee may accrue before cash overtime payments become mandatory, and set standards for determining payment for comp time upon termination of employment. They also establish methods for the treatment of "volunteers," and those employees involved in sporadic and substitute employment in a public agency. The amendments also provide protection against discrimination or adverse action by an employer in retaliation for an employee's assertion of coverage under the FLSA overtime provisions.

Finally, the amendments treat the accrual of comp time by public safety, emergency, and seasonal personnel different from accrual by all other public employees, by allowing a higher ceiling for the former group to accrue comp time than is available for the latter group. The amendments also provide special rules for firefighters and police personnel concerning tour-of-duty practices. (These issues are discussed in greater detail later in this chapter under State and Local Government Employees.)

In 1989, Congress responded to a changing economic climate by passing the "Fair Labor Standards Amendments of 1989," which President George Bush signed into law on November 17, 1989 (Pub. Law 101-157). The legislative history of these amendments indicates that the public was concerned over several related issues. These issues included the fact that the minimum wage had not been increased since 1981, and concern that such an increase could adversely affect employment opportunities for new, essentially untrained/unskilled workers (primarily teenagers). In addition, Congress was responding to concerns from businesses about the credit to be charged against the minimum wage on behalf of workers who received tips. Finally, Congress recognized the administrative and practical difficulties of maintaining two separate tests for determining whether different types of businesses (retail and nonretail) met their respective "annual dollar sales" volume for purposes of FLSA coverage. All these concerns were addressed in the 1989 amendments, which:

- Raised the minimum wage in increments, from $3.35 per hour to $4.25 per hour (see "Minimum Wages" later in this chapter);
- Introduced a subminimum training wage for teenage workers, aged 16–19 (see "Minimum Wages" later in this chapter);
- Increased the amount of "tip" credit that could be applied toward a tipped employee's minimum wage (see "Minimum Wages" later in this chapter); and
- Set a new, uniform "business-volume" (annual dollar sales) threshold for determining whether a business meets the minimum for FLSA enterprise coverage (see "Dollar Volume Test" later in this chapter).

In addition to these major concerns, the FLSA Amendments of 1989 created an exemption to the overtime provisions, not to exceed 10 hours per week, for employees receiving "remedial education" under certain circumstances (see "Overtime" later in this chapter).

Finally, the 1989 amendments extended the protections of the FLSA to employees of the House of Representatives and to employees of the Architect of the Capitol.

INTERSTATE COMMERCE REQUIREMENT

The Act extends coverage over employers based on the nature of the employer's business. The interstate commerce aspect of the employer's business allows the courts to extend the Act's coverage to the "farthest reaches of interstate commerce." (*Overstreet v. North Shore Corp.*)

The courts have established the following principles for determining the appropriateness of extending coverage based on the interstate character of the employer's business:

- If an establishment produces goods for sale in interstate commerce, there is a presumption that all employees who worked in the establishment contributed to the production of the goods. To overcome this presumption, the employer must establish that the functions of

certain employees were segregated from the production of the goods for interstate commerce. (*Guess v. Montague*) However, such segregation will not assist employers in avoiding coverage if their employees qualify under the "enterprise" concept.
- Employers are deemed within the Act's coverage as producing goods for commerce where the employer intends, hopes, or has reason to believe that the goods or any unsegregated part of them will move in interstate commerce. (*United States v. F.W. Darby Lumber Co.; Walling v. Burch*)
- If only a minor part of the employer's business is shipped in interstate commerce or is involved in the production of goods for interstate commerce, the employer may still be covered under the Act where the interstate shipments are "regular and recurrent." (*Mabee v. White Plains Publishing Co.*)

The FLSA prohibits "any person" from introducing into interstate commerce goods produced in violation of the Act's minimum wage and overtime provisions. This prohibition is called the "hot-goods" provision, and it has led to numerous court decisions about what is meant by "person," "introduced," "interstate commerce," "goods," and "produced." The Supreme Court has expanded the meaning of "person" to include allegedly *innocent* secured creditors who have acquired security interests in goods manufactured by debtor-employers in violation of the Act. The Court rejected the argument that the ban on shipping "hot goods" applies only to culpable parties. (*Citicorp Indus. Credit v. Brock*)

EMPLOYER COVERAGE

The FLSA was intended, as remedial legislation, to cover the broadest possible scope of employment situations. To that end, the Act does not define covered employers, but describes them in terms of the amount of business transacted per year. The Act was intended as a statute of general applicability to all "enterprises" in the United States that engage in interstate commerce and meet the established dollar-volume threshold. However, there is one important exception to this presumption of general applicability: the Act does not extend to American Indian tribes or to tribal organizations. The courts have held that extending the FLSA to such entities would violate the tribal immunity guaranteed via treaties with the U.S. government. (*Martin v. Great Lakes Indian Fish & Wildlife Comm'n*)

Dollar-Volume Test

The basic determining factor for employer coverage involves the size of the employer's business. Congress found that the larger the business, the greater its harm to the public by its FLSA violations and the easier it would be to identify and regulate because of its size. Congress therefore established a minimum gross receipts amount—the dollar-volume test—that would serve as the cutoff between covered and noncovered employers.

The 1989 amendments to the FLSA simplified the enterprise coverage test by establishing a uniform $500,000 "business-volume" threshold in place of prior thresholds for retail and nonretail businesses. Under the uniform threshold, effective April 1, 1990, enterprises with annual gross sales exceeding $500,000 are covered by the FLSA if they meet the Act's definition of "enterprise," and if they have at least two employees who engage in commerce or in the production of goods for commerce (see "Interstate Commerce Requirement" for more information).

Small enterprises with less than $500,000 in annual gross sales are exempt from FLSA enterprise coverage. Such firms, however, may still have FLSA obligations with respect to workers covered by the Act on an individual basis.

Excise taxes at the retail level which are separately stated and identified in the customer's bill need not be included in the calculation of gross dollar volume of sales. As a general rule, a tax is "separately stated" where it has been added to the sales slip or invoice or stated orally at the time of sale or visually by means of a poster or other sign reasonably designed to inform the purchaser that the amount of the tax is included in the sales price. (WH Publication 1431, January 1977).

Under the prior coverage rules, certain types of enterprises, i.e., public agencies, hospital and health care facilities, construction and reconstruction businesses, and laundry and dry cleaning establishments, were covered by the FLSA, regardless of their annual business volume (assuming they met other applicable requirements for enterprise coverage). However, the amended rules provide an exemption to small laundry or dry cleaning and small construction/reconstruction businesses by making such enterprises subject to the "business volume" test. The theory underlying this provision is that a small business will not meet the $500,000 threshold, and thus will not fall under FLSA coverage. Coverage of public agencies, hospitals, and health care facilities is unaffected by the 1989 amendments.

"ENTERPRISE COVERAGE"

Under the 1961 amendments to the FLSA, Congress specifically acknowledged the necessity of the enterprise concept for FLSA coverage, to reach subsidiary branches of an employer's operations. The Act defines enterprise as:

> The related activities performed (either through unified operation or common control) by any person or persons for a common business purpose, and includes all such activities whether performed in one or more establishments or by one or more corporate or other organizational units including departments of an establishment operated through leasing arrangements, but shall not include the related activities performed for such enterprise by an independent contractor.

In the absence of the enterprise concept, an employer's subsidiary branches might otherwise be exempt from FLSA coverage, based on the dollar-volume standard. The Act extends coverage to employees, not specifically exempted otherwise, who are employed by certain enterprises engaged in interstate commerce or in the production of goods for commerce.

Where an employer operates several small entities, none of which individually may meet the minimum dollar-volume tests discussed above, the employer may still be covered under the Act by virtue of the enterprise concept of coverage.

The enterprise concept is not independent of the other bases of coverage, because it is still necessary to determine whether the enterprise or two or more of its employees are engaged in interstate commerce or the production of goods for interstate commerce.

However, unlike other bases of coverage, the enterprise concept does not base coverage on the activities of the individual employees: all of the employees in a particular enterprise or establishment may be covered, provided the enterprise and two or more of its employees are sufficiently engaged in interstate commerce or the production of goods for interstate commerce.

The interstate character of the goods as a product that has been moved in interstate commerce is not destroyed by the fact that the product is used to make a different product, which is then sold to intrastate purchasers. And the mingling of the intrastate goods with this product does not negate the product's origin in interstate commerce. (*Wirtz v. Melos Constr. Corp.*)

Although the courts have held that the coverage of the law must be liberally interpreted, they consistently have placed the burden of proving coverage on the employee in an employee-initiated wage suit, and on the Secretary of Labor in a wage-recovery suit or in a suit to restrain violations of the Act. The Act is set up in a way that employees may only sue on their own behalf, and only for the recovery of wages due, while the Labor Secretary may sue on behalf of a class of employees and may obtain injunctive relief in addition to obtaining wages due the employees.

In determining whether a particular business is covered under the enterprise concept, the courts have examined such factors as:

- Related activities of separate business entities; (*Wirtz v. Savannah Bank & Trust Co. of Savannah*)
- The relationship between a "house" agency and the parent organization; (WH AdmOp, Feb. 7, 1962)

- Related activities of conglomerates; (FLSA, Sec. 13(g))
- Work performed by an "independent contractor"; (*Rutherford Food Corp. v. McComb*)
- Work performed for an independently owned retail or service establishment; (*Wirtz v. Charleston Coca-Cola Bottling Co.*) and
- Whether there was a common business purpose, common control, and unified operations. (*Reich v. Circle C Investments;* cf. *Martin v. Universal Alarm Sys.*)

Where the enterprise is engaged in interstate commerce and meets the dollar-volume test, the courts have looked to the "economic realities" of the relationship between the enterprise and the employee. For example, corporate officials who exercise control over areas of employee hiring, firing, training, and compensation have been found to be employers. (*Martin v. W.E. Monk & Co.*) Conversely, an enterprise that authorized and funded, but did not otherwise control, the operation of a service was found not to be an employer. (*Burnison v. Memorial Hosp.*)

EMPLOYER EXEMPTIONS

Not all enterprises are "employers" under the FLSA. Further, not all "employers" that meet the tests for interstate commerce, dollar volume, and "economic realities" are covered under the Act. Congress has authorized several employer exemptions because of concerns that override FLSA compliance. For example, the Act exempts from "enterprise" coverage the "Mom and Pop" establishment that has as its only regular employees the owner or the immediate family member(s) of the owner. This exemption was designed to allow family businesses to operate without concern for the FLSA, and is to be narrowly construed. A business that employed family members at its home base and a large pool of nonfamily members at a separate location is covered by the Act, however, since the exemption is restricted to the income generated by the family members, and may not be extended to the income of the nonfamily employees. (*Martin v. Bedell*)

In addition, common carriers that are covered by the Motor Carrier Act are exempt from FLSA coverage. The Department of Transportation is authorized by the Motor Carrier Act to set hours of work for certain common carriers. Where DOT has exercised this jurisdiction, the FLSA provides that those motor carriers are exempt from coverage. This exemption encompasses employees engaged in activities affecting the safety of operations of motor vehicles engaged in interstate commerce. Also included in this exemption are:

- Drivers who regularly pick up empty containers destined for out-of-state bottling facilities; (*Thomas v. Wichita Coca-Cola Bottling*)
- Drivers who deliver laundry; (*Martin v. Coyne Int'l Enters.*) and
- Field engineers who use their personal vehicles on interstate visits to install computer equipment. (*Friedrich v. U.S. Computer Servs.*)

However, employees who are sent across state lines to purchase miscellaneous items that could have been purchased intrastate were found not to be exempt. (*DeArment v. Lehman*)

The FLSA also exempts agricultural workers employed by an employer who did not, during any calendar quarter during the preceding calendar year, use more than 500 man days of agricultural labor. (*Salinas v. Rodriguez*)

Church-Operated Schools

The existence of schools operated by religious organizations has posed problems for the FLSA. The courts have had to resolve such issues as the following:

- Whether a church-operated school is an "enterprise" for purposes of FLSA coverage;
- Whether individuals who work in such a school are "employees" under the Act; and
- Whether the First Amendment to the U.S. Constitution, which guarantees free exercise of religion, precludes FLSA coverage of such a school.

A federal appeals court ruled that the school is an "enterprise" under the Act and that the history of the FLSA indicates an affirmative intention to treat church-operated schools as enterprises. Rejecting the claim that the individuals who work in the school fall under the Act's exemption for ministerial employees, the court said that the teachers perform no "sacerdotal" function, do not serve as church governors, and do not belong to any clearly delineated religious orders. Finally, the court held that FLSA coverage did not impermissibly burden the church members' exercise of religion under the Constitution. (*Dole v. Shenandoah Baptist Church*)

EMPLOYEE COVERAGE

Employees Engaged in Commerce

In view of the congressional intent to extend the FLSA, as remedial legislation, to the farthest reaches of interstate commerce, Congress and the courts have delineated categories of employees whose employers are involved in interstate commerce. The employees are categorized according to the functions they perform under the "employees engaged in commerce" doctrine:

- Employees in the telecommunications and interstate transportation industries;
- Employees who participate in the distribution of goods that move through channels of commerce; and
- Employees who directly aid or facilitate the operation of instrumentalities of commerce by providing materials or power used by the instrumentalities or by maintaining or reconstructing or repairing them.

Since employees engaged in interstate transportation and telecommunications generally are conceded to be covered by the Act, most litigation under the commerce test of coverage involves the "distribution of goods" and "operation of instrumentalities of commerce" prongs of the test.

However, an employer that operated a telephone answering service attempted to avoid FLSA coverage of its employees via an in-state relay system to the employees. The employees received out-of-state telephone calls that had been forwarded from the employer's in-state clients. The employer argued that the employees received calls that had been placed to its intrastate clients and therefore there was no interstate commerce. The district court ruled that the employees were engaged in interstate commerce, regardless of whether the employer's activities constituted interstate commerce. (*DeArment v. Curtins, Inc.*)

Reflecting the congressional intent to extend the FLSA as broadly as possible, Congress wrestled with one category of employees that pitted two important social goals against one another: illegal aliens. Interestingly, both social goals were embodied in federal legislation designed to regulate employment practices, and these twin goals came into conflict in 1988.

In 1986, the Immigration and Reform Control Act (IRCA) became effective. This statute was intended to restrict the flow of illegal immigration into the United States, which Congress perceived as being fueled by employment opportunities. IRCA provisions have three main objectives:

- To prohibit the employment of illegal aliens;
- To require employers to make a good-faith determination whether potential employees are legal aliens; and
- To penalize employers that fail to make this determination or that make less than a good-faith determination. The penalties range from fines to imprisonment.

An illegal alien working for a motel sued his employer for unpaid wages under the FLSA. The employer argued that IRCA indicated the congressional intent to ban employment of illegal aliens, and that this intent would be thwarted by enforcing the FLSA wage provisions against the employer of an illegal alien.

A U.S. court of appeals ruled, however, that failure to enforce the FLSA in these circumstances would unjustly enrich the employer and would imply that the IRCA stripped employees of statutory rights under the FLSA. The court reasoned that this result would also encourage other employers to take advantage of illegal aliens, knowing that the IRCA would protect them from having to pay wages. Since Congress nowhere indicated an intent that the IRCA would deprive illegal aliens of FLSA rights, the court concluded that illegal aliens are "employees" under the FLSA, even though the IRCA prohibits the employment of such undocumented aliens. (*Patel v. Quality Inn South*)

However, alien detainees working in Immigration Service detention facilities are not "employees" under the Act. The Fifth Circuit observed that the aliens were removed from American industry and are not within the protected group Congress sought to protect under the Act. (*Alvarado Guevara v. Immigration and Naturalization Serv.*)

Cutting against the congressional intent of broad coverage of the FLSA is the complex statutory scheme that exempts many employees covered under other laws such as railway labor, motor carriers, airlines, small telephone exchanges, and water transportation acts, which preempt FLSA coverage in those areas. In addition, the Act contains numerous exemptions and the U.S. Department of Labor is authorized to promulgate regulations regarding exemptions. (See "Employee Exemptions" later in this chapter, for a more detailed discussion.)

"Production for Commerce" Test. Under the "production for commerce" test of coverage, the Act defines "produced" as:

- Employees producing, manufacturing, mining, handling, transporting, or in any other manner working on goods shipped in commerce; or
- Employees engaged in any "closely related process or occupation directly essential" to the production of such goods.

Under these criteria, courts have attempted to define the parameters of "actual production operations" (*Western Union Tel. Co. v. Lenroot*), and to define the meaning of "goods." (*Powell v. U.S. Cartridge Co.*) Section 3(i) of the Act excludes goods "after their delivery into the actual physical possession of the ultimate consumer thereof." Consequently, the courts have also had to address what was intended by the phrase "ultimate consumer." (*Marshall v. Brunner*)

"Fringe" Production Employees

Section 3(j) of the Act provides for coverage of any employee engaged in "any closely related process or occupation directly essential" to production. These fringe production employees were specifically described in the Statement of the House Managers in the 1949 amendments to the Act, which listed some fringe employees who still would be covered under the "closely-related and directly-essential" test. Applying these provisions, the Court of Appeals for the Ninth Circuit ruled that employees of a liquid waste disposal company who regularly remove liquid waste from customers' plants producing goods for interstate commerce, and who perform services for airlines directly related to interstate commerce, are engaged in the production of goods for such commerce under the Act. (*Brennan v. Carrasco*)

Congress intended by these amendments to exclude from FLSA coverage those employees whose work is several degrees or stages removed from the production of goods for interstate commerce. These provisions were interpreted in *Allstate Construction Co. v. Durkin*, where "off-the-road" employees employed by a road contractor in the production of material to repair interstate roads were found to be covered by the Act, even though the material was produced in a state for use on the roads within that state. The U.S. Supreme Court reasoned that these employees were engaged in the production of goods for interstate commerce because "he who serves interstate highways and railroads serves commerce. By the same token, he who produces goods for these indispensable and inseparable parts of commerce produces goods for commerce."

Construction workers on a dam, however, were found not to be involved in an activity that was closely related or directly essential to the production of goods for interstate commerce, according to the Supreme Court, in view of the remoteness of construction from the production of the goods, and the absence of the dedication of completed facilities either exclusively or primarily to such production. The Court also observed that the purpose of the dam—to provide water to a locality—could not be regarded as the production of goods for commerce. (*Mitchell v. H.B. Zachry*) This case illustrates the fact that the employer may meet the dollar-volume test and be engaged in interstate commerce, only to be excluded from coverage because its employees do not produce the type of goods that the Act was intended to cover.

EMPLOYEE EXEMPTIONS

The Act contains a complex scheme of exemptions for employees and employers in certain specified industries. In addition, the Act also carves out specific exemptions for employees having certain responsibilities, where coverage of the employee is thought to be inconsistent with the Act's purpose. These employees fall under one or several of the exemptions for executive, administrative, or professional employees, depending on job duties. These three classes of exemptions are collectively referred to as the "white collar exemptions." Each exemption carries with it a specific set of criteria, or test, that must be met for the employee to fall within the exemption. (See Appendix B for a summary of white-collar exemptions.)

Some employee exemptions suspend only the overtime requirements, while others suspend only the minimum wage and equal pay requirements. Still others suspend two or all four standards—minimum wage, overtime, equal pay, or child labor. Exemptions may apply to all the employees in an establishment, or only to certain individuals. As an added complication, the exemptions frequently overlap. (See Appendix C for a summary of FLSA exemptions from minimum wage and overtime requirements.)

In addition, the U.S. Department of Labor is authorized to promulgate regulations implementing the FLSA. Since 1991, the DOL has passed regulations that:

- Exempt from overtime employees who participate in nonjob specific remedial education programs offered by their employers;

- Classify computer systems analysts and computer programmers as executive, administrative, and professional employees (exempt from minimum wage and overtime); and
- Modify the "salary basis" test for exempt employees in the public sector (see "State and Local Government Employees" later in this chapter for a more complete discussion of this group of employees).

All the exemptions under the Act are subject to a rule of "strict construction"; that is, any doubt must be resolved in favor of the employee's coverage. (*Calaf v. Gonzalez*) The burden of proving that a particular exemption applies lies with the employer who asserts it. (*Coast Van Lines, Inc. v. Armstrong*)

White-Collar Exemptions

The Act expressly exempts "executive, administrative, and professional" employees from its minimum wage and overtime provisions. The Act charges the Secretary of Labor with responsibility to define and limit these exempt categories.

An executive employee is limited to one whose duties "include some form of management authority—to persons who actually direct the work of other persons." To qualify as an "exempt executive" employee under the Department of Labor regulations, the employee must:

- Have as his primary duty the management of (*a*) the enterprise in which he is employed or (*b*) a customarily recognized department or subdivision of the enterprise;
- Regularly supervise the work of two or more full-time employees;
- Have the authority to hire, discharge, and promote, or effectively to recommend such action;
- Regularly exercise discretion in the course of his primary duty;
- Spend at least 80 percent of the workday engaged in the primary duty and receive a stipulated amount of pay per week. This stipulated amount per week is either $155 (under the "long test") or $250 (under the "short

test"). The regulations were drafted with an eye to expeditious determinations. To that end, individuals who are proffered as executives will be examined under a more detailed set of factors if they are paid less than $250 per week, and under a more streamlined test if they earn more than $250 per week. (The tests have not been revised for many years and, for all practical purposes, no executive earns less than $250 per week. Therefore, the long test has very little applicability. However, the Labor Department is considering changes in these dollar amounts.)

The courts have held that an employee must meet all the applicable tests to qualify for the exemption. (*Wirtz v. C.&P. Shoe Corp.; Wirtz v. Williams*) The employee's job title is not controlling, but the duties involved determine whether the executive exemption should apply. (*Associated Builders v. Brennan*) In addition to receiving the minimum-dollar amount specified in the regulations, the employee must be paid on a "salary basis." The Wage-Hour Administrator has stated that this means the employee must receive his full salary for any week in which he performs any work, regardless of the number of hours worked. Recent developments in the "salary basis" test have illustrated the complexity of this standard.

SALARY BASIS TEST

As noted above, the Wage-Hour Administrator has established that an exempt employee must receive a full "salary" for any week in which he performs any work to retain the exemption. Where an exempt employee is absent for one or more entire days, and has no leave on the books or is authorized to take leave without pay, the employer may deduct from the employee's salary that percentage of days missed from the total workweek. Typically, an employee who works a five-day workweek and is absent without leave for one day may have his salary deducted by 20 percent (one-fifth of the time covered by the salary).

Where an exempt employee takes leave without pay and is absent for less than a full day (i.e., a partial day absence), the courts have ruled that an employer's deduction from salary for a "partial day absence" violates the salary basis test. An employer that provides environmental engineering, architectural, scientific, and planning services to various industrial clients followed a written practice of deducting for "partial day absences" from its highly paid employees, including engineers, accountants, architects, scientists, supervisors, and administrators, when these employees took leave without pay. Although the employer classified these employees as exempt from the FLSA overtime provisions, the U.S. Court of Appeals for the Second Circuit ruled that the employees did not receive a true "salary" under the FLSA regulations promulgated by the Department of Labor. The appeals court noted that the FLSA regulations authorized an employer who made an "inadvertent" deduction from an exempt employee's salary to retroactively restore that exemption by returning to the exempt employee the amounts inadvertently deducted. However, in this case, the appeals court ruled, the employer's deductions were not inadvertent, and therefore, the "window of correction" was not available to this employer. (*Martin v. Malcolm Pirnie Inc.*; see also *Klein v. Rush Presbyterian-St. Luke's Medical Center*)

The *Malcolm Pirnie* decision indicates that the mere possibility that an exempt employee's salary is subject to docking for partial day absences means that all exempt employees in the same classification whose salaries are subject to docking for partial day absences do not receive a true "salary" and, therefore, are not exempt from overtime (regardless of whether docking actually occurred). In addition, the "window of correction" will be strictly construed and is available only to inadvertent deductions. Following *Malcolm Pirnie*, two exceptions to the salary basis test have been created (one statutory and one regulatory):

- FLSA-exempt employees who take "unpaid intermittent leave" or "leave on a reduced leave schedule" authorized by the Family and Medical Leave Act of 1993 (FMLA) will not lose their FLSA exempt status, even

where the employer deducts from their "salary" for partial day absences, if the leave qualifies as FMLA leave; and
- FLSA-exempt employees in state and local governments may incur "salary" deductions for partial day absences, without losing their exempt status, under certain circumstances, pursuant to a different "salary basis" regulation promulgated by the DOL in 1992 (see "State and Local Government Employees" later in this chapter for a more complete discussion of this issue; see also "Family and Medical Leave Act" in Chapter 9 for a more detailed discussion of this law).

The salary aspect of the executive employee exemption is complicated and may involve such factors as offsets for jury duty or military leave, salary plus bonus calculations, bona fide reductions not intended to circumvent the salary basis requirements, offsets as credit for board and lodging, and other issues. Specific problems should be addressed to the local office of the U.S. Department of Labor, Employment Standards Administration, Wage-Hour Division. (See Appendix D.)

Finally, the regulations provide that an employee who is in "sole charge" of a particular operation is to be deemed an "executive" employee. In addition, an employee may fall under an executive, administrative, and professional exemption simultaneously. (*Legg v. Rock Prods. Mfg. Corp.*, WH-463, WH AdminOp, Aug. 21, 1978)

The second white-collar exemption removes the administrative employee from protection of the minimum wage and overtime provisions of the FLSA. The salary tests are similar to those that apply to the executive employee. The administrative employee must:

- Perform office or nonmanual work directly related to management operations;
- Regularly exercise discretion beyond clerical duties;
- Perform specialized or technical work, or perform special assignments with only general supervision; and

- Spend at least 80 percent of work time on exempt work. Retail-service employees must spend at least 60 percent of work time on exempt work.

The phrase "directly related to management policies or general business operations" contained in the regulations may cover the responsibilities of a wide variety of employees who carry out major assignments in conducting the business or whose work affects business operations to a substantial degree. The Wage-Hour Division warns that job titles will not control.

Highly paid *administrative employees* (those earning over $250 per week on a salary basis) are exempt if they meet all the criteria of the short test:

- The employee's position must include work requiring the exercise of independent judgment and discretion; and
- The employee's primary duty is office work or work that is not of a manual nature, and is directly related to management policies or to general business operations of the company or its customers. The Wage-Hour Administrator has issued an Explanatory Statement concerning the meaning of "administrative employee" under the regulations.

The last white-collar exemption is the professional employee category, which covers a wide variety of occupations from law and medicine to writing, acting, and other artistic professions. Elementary and secondary school teachers are covered under this exemption by virtue of the 1966 amendments to the Act. As with other white-collar employees, the professional employee is exempt from both the minimum wage and overtime provisions of the Act.

A former senior research associate in a chemical development department who earned more than $250 per week brought suit against his employer claiming he should have been paid overtime during the two years preceding his dismissal because he did not consider his status as that of a professional employee. A federal district court in Pennsylvania found to the contrary because the associate was engaged in a learned profession and had as his primary duty the "performance of work . . . requiring knowledge of an advanced type in a field of science or learning" under the regulations. In addition, he was part of a research team that investigated and evaluated new syntheses for pharmaceutical products, he had discretion to exercise professional judgment, and he did not contest the employer's evidence, which proved that he was fully qualified to perform professional work. (*Molinari v. McNeil Pharmaceutical*)

A newspaper employee who wrote radio and television commentary and criticisms was found to be within the professional employee exemption, since he primarily performed tasks that relied on his creativity, initiative, imagination, talent, and flair. (*Lewis v. News World Communications;* but see *Sherwood v. Washington Post*)

As with administrative employees, the professional-employee exemption is available if the employee is paid on a salary basis and the salary meets the minimum-dollar amount specified in the regulations for 40 hours of work per week. Lawyers and doctors actually practicing in their fields need not meet the minimum-dollar amount.

"Long Test." The Wage-Hour Division has devised an elaborate test ("long test") for determining whether low-paid (between $155 and $250 per week) white-collar employees qualify for exempt status. It has also devised a streamlined test ("short test") for higher-paid employees (more than $250 per week). For each category of exempt employee (executive, administrative, professional), there is a separate long test and short test. (Ed. note: These tests share some common criteria, but differ in significant ways. Consult Appendix B in this Primer for more information.)

Because the minimum-dollar amounts under both the long and short tests were devised many years ago, the long test is not in use for any practical purpose. Nevertheless, it has historical significance. Under the long test, a low-paid white-collar employee is required to have as his primary duty work that either:

- Requires advanced knowledge in a field of science or learning, of a type customarily acquired by a prolonged course of specialized study; or
- Is original and creative in character in a recognized field of artistic endeavor, so that the result depends primarily on the employee's invention, imagination, or talent.

Since this description is fraught with subjective, ill-defined phrases, the Wage-Hour Division has attempted to provide guidance by issuing a plethora of Administrative Opinions.

"Short Test." For white-collar employees earning more than $250 per week on a salary basis, the short test requires that an exempt employee must:

- Have as his primary duty the performance of work requiring advanced knowledge in a field of science or learning, including work that requires the consistent exercise of discretion and independent judgment; or
- Have as his primary duty the performance of work requiring invention, imagination, or talent in a recognized field of artistic endeavor.

The short test is truly shorter than the cumbersome and ambiguous long test. To facilitate matters, the Wage-Hour Division has issued a chart of professions whose employees fall within the exemption. Such professional employees include registered or certified medical technologists, registered nurses, computer systems analysts, and supervisory programmers.

Nonemployees

In addition to employees and exempt employees, the Act recognizes "nonemployees" as individuals who do not qualify for employee status. For example, apprentices are regarded by the Wage-Hour Division as nonemployees, because apprentices are not what Congress intended to cover by the word employee. According to the Division, an apprentice is a person at least 16 years old (or older, if required by state or federal law) who is employed to learn a skilled trade pursuant to the terms of a *written* apprenticeship agreement with the employer. (Regulations covering employment of apprentices appear at 29 C.F.R. 521.) Trainees for work on railroads are not employees, according to the U.S. Supreme Court, since two important qualifications are lacking: (*a*) any benefit to the employer and (*b*) compensation or an intent that the services rendered be paid for. (*Walling v. Portland Terminal Co.*)

A major category of nonemployee is the independent contractor. Certain jobs may be performed with an independence in judgment that is contrary to an employer-employee relationship which is characterized by the employer's direction of the employee on the job. This is one of the wide range of factors the courts examine to determine whether a particular individual is an employee or an independent contractor. The determining factors include:

- The extent to which the services rendered are an integral part of the employer's business;
- The permanency of the relationship;
- The amount of the individual's investment in facilities and equipment;
- The individual's opportunity for profit or loss;
- The degree of independent business organization and operation;
- The nature and degree of control exercised over the individual by the employer; and
- The degree of independent initiative, judgment, or foresight used by the individual providing the service. (*Dole v. Snell*)

This set of criteria for independent contractor status has come to be known as the "economic realities" test. The courts have applied these factors in a way that no one factor will be regarded as determinative; rather, all must be weighed in order to decide the economic realities of the situation. (*Brock v. Lauritzen Farms*) Central to a court's decision is whether the worker is *economically dependent* upon the business to whom he or she renders services. (*Usery v. Pilgrim Equip. Co.*) The difficulty with independent contractors is that they receive, and expect to receive some compensation for their efforts. The *de-*

pendency on the employer is the litmus test for determining whether a particular individual is an independent contractor or an employee. The language of the Act defines "employ" as "to suffer or permit to work," and the courts have adopted a common sense understanding of the term, with respect to a claimed independent contractor, in the context of the relationship that existed at the time. (*Walling v. Jacksonville Terminal Co.*)

Applying the economic realities test, the courts have rejected claims of "independent contractor" status and found that the following groups of workers are statutory "employees" under the FLSA:

- Dancers in an upscale topless nightclub, where the nightclub owner exercised control and the dancers neither invested in the club nor had an opportunity for profit or loss; (*Martin v. Priba Corp.; Reich v. Circle C Invs.*)
- Seamstresses who worked at home, even though the employer exercised no control over the manner in which they worked and they could perform work for others; (*Martin v. Albrecht*) and
- A maintenance laborer who worked for an apartment management company, even though he was not directly controlled by the company and could accept work from others. (*Hageman v. Park West Gardens*)

Migrant farm workers have occasionally been the subject of independent contractor disputes. An additional complexity in such cases is the presence of the farm labor contractor, who stands between the farm worker and the farm owner. The courts have had no difficulty finding an employer-employee relationship involving the farm worker and both the contractor and the farm owner. (*Hodgson v. Griffin & Brand of McAllen, Inc.*)

Trainees are another category of nonemployee. The U.S. Wage-Hour Administrator applies a six-part test to determine whether a particular individual falls into this category. The individual must meet *all* six factors:

- The training, even though it includes actual operation of the employer's facilities, is similar to that which would be provided in a vocational school;
- The training is for the benefit of the trainee;
- The trainee does not displace regular employees, but works under closer supervision;
- The employer providing the training gains no immediate advantage from the trainee's activities—on occasion, the employer's operation may in fact be hindered;
- The trainee is not guaranteed a job at the completion of his training; and
- The employer and the trainee understand that the employer is not obligated to pay wages during the training period.

The six-factor test for determining whether a trainee is an employee under the FLSA is not an "all-or-nothing" standard, but should be used to assess the "totality of the circumstances." Firefighter trainees were not employees, where the training is similar to that given in a vocational school, the training is for the trainee's benefit, the trainee does not displace regular employees, the employer gains no immediate advantage from the trainee's activities, the trainee is not necessarily entitled to a job at the completion of training, and the parties understand that the trainee will not be paid. (*Martin v. Parker Fire Protection Dist.*)

Typically, a graduate research assistant and a senior in college who are required to do on-the-job training as part of their course work are regarded as "trainees." (WH AdminOp, June 7, 1967, and WH-20, Mar. 31, 1970)

On the other hand, employees who volunteered to participate in the employer's display model program were found to be "employees" for purposes of this work, since the time spent was primarily for the benefit of the employer. (*Martin v. Conagra, Inc.*)

Airline trainees for the position of flight attendant have given rise to much litigation, with the courts holding that these trainees are not employees under the FLSA. (*Donovan v. American Airlines*)

Historically, the courts rejected claims that prison inmates were "employees," because of the unique relationship between the inmates and the prison system, which requires the inmates to work. (*Gilbreath v. Cutter Biological Inc.*) Consistent with this approach, the Seventh and Ninth Circuits have ruled that prison inmates are not "employees" under the FLSA, since inmate labor is different from labor exchanged for wages in a free market, and therefore, the relationship is penological, not pecuniary. Because inmates work as part of the prison's requirement that they work, the courts reasoned, the economic reality is that their labor belongs to the state. (*Vanskike v. Peters; Hale v. Arizona*)

Other categories of individuals who may perform work for an employer but who are exempt from FLSA coverage include volunteers, handicapped workers, outside salespersons, mental patients or patient workers at rehabilitation facilities, and certain agricultural laborers.

HOURS OF WORK

Prior to determining whether an employee is entitled to minimum wages or overtime or both, it frequently becomes necessary to establish that the employee was engaged in compensable activity or that the time reserved for the employer was compensable time.

Where the issue is whether the activity engaged in was compensable, the courts generally examine whether the employer knew that the employee was engaged in such activity, whether the employee was specifically ordered to refrain from such activity, and whether the activity benefited the employer. (*Mitchell v. Caldwell; Davis v. Food Lion*)

For example, the Secretary of Labor brought suit to recover allegedly unpaid wages on behalf of employees who worked at satellite pumping stations located in isolated areas substantially removed from any community. The U.S. Court of Appeals for the Fifth Circuit found that the employees spent "on-call" time with their families, that they were only rarely required to respond to employer needs, and that they were fully aware of the employer's on-call time policy when they were hired. Applying the well-accepted rule concerning on-call time, the court declared that these employees were "waiting to be engaged," and were not "engaged to wait." (*Brock v. El Paso Natural Gas Co.*; see also *Paniagua v. Galveston, Tex.*; *Owens v. Local 169*; and *Birdwell v. City of Gadsden*)

An agreement between chauffeurs and the limousine service that employed them entitled the chauffeurs to compensation for time spent waiting for an assignment. However, they were not entitled to compensation for time spent waiting *away* from the employer's premises or outside of the terms of the agreement, since this time was spent primarily for the chauffeurs' rather than the employer's benefit. (*Caryk v. Coupe*; and see *Martin v. Ohio Turnpike Comm'n*)

Idle time that a casino required its employees to spend at the casino was compensable, because the principal benefit inured to the casino and the employees were not completely free to use the time for their own purposes. (*Brock v. Claridge Hotel & Casino*)

Physician assistants are entitled to compensation for "on-call" time spent waiting for calls to provide emergency medical services to prison inmates, because they could not use this time effectively for their own purposes. They were required to respond within 20 minutes to any of seven facilities within an eight-mile radius, and the number of calls received ranged from 10 to 12 per weekday and up to 24 per weekend shift. The assistants were unable to shower, eat in restaurants, entertain guests, perform yard work, or attend sporting events during on-call hours. (*Casserly v. Colorado*)

Whether the meal periods of law enforcement personnel are compensable depends on the circumstances (*Lamon v. City of Shawnee*; cf. *Armitage v. City of Emporia*) and the standard applied. ("predominantly-for-the-benefit-of-the-employer" or "completely-relieved-from-duty"; see *Henson v. Pulaski County Sheriff Dep't*) Within a law enforcement agency, the off-duty activities of a canine officer have also been found to be compensable. (*Truslow v. Spotsylvania County Sheriff's Dep't*; *Nichols v. City of Chicago*)

Some city firefighters are entitled to compensation for on-call time (*Renfro v. City of Emporia*), but others may not be, depending on exigent circumstances. (*Clay v. City of Winona*)

The most common disputes over whether certain time is compensable involve activity that occurs before ("preliminary") or after ("postliminary") the employee's principal work activity. If such work is part of an employee's principal activity, then it is compensable. If such work is not, then it is usually found to be noncompensable. Disputes involving preliminary and postliminary activities fall under the Portal-to-Portal Act. (For information concerning preliminary and postliminary activity, see the introduction to "Preliminary and Postliminary Activities," Chapter 3.)

MINIMUM WAGES

The "Fair Labor Standards Amendments of 1989," signed by President George Bush in November 1989, affected the minimum wage in three important respects: it raised the minimum wage in increments from $3.35 to $4.25; it created a "sub-minimum" training wage for teenagers; and it raised the percentage of the amount of money received by employees in the form of tips that could be credited against minimum wages due those employees. Those changes are:

Minimum Wage Hike. The two-step hike in the federal minimum wage was phased in through two 45-cent installments to help ameliorate the economic impact on employers. The first increase, from $3.35 per hour to $3.80 per hour, became effective on April 1, 1990. The second increase, to $4.25 per hour, became effective on April 1, 1991. These rates apply to all 50 states and U.S. territories and possessions, except American Samoa, where minimum wages are set by the Secretary of Labor based on recommendations from Special Industry Councils. However, a special phase-in schedule applies to certain industries in Puerto Rico.

Tip Credit Increases. The 1989 amendments allowed employers of tipped employees to count tips as covering a greater portion of the required federal minimum wage. After March 31, 1990, the amendments increased the permitted tip credit from 40 percent to 45 percent, and to 50 percent after March 31, 1991.

Aside from setting limits on the amount of money that can be offset against minimum wages due tipped employees, the FLSA also provides rules for averaging wages over a given period of time to comply with the minimum wage requirements. However, the old rule still applies that the credit may not exceed the value of the tips actually received.

Exceptions to the minimum wage are made for learners, apprentices, messengers, and superannuated workers. However, an employer should obtain a certificate of exemption from the Wage-Hour Division before paying the reduced rate. In addition, certain industries and occupations are exempt from the minimum wage requirement; the Wage-Hour Division should be consulted for such information.

In 1986, the FLSA was amended to simplify the administration of sheltered workshops. Prior to this legislation, handicapped workers were exempt from the minimum wage provisions, and sheltered workshop employers were required only to pay their handicapped workers at least 50 percent of the minimum wage. The 1986 amendments eliminated separate certification requirements for various categories of handicapped workers and based all wages on individual productivity.

The Wage-Hour Administrator has established rules for computing and paying the minimum wage, the unit of time over which the minimum wage may be averaged, the types of deductions permitted, the effect of piece rates or bonuses, and other matters. Although the Act requires employers to maintain adequate and accurate records, the employer may decide for itself *how* to maintain its records if it is able to provide the Administrator with basic data on the subjects specified above concerning minimum wages.

The two main sources of difficulty in administering this part of the Act concern the length of time over which wages may be averaged to comply with the minimum wage and which deductions may be legally made from employees' wages.

Employees receive pay in various forms: hourly, fixed weekly, fixed monthly, fluctuating workweek, piece rates, bonuses, and commissions. Since the Act sets $4.25 as the minimum for each hour, an hourly paid employee must receive this rate for all hours worked. An employer may not "juggle" the books to pay the employee less than this rate for some hours and more than this rate for other hours in the workweek, even if the average hourly rate meets the minimum wage rate.

A fixed weekly salary is determined by the number of hours worked during a week divided by the actual compensation received. This amount must equal or exceed the minimum hourly wage rate. For a fixed monthly rate, or for any fixed rate that exceeds one week, the employer must translate the salary into a weekly wage rate and satisfy the fixed weekly salary standard set forth above. Under this formula, the fixed monthly salary is multiplied by 12 (months) and divided by 52 (weeks per year) to ascertain the weekly rate; the bimonthly salary is multiplied by 24 (bimonthly periods) and divided by 52 (weeks per year) to determine the weekly rate under the payment schedule.

For employees who are paid on a piece-rate basis, or for those paid under an incentive plan, the salary must meet the average hourly minimum wage rate for all hours worked in the week, although the employee may not earn the mininum wage for every hour worked.

Where there is a mixed rate, such as where an employee receives an hourly rate for some hours worked and a piece rate for other hours in the same week, the hourly rate must be at least the minimum and the piece-rate wages must average at least the minimum for the piece-rate hours.

The minimum wage required by the FLSA must be paid in cash or "facilities furnished" and not in scrip, tokens, or anything else that is not readily convertible into money, at face value. The Wage-Hour Administrator treats any kickbacks that reduce the employee's wages below the hourly minimum as illegal.

Under the Act, employers are entitled to deduct from an employee's wages the "reasonable cost of fair value (not retail value) of meals, lodgings, and other facilities" provided to employees, provided the employer satisfies the conditions listed below. The Wage-Hour Division has defined "other facilities" used in Section 3(m) of the Act as being "like board or lodging," such as:

- Meals furnished at company restaurants or cafeterias;
- Housing furnished for dwelling purposes;
- General merchandise furnished by company stores and commissaries;
- Fuel;
- Electricity and other utilities for the employee's noncommercial use; and
- Transportation for the employee between home and work, where the travel time is noncompensable under the Act, and the transportation is not an incident of and necessary to the employment.

Such facilities may be considered wages paid to the employee only if they are customarily furnished by the employer. Employee discounts at retail establishments may not be considered part of the wage, since these discounts simply accommodate employees by reducing the prices of purchases they make. (WH AdminOp, Oct. 5, 1961)

In order for the employer to deduct the reasonable cost or fair value of meals, lodging, and other facilities from employees' minimum wages, the employer has the burden of establishing that:

- The facilities were furnished for the employees' benefit;
- The employees were told that the value was being deducted from their wages;
- The facilities were of a kind customarily furnished by the employer; and
- The employees accepted the facilities voluntarily.

Reasonable cost to the employer may not include any profit to any other "affiliated persons" such as:

- Spouse, child, parent, or other close relative of the employer;

- Partner, officer, or employee in the employer's organization;
- Parent, subsidiary, or other closely connected operation of the organization; and
- An agent of the employer's organization.

An employer may make other deductions from minimum wages, such as taxes, uniform cleaning, credit union loans, payroll savings plans, insurance premiums, and voluntary contributions to church, charitable, or other institutions. Illegal deductions include those for meal periods, breakage of merchandise, cash register shortages, and theft losses. However, where there is a debt that the employee owes the employer, a deduction to remove this indebtedness will be allowed, but only if the deduction does not reduce the employee's wages below the minimum wage rate. (*Brennan v. Veterans Cleaning Serv.*) (State minimum wage requirements appear in Appendix E.)

Although minimum wage violations generally arise as a result of an employer's failure to pay the requisite amount, at least one large employer ran afoul of the FLSA by failing to "pay" pursuant to the Act. California state officials, operating under a budget impasse that precluded the state from paying paychecks, issued paychecks 14 to 15 days late. This delay was found to constitute a violation of the FLSA's minimum wage provisions, since "unpaid minimum wages" occurred when the regular payday passed without employees receiving pay. (*Biggs v. Wilson*)

During a subsequent budget impasse, California state officials paid state employees with "registered warrants" to avoid the minimum wage violation involved in the prior budget impasse. But because the registered warrants are not payable on demand, and thus have limited negotiability, they did not constitute "cash or its equivalent" and the payments violated the FLSA. (*Parr v. California*)

OVERTIME

The FLSA requires the payment of overtime at a rate of one-and-one-half times (or time-and-a-half) the employee's regular rate of pay for all hours worked in excess of 40 per week. The Act does not establish a daily maximum hours limit, after which overtime would be required. Overtime need be paid over to the employee only on the regular payday for the workweeks in question. (Appendix F sets for the Wage-Hour Division's explanation of how to calculate overtime via its coefficient table.)

The question occasionally arises whether the employer authorized the employee to work the overtime for which he seeks compensation. The Act authorizes overtime if the employer "suffered or permitted" the employee to work the overtime hours. If the employer knew the employee was working the additional hours or if the overtime appeared on the payroll records, the employer will be presumed to have suffered or permitted the employee to perform the overtime work. If the circumstances indicate that the employer knew or should have known that the employee was working overtime for the employer's benefit, then the employer may be liable for those hours. (For a detailed discussion of compensable time, see "Hours of Work" earlier in this chapter.)

Since overtime is calculated based on the employee's regular rate of pay, it often becomes crucial to determine that regular rate. Items usually included in this rate are:

- Wages, salary, commission, or piece rate;
- Incentive bonuses;
- Shift premiums;
- Cost-of-living allowances;
- Premiums for hazardous duty or "dirty" work; and
- Other payments that are regarded by the employee as part of his regular compensation.

Types of compensation usually excluded from overtime, as not being part of the regular rate of pay, include:

- Premium pay under union contracts for work on Saturdays, Sundays, and holidays;
- Pay for time not worked, for example, vacations, sick leave, and holidays;
- Contributions to a pension or insurance plan;

- Outright gifts;
- Bonuses that are completely discretionary with the employer;
- Distributions from a profit-sharing plan that meets the Wage-Hour Administrator's regulations;
- Contributions to a bona fide thrift or savings plan that meet the Wage-Hour Administrator's regulations; and
- Longevity pay directly related to years of service, since this is considered to be a "gift." (*Moreau v. Klevenhagen*)

The FLSA requires that the "regular rate of pay" be more than one-and-one-half times the applicable minimum wage. An employer that paid its banquet waiters at least $14 per hour (consisting of an hourly wage plus a percentage of the service charge applied to banquet bills) was found to have complied with the Act. (*Mechmet v. Four Seasons Hotels*)

On the other hand, a premium payment to employees for evening and night shift work was not, in all cases, one-and-one-half times the employee's regular rate and, as a result, could not be excluded from the regular rate for purposes of calculating required overtime pay. (*Brock v. Wilamowsky*)

Where firefighters' salaries provided compensation for all hours worked, the employer calculated the regular rate by dividing the salaries only by the firefighters' straight-time hours. The firefighters challenged this practice, but the court ruled that "regular rate" excluded the *number* of hours of vacation and paid time off, but included *amounts* paid for time not worked. This formula greatly increased the firefighters' overtime pay. (*Aaron v. City of Wichita, Kan.*)

As mentioned earlier, the method of payment determines the overtime calculation. Where an employee performs more than one job for the employer, or is paid partially on an hourly rate and partially on a piece rate, or on a commission basis, the overtime rate will vary according to what the employee's regular rate is determined to be. (State maximum hours and overtime requirements appear in Appendix G.)

The FLSA Amendments of 1989 created a new exemption to the overtime provisions, not to exceed 10 hours per week, *in the aggregate,* for employees receiving "remedial education" that is:

- Provided to employees who lack a high school diploma or educational attainment at the eighth-grade level;
- Designed to provide reading and other basic skills at an eighth-grade level or below; and
- Does not include job-specific training.

Fluctuating Workweek

An important variation on the standard overtime situation involves the employee whose workweek fluctuates. In order for the employer to comply with the Act's overtime provisions where the employee works irregular hours that fluctuate from week to week, there must exist an agreement—preferably written—that provides at least for the FLSA minimum wage, for overtime at the statutory rate for all hours worked per week, and for a weekly wage guarantee for not more than 60 hours calculated according to the rate specified in the agreement.

These agreements, called Belo agreements, are named after the 1942 U.S. Supreme Court decision in *Walling v. A.H. Belo Corp.* Belo agreements require two essential elements:

- Neither the employer nor the employee can anticipate or control with any certainty the number of hours worked from one week to the next; *and*
- The employee's workweek must fluctuate both *above and below* the FLSA overtime limit of 40 hours per week.

The failure of an employee's workweek to dip below the 40-hour mark will constitute a failure to meet the "irregular hours" requirement of the Belo plan. (*Donovan v. Tierra Vista*)

The Belo agreements allow employers to control labor costs and limit overtime expenses, while guaranteeing the employee a fixed weekly pay regardless of the irregular hours worked. Where the agreement fails to meet the Belo requirements, the employer will be required to pay overtime based on fixed pay for fluctuating hours.

An employee whose hours fluctuated from week to week, but never less than 40 hours per week, received overtime at a fixed rate for all hours worked plus one-half his hourly rate for all hours over 40. The employer relied on an FLSA regulation that authorizes an employer and an employee to agree that overtime will be paid at 50 percent of the employee's "regular hourly rate." Although the Act requires that overtime equal 150 percent of an employee's "regular rate," the court held that the FLSA regulation was a permissible construction of the Act's overtime language. (*Condo v. Sysco Corp.*)

STATE AND LOCAL GOVERNMENT EMPLOYEES

Congress amended the FLSA to allow a proper "fit" of the Act over previously noncovered employees of state and local governments, following the U.S. Supreme Court's decision in *Garcia v. San Antonio Metropolitan Transit Authority*.

The Fair Labor Standards Act Amendments of 1985 allow for the payment of compensatory (comp) time off in lieu of cash payments for overtime work, and provide standards for determining payment of comp time upon termination of employment for state and local government employees. The amendments also provide for the treatment of volunteers and sporadic employment and substitute employment in a public agency, compensatory time limits, and protection against discrimination or adverse treatment in retaliation for an assertion that an employee is covered by the FLSA overtime provisions.

Special Rules For Exempt Employees

The FLSA exempts from certain pay requirements those individuals who qualify as "executive, administrative and professional" (EAP) employees. Under traditional (i.e., pre-*Garcia*) FLSA rules, a private sector employer who alleged that an individual was an EAP-exempt employee had to meet both a "duties test" (i.e., the employee performed EAP duties at least 80 percent of the workweek) and a "salary basis test" (i.e., the employee received a true *salary*, which did not fluctuate with the quantity or quality of work performed within the workweek). Many of the cases involving the EAP exemption involved disputes over whether the employee actually performed EAP duties for at least 80 percent of the workweek and whether the employee received a true salary, which was not subject to reduction or deduction based on quantity or quality of work.

Following *Garcia*, public employers soon realized that their EAP-exempt employees, like all public sector employees, were subject to having their pay reduced for absences when no leave was available. This practice, frequently embodied in state or local law, reflected the philosophy that an employee who is paid from the public treasury (i.e., taxpayers' money) should not be paid for time not worked. If an employee had exhausted his or her accrued leave and was absent, his or her pay would be deducted for the time not worked and not covered by leave.

This practice created problems for public employers with regard to their EAP-exempt employees, particularly if the EAP employee was absent for less than a full day. FLSA case law developed prior to *Garcia* had long prohibited the practice of deducting from an EAP employee's salary for a "partial day absence." If an employer made a deduction from an EAP-exempt employee's salary for a partial day absence that was not covered by accrued leave, the courts had ruled that the employee did not receive a true *salary*, and therefore, the employee was entitled to overtime because he or she was not an EAP-exempt employee under the FLSA.

However, public sector employers observed this practice of deducting from employees' salaries for partial day absences, on the theory that public funds should not be paid to employees for time not worked and not covered by leave. Theoretically, this meant that no public employee received a true salary (because all employees were subject to having their pay deducted for partial day absences), and therefore, no public employee was exempt from the FLSA.

From 1987 to 1992, several courts in various parts of the United States struggled with the inability of the FLSA private sector rules to "fit" properly over the newly covered public sector employers and employees. (*Abshire v. Kern County, Cal.; Alex v. California; Hilbert v. District of Columbia; Thomas v. Fairfax*

County, Va.) In 1992, the U.S. Department of Labor promulgated new regulations that allow public employers to follow a practice of deducting from EAP employees' salaries for partial day absences, without losing the exemption, where:

- The employee is paid "according to a pay system established by statute, ordinance, or regulation, or by a policy or practice established pursuant to principles of public accountability";
- The employee accrues personal leave and sick leave under the system, which also requires the employee's pay to be reduced or the employee to be placed on leave without pay for absences of less than one day due to personal reasons or illness or injury; and
- The employee does not use leave because (*a*) permission for leave was not sought or was denied; (*b*) accrued leave has been exhausted; or (*c*) the employee elected to take unpaid leave.

The regulation also provides that deductions from pay due to a budget-required furlough will not affect the employee's salaried status, except in the week in which the furlough occurs. The regulation has prospective effect only. (See Appendix K, "Salary Basis Test for Public Sector Exempt Employees," for the contents of the regulation.)

The amendments treat differently accrual of comp time by public safety, emergency, and seasonal personnel, and accrual by all other public employees. They also provide special rules for firefighters and police personnel concerning tour-of-duty regulations.

In *Garcia*, the Supreme Court rejected a claim that the Tenth Amendment to the U.S. Constitution precluded the federal government from extending the FLSA to the states. More recently, states have challenged FLSA coverage by raising the Eleventh Amendment's grant of immunity. In *AFSCME v. New Mexico Corrections Dep't*, a federal district court ruled that the Eleventh Amendment barred the state employee's FLSA suit against the state employer. (But see *Gilbreath v. Cutter Biological, Inc.; Brinkman v. Department of Corrections*)

Finally, an important difference exists between overtime pay practices in the federal government and all other overtime pay practices—the "good-faith" defense. Specifically, the FLSA provides that an employer who violates the Act's overtime provisions may seek to have the liability reduced by pleading that it relied in "good faith" on a "written administrative regulation, order, ruling, approval, or interpretation" of the Department of Labor's Wage-Hour Administrator. However, since the federal government operates under regulations promulgated by the Office of Personnel Management, rather than the Wage-Hour Administrator, one court has ruled that the good-faith defense is not applicable to the federal government. (*Berg v. Newman*) For more information on the good-faith defense, see Chapter 3 under that heading.

Comp Time Limits

Comp time may be paid in lieu of overtime, but it must be computed on the basis of time-and-one-half for each overtime hour worked.

Public safety, emergency, and seasonal employees may earn up to 480 hours of comp time before cash payments are required; under the time-and-one-half measure, this means that these employees can only work 320 actual overtime hours before becoming eligible for cash payments. All other state and local workers may accrue up to 240 comp time hours, or 160 overtime hours actually worked. Volunteers to state and local governments who receive no compensation or varying forms of compensation (e.g., expense reimbursements or a "nominal fee") are not considered employees under the Act. The hours in which public employees perform occasional or sporadic part-time work that is different from their regular assignments will not count toward overtime calculations.

Section 7(o) of the FLSA requires a government employer to enter into a comp-time agreement prior to electing comp time for its employees. A federal district court was presented with the "difficult question": when a public agency or political subdivision of a state does not have a collective bargaining agreement, memorandum of understanding, or any other agreement between itself and its employees' designated representative regarding compensation for the employees' overtime work, does Section 7(o) of the Act *compel* the public agency to compensate such employees monetarily, rather than with time off, for the overtime hours worked?

Responding in the affirmative, the court observed that the city determined, "in its sole discretion," which employees would receive comp time and which would receive wages. In addition, the court rejected the city's sole defense that state law bars the type of agreement contemplated under Section 7(o) as being without merit. (*Wilson v. City of Charlotte*)

According to the U.S. Court of Appeals for the Tenth Circuit, if the employees are represented, the following rules apply:

- The employer may not use agreements it obtained from employees to pay comp time instead of wages, even where it has a history of paying comp time;
- The employer may not withhold recognition of the employees' representative, where they have designated this representative in a letter and petition to the employer;
- The employer may not rely on the Tenth Amendment to the U.S. Constitution to refuse to bargain with employees' designated representative, since Section 7(o) of FLSA is constitutional; and
- The employer may only use a comp-time agreement obtained through the representative. (*Firefighters (IAFF) Local 2203 v. West Adams County*)

Where no agreement has been reached, the courts are divided concerning what actions the government employer may take. One court ruled that the employer may negotiate directly with the individual employees. (*Wilson v. Charlotte*) Another court ruled that the employees' collective designation of a representative precludes individual agreements. (*International Ass'n of Firefighters, Local 2203 v. West Adams County Fire Dist.*) There is more agreement for the proposition that state or local law must provide some formal mechanism for recognizing the employees' designation of a representative. (*Wilson v. Charlotte*)

However, the U.S. Supreme Court ultimate resolved an apparent conflict between two FLSA provisions concerning compensatory time, where the employees had designated a representative for purposes of negotiating a compensatory-time agreement but state law prohibited the government agency from engaging in such bargaining. The Court determined that deputy sheriffs did not have a representative with *lawful authority* to negotiate for them, since state law prohibits the county from entering into an agreement with the deputies' union. Therefore, the county sheriff's department was not required to give its deputies the option of getting overtime in lieu of compensatory time, since the county's pay system constituted a valid agreement between the county and the individual deputies. (*Moreau v. Klevenhagen*).

Where state law prohibits a government employer from entering into agreements with employees' representative, Section 7(o) of the FLSA preempts this prohibition. (*Abbott v. Virginia Beach*)

Tour of Duty for Fire and Police Personnel

The FLSA allows state and local government employers to establish a longer work period than the normal seven-day week for purposes of computing overtime pay for law enforcement personnel and firefighters. One court has ruled that the law enforcement personnel of Native American tribes are exempt from these provisions, even though the Act is silent as to these individuals. (*Reich v. Great Lakes Indian Fish & Wildlife Comm'n*) Finally, the Act provides a complete exemption from overtime pay for police or firefighters employed by public agencies with fewer than five employees.

Under the special overtime rules, a public employer may establish a work period or "tour of duty" for its firefighters or police officers of up to 28 consecutive days. Overtime eligibility for firefighters begins once they work more than 212 hours during a 28-day work period (based on a 7.57-hour workday). Public employers may use a shorter tour of duty for firefighters and police officers, provided that the maximum hours are reduced proportionally. For example, firefighters on a 14-day tour would be eligible for overtime after 106 hours. Under these rules, the shortest permissible work period is seven days, during which a firefighter may work 53 hours and a police officer may work 43 hours (based on a 6.11-hour workday). (Appendix H reproduces the Overtime Compensation Rules for police officers and firefighters of state and local governments.)

A county did not violate the FLSA when its firefighters, who worked a 21-day work period, were paid pursuant to a plan that averaged payments of straight time and overtime with each bi-weekly paycheck, even though they did not earn specific amounts paid bi-weekly, where:

- The plan complied with the collective bargaining contract;
- Averaging of straight-time payments is permissible under the Act; and
- The overtime payments, which must be paid on the next regularly scheduled payday, were either paid during the work period and in advance of the time when they were payable, or were paid at the end of the work period. (*Mullins v. Howard County*)

Where the municipal employer had adopted a work period of no less than seven and no more than 28 days, the FLSA would not require overtime until 43 hours had been worked. However, the municipal employer had entered into a collective bargaining contract with the police union that required overtime pay after 40 hours of work. The court ruled that the employer's failure to pay overtime until 43 hours had been worked may have violated the union contract, and whether this practice violated the FLSA was an issue for the jury. The police officers' entitlement to overtime depended on whether the city had adopted a work period that would entitle the city to the special overtime provisions for police and firefighters. The court rejected the police officers' argument that the city had waived coverage of the special provisions for police and firefighters, on the ground that parties cannot contract out of the FLSA. (*Birdwell v. City of Gadsden, Ala.*)

Recent court cases have wrestled with the question whether paramedics fall within the FLSA "tour of duty" provisions for law enforcement and firefighters. In one case, the court ruled that ambulance work that was not directly connected to firefighting or police activities was not within the Act's "tour of duty" provisions. (*Littlefield v. Old Orchard Beach*) However, another court held that ambulance duties should be regarded as substantially related to police and firefighter activities, and only those ambulance activities that are completely unrelated to firefighting or law enforcement should be deemed outside the "tour of duty" provisions. (*Wouters v. Martin County, Fla.*; see also *Ball v. District of Columbia*)

RECORDKEEPING

The Act requires employers to maintain adequate records of all hours worked, all employees, the wages received, and other terms and conditions of employment. Where records were inadequate or nonexistent, courts have ruled that:

- Employers must "disprove" the evidence of hours worked by the employee; (*Skipper v. Superior Dairies, Inc.*)
- Employers may not claim that there is no evidence of the precise amount of time worked; (*Wirtz v. First State Abstract & Ins. Co.*)
- An employer's failure to rebut the employee's evidence based on employee testimony allows a court to establish the hours actually worked; (*Wirtz v. Durham Sandwich Co.*)
- An employee may establish by "just and reasonable inference" the amount of hours worked in the absence of employer records. (*Anderson v. Mt. Clemens Pottery Co.*; *Duchon v. Cajon Co.*)

An employer did not violate the overtime provisions when it refused to compensate an employee for five minutes of overtime work, according to a federal appeals court, since the employer had a policy of compensating overtime work only if it constituted at least six minutes per week. The appeals court held that nonpayment for the five-minute segment was a *de minimis* (i.e., trifling) violation. The amount of overtime for which the employee would not be paid accrued over a period of one year, the court noted, but did not constitute a substantial measure of his time and effort. (*Brandon v. United States*)

There is no required format for maintaining records, so long as the information is accurate and complete. Employers are advised to retain these records for six years, which is the general statute of limitations adopted by Congress in Title 28 of the U.S. Code (28 U.S.C. Sec. 241(a)). Although the Portal-to-Portal Pay Act establishes a three-year limitations period for willful violations, an administrative proceeding may reach back six years to the employer's records.

Finally, the Act requires the display in a prominent place of the FLSA poster that states the minimum wage, overtime, and equal pay requirements of the Act, and how an employee may pursue wages due and the exercise of other statutory rights. The Wage-Hour Division provides copies without charge.

CHILD LABOR

The employment of minors is regulated by the FLSA and by many state laws. Section 12 of the FLSA prohibits the use of "oppressive" child labor and bans the shipment of any such "hot goods" produced by such oppressive child labor. In addition, employers may be personally liable for child-labor violations and may face fines, levied on a daily basis, along with the corporation which may be fined daily for its violations. (*McLaughlin v. McGee Bros.*)

The Act also requires that if minors are employed, they must be above 18 years old in any "hazardous" occupation, as defined by the U.S. Department of Labor. In other cases, the minors must be above 14 or 16, depending on the type of employment and by whom employed. For example, the child-labor restrictions in the FLSA may apply to employees of small newspapers, railroads, or airlines, even though the employees in such establishments are exempt from the minimum wage and/or overtime requirements.

ENFORCEMENT

Congress provided that the Act would be enforced only through lawsuits, initiated either by the Secretary of Labor or by private individuals. The Act provides for the following actions:

- Suits by the Secretary of Labor to collect unpaid minimum wages and overtime pay due employees and an equal amount in liquidated damages;
- Suits by the Secretary for injunctions to restrain employers from violating the law. The 1961 amendments to the Act granted jurisdiction to the federal courts to order payment of back wages in such an injunction action, and as part of such an order, a federal court may enjoin the interstate shipment of goods produced by employees not paid in accordance with the Act's wage requirements (hot goods injunction);
- Suits by employees themselves to recover any back wages due them under the Act, an equal additional amount as liquidated damages, and attorneys' fees and court costs; and
- Criminal actions by the U.S. Department of Justice against "willful" violators of the Act. Conviction in such an action may lead to a fine or, in the case of a second offense, imprisonment.

The primary responsibility for enforcing and administering the FLSA rests with the Wage and Hour Division of the Labor Department. The Division makes inspections and investigations to determine compliance with the Act, issues rules, regulations, and interpretations, and makes determinations on requests for exemptions.

CIVIL MONEY PENALTIES

The 1989 amendments to the FLSA authorized the Wage and Hour Division to promulgate regulations to enforce the Act via "civil money penalties (CMPs)." The civil penalty regulations, which became effective in November 1992, permit the

Wage and Hour Division to seek penalties of up to $1,000 per violation for repeated and willful violations of the Act. Under the Division's policy, each individual employee can be treated as a separate violation. If an employer erred in computing overtime for 10 employees, the fine could be $10,000, regardless of the back-pay liability.

Since the implementation of this new policy, enforcement actions at the administrative level have resulted in fines for minor offenses averaging $10,000. According to one source, most fines are in the $10,000 to $40,000 range under the Division's enforcement formula. The CMPs may prove to be the Division's most potent tool for enforcing the Act. (See Appendix L for full text of the regulations.)

In addition, the FLSA requires the Secretary of Labor to conduct certain studies and reports and to present the results to Congress. These provisions require the Secretary to:

- Investigate whenever he has reason to believe that, in an industry subject to the Act, foreign competition has resulted or is likely to result in increased unemployment in the United States. Should the Secretary determine that increased unemployment has resulted or is likely to result, he then must make a full report of his findings and determinations to the President and to Congress;
- Conduct studies on the justifications or the lack thereof for each of the exemptions provided by Section 13(a) and (b) of the Act. The studies are to include an examination of the extent to which employees of "conglomerates" are subject to these exemptions and the economic effect of their inclusion in such exemptions;
- Study and report to Congress biennially on ways to prevent curtailment of employment opportunities for disadvantaged minorities, youth, and the elderly; and
- Report to Congress annually on the economic impact of the FLSA—the so-called (Section) "4(d)" reports.

Finally, employers may be liable for amounts found due as underpayments, plus an equal amount as liquidated damages, plus attorneys' fees and court costs. Employers who are found to have "willfully" violated the Act (with the knowledge that the Act was "in the picture") (*Coleman v. Jiffy June Farms*) may be fined up to $10,000, imprisoned up to six months, or both. Employers may also be liable for punitive damages in suits filed by the Secretary of Labor (*Martin v. American Int'l Knitters*) or suits filed by former employees. (*Travis v. Gary Community Mental Health Center*)

STATUTE OF LIMITATIONS

Under the FLSA, an aggrieved employee has two years from the date of the alleged violation to file an action. In civil rights and other litigation, a body of case law has developed as to when the right to file accrues. The courts have had to choose between the time when the employee receives notice of the adverse decision, or when the decision is implemented. Generally, the courts have held that the time when the employee receives notice is the time when his right to file an action accrues. (*Delaware State College v. Ricks*)

In the context of FLSA litigation this conflict of when the right to bring an action accrues has not been an area of contest. However, the prudent employee will file an action as soon as he or she learns of the alleged violation in order to preserve his or her rights.

Under the Portal-to-Portal Pay Act, the limitations period for filing an FLSA action is extended to three years if the employee can show that the employer engaged in a "willful" violation of the FLSA. It should be noted that such a finding will be persuasive, if not conclusive, as to any good-faith belief defense to the imposition of liquidated damages liability on the employer. (See Chapter 3 for further information on this subject.)

Finally, there is a general six-year limitations period enacted by Congress in 1966 under Title 28 of the U.S. Code (28 U.S.C. Sec. 241(a)) to an administrative action before a federal agency. In those cases where the Portal Act does not apply, the six-year period controls. (*Glenn Elec. Co. v. Donovan*)

LIQUIDATED DAMAGES

The Act provides that employers who violate the minimum wage and/or overtime provisions of the FLSA are liable for these wages, plus liquidated damages equal to the unpaid wages. Under the Act, the liquidated damages are mandatory; once the employer is found to have violated the Act's wage provisions, the employee stands to collect twice the amount of the unpaid wages. The employee may also collect costs and reasonable attorneys' fees. The employer's liability can therefore be quite extensive.

An employer was found liable for liquidated damages based on the facts that the employer:

- Failed to pay FLSA overtime;
- Violated the state minimum wage law;
- Failed to maintain adequate records of hours worked; and
- Showed "manifest" bad faith in failing to maintain records and pay statutorily required amounts. (*Caryk v. Coupe*)

The Portal Act provides that courts may use discretion in awarding liquidated damages, if the employer can show that it had a good-faith belief based on reasonable grounds that its conduct did not violate the Act. Under this good-faith belief defense, the court may reduce or deny entirely an award of liquidated damages that is otherwise mandatory under the FLSA. (For further discussion of this issue, see Chapter 3.)

3
PORTAL-TO-PORTAL PAY ACT

Congress passed the Portal-to-Portal Pay Act (Portal Act) in May 1947 as an amendment to several statutes. The Portal Act was created as a result of the U.S. Supreme Court's decision in *Anderson v. Mt. Clemens Pottery Co.* in which the Court examined a situation involving nonpayment for time employees spent walking to and from their workplaces within the employer's compound. Studies indicated that it took approximately 14 minutes for employees to enter the premises, punch in, walk to their respective worksites, put on uniforms, and begin working. The employer credited the employees for time worked in a manner that resulted in their being compensated for 56 minutes less *per day* than the time recorded by the time clocks.

The Supreme Court held that the time necessarily spent by the employees walking to work on the employer's premises, following the punching of the time clocks, was working time within the scope of the FLSA overtime provisions. The time employees spent pursuing "preliminary" activities after arriving at their places of work, such as putting on aprons and overalls, removing shirts, taping or greasing arms, putting on finger cots, preparing equipment for productive work, turning on switches for lights and machinery, opening windows, and assembling and sharpening tools, was also working time within the scope of the Act's overtime provisions.

The Court ruled that time spent by employees must be counted as work time under the FLSA whenever all of the following conditions are present:

- Physical or mental exertion by the employee (whether burdensome or not);
- Exertion controlled or required by the employer; and
- Exertion pursued necessarily and primarily for the benefit of the employer and its business.

These standards were first applied by the Court in cases involving underground travel time of iron and coal miners. (*Tennessee Coal, Iron & R.R. v. Muscoda Local 123; Jewell Ridge Coal Corp. v. Mine Workers Local 6167*) However, *Mt. Clemens Pottery* represented the first application of these criteria in a manufacturing environment. This prework activity, literally from the entry "portal" of the workplace, to the exit "portal" off the employer's premises at the end of the shift, became known as preliminary activity (and the courts now recognize its counterpart—postliminary activity) in issues involving compensable time under the FLSA.

PRELIMINARY AND POSTLIMINARY ACTIVITIES

The most common disputes over whether certain time is compensable involve activity that occurs before ("preliminary") or after ("postliminary") the employee's principal work activity. If such work is part of an employee's principal activity, then it is compensable. If such work is not, then it is usually found to be noncompensable. Such activities include:

- Walking, riding, or traveling to and from the actual place of performance of work;
- Checking in or out and waiting in line to do so;
- Changing clothes;
- Washing up, showering, or bathing; and
- Retrieving or returning tools of the trade.

These activities can be regarded as part of the principal activity or can be found to be incidental to that activity, depending on the facts of each case. For example, miners who must travel substantial distances underground before beginning work are more likely to be credited for such travel time than are individuals walking from the parking lot to the factory.

In *Mt. Clemens*, the Court also held that these preliminary activities must be included in overtime computations under these rules, unless such time is so inconsequential as to fall within the rule on trifles. Today this rule is known as the *de minimis* rule.

Once it has been shown that an employer has violated the FLSA, the employer is liable for damages for those violations. The damages can be augmented if the violations are "willful" (see "Willful Violations" later in this chapter), but at a minimum, the employer must compensate the employee for all unpaid minimum and overtime wages due. But what happens if the records are inaccurate or nonexistent? The Supreme Court in *Anderson v. Mt. Clemens* established the principle of a "reasonable inference"; that is, whatever may be reasonably inferred from the type of work practices that exist in the relevant industry will be held against the employer.

This "reasonable inference" standard was the basis for a federal appeals court's decision to affirm the imposition of damages liability under the Portal Act on an employer that violated wage and recordkeeping provisions of the FLSA. Although the damages were only an approximation, the appeals court reasoned, the employer failed to negate the reasonable inferences to be drawn from the Secretary of Labor's evidence concerning the extent of uncompensated work performed for the employer. (*McLaughlin v. Ho Fat Seto*)

The effect of the *Mt. Clemens* decision was explosive. In the months following the decision, the courts were flooded with what were called portal-pay suits, involving an estimated five billion dollars in back pay and liquidated damages. The impact was nationwide.

BASIC PURPOSE

Congress responded to *Mt. Clemens* by passing the Portal-to-Portal Pay Act, which affected not only the FLSA but also the Walsh-Healey Act and the Davis-Bacon Act. The basic objective of the Portal Act was to relieve employers from the unforeseen liabilities of the *Mt. Clemens* decision. The most significant aspects of the Portal Act's changes are:

- The Act banned future suits by employees to recover back pay for activities that take place before the start or after the completion of an employee's "principal activities," unless these preliminary or postliminary activities must be paid for under a contract, custom, or practice in the plant;
- Actions brought by unions or other representatives of employees on their behalf were prohibited. However, actions by employees on behalf of additional employees similarly situated were still permitted, provided each participant gave his consent in writing; and
- A two-year statute of limitations was established on all claims under the FLSA and the Walsh-Healey and Davis-Bacon acts. The limitations period is calculated back from the date the action is filed in court. This means that only violations occurring within two years (three years if the court finds willful violations) of the date the action is filed will be heard.

An action *accrues*, for purposes of the two-year limitations period, when the employee becomes or should become aware of the violation. Accrual of an action is determined so that a prospective calculation can be made, from the date the employee learns of the violation to two years forward from that time. For example, if a violation occurred in December 1984, then the employee must bring the action by December 1986 or he is "time-barred" by the two-year statute of limitations.

The limitations period theoretically protects the employer from having to defend against "stale" claims where the evidence and/or witnesses are no longer available for the employer's best defense. On the other hand, the accrual rule is intended to encourage aggrieved employees to bring timely claims.

Courts have readily accepted the theory of the "continuing violation," which consists of an employer's repeated violation of the Act for a period of time. Each new violation renews the accrual date, so that the two-year period begins to run from the date of the most recent violation.

WILLFUL VIOLATIONS

The Portal Act was amended in 1966 to provide that where a cause of action arises out of a willful violation of the FLSA, the action may be commenced within three years after the *accrual* of the cause, when the employee knew or should have known of the violation. This extension of the limitations period from two to three years also extends any back pay due by a significant degree (an additional year of unlawfully withheld wages), and also exposes the employer to substantially greater liquidated damages liability. An employer who has not engaged in any willful violation of the FLSA may face up to two years of back-pay liability. If the employer is found to have committed willful violations, the monetary liability is potentially three times the amount facing the nonwillful violator (three years of back pay plus an equal amount as liquidated damages equals six years of back pay).

Consequently, the determination of what is a willful violation has taken on additional importance to contesting parties, and to the courts that must attempt to formulate clear, predictable, and fair standards for determining when a willful violation has occurred.

The first important pronouncement of what was meant by the term "willful" in the context of the FLSA arose in the case of *Coleman v. Jiffy June Farms.* In this case, the Court of Appeals for the Fifth Circuit said that an employer willfully violates the FLSA where the employer "knew or suspected that his actions might violate the FLSA. Stated most simply . . . [D]id the employer know the FLSA was *in the picture*?" (Emphasis supplied.) This came to be known as the "in the picture" standard for determining willfulness.

In 1988, the Supreme Court rejected the "in the picture" standard, reasoning that this approach imposed liability even if the employer was merely negligent. Since employers are required by law to post notices about the applicability of the

FLSA, the Court observed, employers knew that the Act was "in the picture" in virtually every case in which FLSA violations were alleged. Under these circumstances, the Court concluded, every violation of the Act would lead to a finding of a willful violation because the Act was "in the picture" in every case. This was not what Congress intended by referring to "willful" violations, the Court declared. (*McLaughlin v. Richland Shoe Co.*)

Having rejected the "in the picture" standard, the Court had to establish what standard would be appropriate for determining whether a violation was "willful." The Court first acknowledged that the Portal Act's imposition of liquidated damages liability was intended to be punitive, in view of the congressional perception that willful violations are more culpable than negligent violations.

Turning to a decision it rendered under the Age Discrimination in Employment Act (*Trans World Airlines v. Thurston*), the Court examined its formulation of what constitutes a "willful" violation under the Age Discrimination in Employment Act (ADEA): a "willful" violation requires a showing that the employer "knew or showed reckless disregard" for whether its conduct was prohibited by the Act. This standard appeared workable, but the Court had a third standard to examine.

In *Laffey v. Northwest Airlines,* the U.S. Court of Appeals for the District of Columbia ruled that a violation of the FLSA is willful if the employer recognizes it might be covered by the Act and acts without reasonable basis for believing that it was complying with the Act. The Supreme Court reasoned, however, that this standard would permit a finding of willfulness based on mere negligence or on a good-faith but incorrect assumption about a pay plan. On that basis, it rejected this intermediate standard.

The only remaining standard—the *Thurston* "knew or showed reckless disregard" standard developed under the ADEA—was adopted by the Court for use in FLSA cases as well.

The 1966 amendments also removed the two-year time limit from injunction actions brought by the Secretary of Labor, unless the Secretary also seeks an order requiring payment of back wages. And there is no time limit on contempt proceedings for violation of an injunction issued in an earlier proceeding.

Finally, there are two generally applied limitations periods that also affect actions under the FLSA. There is a five-year limitations period on criminal actions brought by the federal government, and this period applies to criminal actions brought by the government under the FLSA.

There is also a general six-year limitations period for administrative proceedings and a general six-year period for lawsuits that were not affected by the Portal Act. (*Glenn Elec. Co. v. Donovan*)

OTHER PROVISIONS

The Portal Act amended the FLSA and the Walsh-Healey and Davis-Bacon acts in other significant ways. In addition to the limitations-period changes discussed above, which control all three statutes, the Portal Act also amended these laws in the areas of:

- Barring future suits for back pay for preliminary or postliminary activities, unless these activities are otherwise to be compensated at the worksite;
- Barring representative suits, except where the employees sue on behalf of themselves and other employees similarly situated. However, joining in such a suit requires the employee affirmatively to "opt-in" to the lawsuit, in writing;
- Establishing a good-faith defense to any liability under the Act, as to back pay and liquidated damages. The employer must plead and prove that it acted in good-faith reliance on and in conformity with a written administrative regulation, order, ruling, approval, interpretation, practice, or enforcement policy issued under the respective statute. Under an FLSA claim, the employer must point to a ruling of the Wage-Hour Administrator; under Davis-Bacon Act claims, the employer must refer to a ruling or order of the Secretary of Labor;

and under Walsh-Healey Act claims the Labor Secretary or any federal official designated by him in administering the Act may be the source of an order or ruling on which the good-faith defense may be based;
- Granting courts hearing FLSA actions discretion to deny or reduce liquidated damages if the employer acted in "good faith" and had "reasonable grounds" for believing that no violation of the Act was being committed; and
- Relieving employers of all retroactive liability that arose as a result of the Wage-Hour Division's definition of the term "area of production" within the meaning of the FLSA's agricultural processing exemptions.

Shortly after the Portal-to-Portal Pay Act was passed, the Wage-Hour Division issued a detailed Interpretative Bulletin setting out its interpretation of the Act. According to the Division, the Act's legislative history indicates that a strict construction of the statutory terms is warranted, and that the Act was not intended to modify the general policy of the FLSA as remedial legislation. The Portal Act in fact was intended to relieve employers in certain situations where liability was both unforeseen and catastrophic. The Bulletin counsels that the FLSA is to be liberally interpreted to foster the congressional policy of establishing fair labor standards, and that the FLSA exemptions are to be narrowly construed for the same reason.

GOOD-FAITH DEFENSE

Perhaps the most heavily litigated aspect of the Portal Act involves the good-faith defense contained in Sections 9 and 10 of the Act because a finding that the employer acted in good faith when it violated the FLSA precludes any determination that the violation was willful. A willful violation, as we have seen, entitles the prevailing plaintiff to an award of liquidated damages equal to the amount of the unpaid wages, and exposes the employer to an extended limitations period from two to three years. Of course, this exacerbates the employer's monetary liability for back wages from two years to potentially six years.

The good-faith defense provides the employer with a shorter limitations period for back-pay liability, and it grants the courts *discretion* to deny or reduce any liability for liquidated damages. However, the court must find that the employer's violation occurred in good faith, that it had reasonable grounds for believing that no violation was being committed.

The Act defines "good faith" as compliance with a written administrative regulation, order, ruling, approval, or interpretation, or any administrative practice or enforcement policy issued by the specified official administering the FLSA, the Walsh-Healey Act, or the Davis-Bacon Act. Such writing or practice will provide a complete defense to any claim of willful conduct under the language of the Act.

The good-faith defense protects government employers, as well as private sector employers, even though this provision of the Act was not changed when the FLSA was amended to apply to the federal government and the Civil Service Commission was vested with authority to oversee the government's compliance with the FLSA's overtime provisions. A federal district court has reasoned that Congress sought to provide federal employees with as much, but not more, protection than counterparts in the civilian economy enjoyed, and to deny government employers this defense would frustrate the purposes of the Act. (*Palardy v. Horner*)

It appears from a review of the case law decided under the Portal Act that the good-faith defense is most frequently contested when there is no written administrative regulation, order, ruling, or the like, and the employer has proffered some evidence that its actions were reasonably based. Such evidence could take the form of a written opinion from privately retained legal counsel in an unsettled area of law. The employer must show that it *received* such advice, and that it relied in good faith *on that advice*. A post hoc awareness of the existence of such a writing is insufficient to demonstrate that the employer in fact relied on that advice in selecting its course of action.

The Wage-Hour Division's Interpretative Bulletin discusses the good-faith defense in detail, and is the most thorough and reliable discussion of this aspect of the Portal Act available.

In construing this defense, the Division emphasizes that the employer's action must have been (*a*) in conformity with the ruling, administration opinion, order, and the like; (*b*) in reliance on the ruling; and (*c*) in good faith. An action may not be considered to have been "in conformity with" the administrative ruling or interpretation, unless it is in *strict* conformity with that determination, according to the Interpretative Bulletin. An erroneous belief by the employer that it acted in conformity with the ruling would not be sufficient to meet the good-faith defense prerequisites. Actual and substantial conformity is required.

Likewise, it is pointed out in the Bulletin, an employer's action may not be considered to have been "in reliance on" an interpretation or ruling unless the employer had actual knowledge of the ruling or interpretation at the time of the employment decision, and in fact, relied upon *that* ruling.

As to the final requirement, the Division's position is that good faith is not the actual state of mind of the employer, but an objective test as to whether the employer, in acting or omitting to act as it did, and in relying upon the regulation, order, ruling, and the like, acted as a "reasonably prudent man would have acted under the same circumstances." Part II of the Bulletin also defines the terms "regulation and order," "interpretation," "ruling," "approval," and "practice or enforcement policy."

Following the 1985 amendments to the FLSA, government employers were faced with a host of questions concerning employees whose status under the Act was unclear. Where these government employers acted in good faith, based on reasonable, objective evidence, they did not incur liquidated damages. For example, a city employer declined to pay overtime to its fire department employees on two grounds:

- The paramedics were classified as fire protection employees, and thus exempt under federal regulations (29 C.F.R. Section 553.215) from a 40-hour workweek; and

- The fire department employees were executive employees exempt from overtime under the "salary basis" test under the regulations (29 C.F.R. Section 541.1(f)).

Declining to impose liquidated damages in both cases, the federal district court ruled in the first dispute that there was no clear legal precedent advising the city that its conduct was manifestly condemned under law, the standards found in the regulations were ambiguous, and application of the regulations to the paramedics was a question for the jury. (*Bond v. City of Jackson*)

In the second case, the court ruled that the city acted in good faith and reasonably believed that it did not violate the Act. The court noted that the city earnestly sought to determine its obligations, and the city offered proof in court as to the *bona fides* of its efforts and of its belief. Finally, the fact that the court submitted the question whether these employees were managers or supervisors to the jury indicates that the city had a reasonable basis for its belief. (*Wright v. City of Jackson*)

OPM REGULATIONS

The FLSA has covered private sector employees since 1938, and employees of the federal government since 1974. The Department of Labor (DOL) is responsible for promulgating and enforcing FLSA regulations over private sector employees (and following *Garcia*, for state and local government employees). The Office of Personnel Management (OPM) is responsible for promulgating and enforcing FLSA regulations over federal government employees. Following the *Garcia v. San Antonio Metropolitan Area Transit Authority* decision in 1985, this two-track system of regulatory enforcement occasionally has led to confusion, FLSA violations, and court challenges in wage-hour enforcement. This activity has been most evident in the area of liability for violations (i.e., the penalties employers face for violating the Act), particularly with reference to the OPM regulations under the FLSA.

Two court decisions illustrate important distinctions between the OPM regulations and the DOL regulations concerning the "good faith and reasonable basis" defense to FLSA violations. As noted earlier, the FLSA provides that an employer who violates the Act's overtime provisions may seek to have the liability reduced by pleading that it relied in "good faith" on a "written administrative regulation, order, ruling, approval, or interpretation" of DOL's Wage-Hour Administrator.

In the first case, civilian electronic technicians employed by the U.S. Air Force successfully challenged the Air Force's determination that the technicians were FLSA-exempt employees. However, the district court, which ruled for the technicians, also declared that the Portal Act's good-faith defense shielded the Air Force from overtime liability. On appeal, the U.S. Circuit Court observed that when Congress extended the FLSA to federal employees in 1974, it did not amend the Portal Act to provide a good-faith defense to the federal government for relying on OPM regulations. The appeals court ruled that the good-faith defense is only applicable in reliance on Wage-Hour Administrator guidance, and therefore, is not applicable to the federal government. (*Berg v. Newman*)

In the second case, another court examined a municipality's good-faith actions to resolve questions and the "reasonableness" of that city's claimed "reasonable basis" for acting in a particular manner. City officials attended seminars and conferences, sought and received DOL guidance, and organized a multi-agency "FLSA Working Group" to ascertain the exempt status of the employees in question. The city ultimately concluded that the employees were exempt based on language in the OPM regulations.

The court noted that the city made substantial good-faith efforts to determine whether the employees in question were FLSA exempt. The court found, however, that the city's reliance on OPM regulations was not "reasonable," since the regulations governed *federal* workers and the city should have relied on DOL regulations governing state and local government employees. The court concluded that the city had not met the "reasonable basis" requirement of the good-faith defense. (*Westfall v. District of Columbia;* see also *Martin v. Albrecht*)

4
EQUAL PAY ACT

On June 10, 1963, President John F. Kennedy signed the Equal Pay Act, which was designed to eliminate wage differentials based on sex. The Equal Pay Act (EPA) amended Section 6 of the Fair Labor Standards Act (FLSA) and shares the FLSA's minimum-wage coverage standards, with certain exceptions.

In 1977, Congress passed the Reorganization Act of 1977, authorizing President Jimmy Carter to "reorganize" and streamline certain federal government agencies. Under Reorganization Plan No. 1 of 1978, the Equal Employment Opportunity Commission (EEOC) was given authority, previously vested in the Department of Labor, to enforce the EPA and the Age Discrimination in Employment Act (ADEA). Executive Order 12144 (1979) implemented the transfer of authority. (See Appendix I for a directory of EEOC offices.)

The EEOC adopted regulations established by its predecessor, the Labor Department's Wage-Hour Division, for recordkeeping under the EPA. While the Act was under the authority of the Wage-Hour Division, the Wage-Hour Administrator had issued numerous Administrative Opinions and an Interpretative Bulletin concerning agency policy toward enforcing the EPA.

Upon assuming responsibility for this new task, the EEOC stated that an employer who acted in good-faith reliance on and in conformity with any written interpretation by the

Wage-Hour Administrator may establish a good-faith defense to liquidated damages liability under the EPA, in line with Section 10 of the Portal-to-Portal Pay Act (Portal Act), as it modifies the FLSA. The Commission cautioned, however, that an employer could not establish a good-faith defense where it relied on any interpretation contained in the regulations promulgated under the EPA that had been rejected by the courts.

MAJOR PROVISIONS

The EPA, incorporated into the FLSA, requires that male and female workers receive equal pay for work requiring equal skill, effort, and responsibility, and performed under similar working conditions. The Act's coverage is essentially the same as that of the minimum-wage provisions of the FLSA. An employer covered by the FLSA's minimum-wage provisions is most likely to be covered by the EPA. However, the EPA does not share the FLSA's exemption from coverage for certain categories of employees, such as executive, administrative, and professional employees and outside salesmen. These categories are covered by the EPA. The EPA provides specific exemptions from liability where wage differentials are:

- Based on any factor other than sex;
- Paid pursuant to a bona fide seniority system;
- Paid pursuant to a bona fide merit system; and
- Paid pursuant to a system that measures earnings by quantity or quality of production.

In equalizing past wage disparity based on sex, an employer may not lower the wages of the higher-paid worker to those of the lower-paid worker. In attempting to cure a pay disparity between a female temporary custodian who received less than male temporary custodians, a school district violated the Act when it lowered the male rate to the female's rate. (*EEOC v. Romero Community Schools*) As with the FLSA, unpaid wages may expose an employer to liquidated damages for willful violations, and to attorneys' fees and costs.

In applying the test of "equal pay for work requiring equal skill, effort, and responsibility, performed under similar working conditions," the courts have discerned a number of crucial questions that must be answered. The litigants must present the question of which jobs are properly to be compared ("comparators"), when equal salaries may not constitute equal "pay," and whether equal work is being performed under "similar" working conditions, among others. The plethora of variables makes this area of wage-hour law particularly fertile.

For example, a federal appeals court, affirming the district court, has ruled that a female former college professor was not assigned a heavier instructional workload than male professors. The female professor alleged that the heavier workload precluded her from coaching extramural activities, but the appeals court observed that she attempted to compare herself with five male "comparators" who were primarily assigned administrative duties. (*Berry v. Board of Supervisors, LSU*)

A male production machinist did not establish a prima facie case based on his claim that the employer improperly paid him less than it paid comparable female clerical workers whose jobs allegedly involved less skill, effort, and responsibility. The appeals court ruled that the Equal Pay Act only prohibits employers from paying employees less for "equal work." (*Beavers v. American Cast Iron Pipe Co.*)

Wage comparisons are made only between wages paid to employees of the opposite sex within the same establishment, rather than between members of the same sex, or between employees within different establishments. The EPA meaning of establishment follows the FLSA definition: a "distinct physical place of business" and not "any entire business or enterprise" that might encompass separate places of business. (29 C.F.R. Sec. 1620.9) However, in determining an employer's obligations under the EPA, employer and establishment are not synonymous terms. An employer may have more than one establishment in which it employs workers within the meaning of the Act. In such cases, the legislative history makes clear that there shall be no comparison between wages paid to employees in different establishments. (20 C.F.R. Sec. 1620.7)

The courts and the EEOC have attempted to provide definitive answers to the meaning of equal "pay" (i.e., "wages"), equal "work," equal "skill," equal "effort and responsibility," and the effect of additional duties on this evaluation. The Wage-Hour Administrator had previously called for a "practical" approach to the interpretation and application of the "similar working conditions" criterion. The regulations currently control this element of the equal pay standard. (29 C.F.R. Sec. 1620.13; *Maguire v. Trans World Airlines*)

ENFORCEMENT

Prior to the 1978 transfer of enforcement authority to the EEOC, the Commission solely administered equal pay issues under Title VII of the Civil Rights Act of 1964. Under Title VII, the Commission is required to attempt informal methods of conciliation before resorting to litigation. Congress failed to specify in the Reorganization Act of 1977 whether the same philosophy of conciliation-before-litigation applied to EPA enforcement.

A federal district court decided in 1982 that the Commission was indeed required to engage in good-faith conciliation efforts before it could bring an action under the EPA. (*EEOC v. Home of Economy, Inc.*) Imposing the conciliation requirement fulfills the congressional intent embodied in the Reorganization Act of 1977 that the EEOC's enforcement functions "should not be limited" to the functions related to equal pay administration previously vested in the Secretary of Labor, the Wage-Hour Administrator, and the Civil Service Commission (currently the Office of Personnel Management). The court reasoned that the Commission should act as a conciliator before it acts as a litigator under the EPA, in conformity with its conduct under Title VII.

Arbitration

Can an employment agreement's arbitration provision bar a former employee's lawsuit alleging that the employer violated the EPA? A female former stock broker filed an EPA action

Equal Pay Act

following her layoff and the employer argued that the broker signed an employment agreement containing an arbitration clause. A federal district court stayed the lawsuit, pending arbitration, in view of her failure to show that Congress intended to bar arbitrators from hearing such claims.

The U.S. Court of Appeals for the Second Circuit dismissed the broker's appeal, on the ground that the party who has been compelled to arbitrate can argue that the arbitral forum was the incorrect one when the arbitration award is before a federal court for enforcement. Therefore, according to the appeals court, the decision as to the correct forum can be reviewed and upholding the lower court's stay was proper. (*Steele v. L.F. Rothschild & Co.*)

COVERAGE

Employees

As with the FLSA, the EPA covers employees engaged in interstate commerce, employees who participate in the distribution of goods that move through channels of commerce, and employees who directly aid or facilitate the operation of instrumentalities of commerce. This last group includes such instrumentalities as railroads, highways, waterways, and airports.

The Act also applies to employees engaged in the production of goods for interstate commerce, such as:

- Employees producing, manufacturing, mining, handling, transporting, or in any other manner working on goods shipped in commerce; and
- Employees engaged in any "closely related process or occupation directly essential" to the production of such goods.

The "closely related" and "directly essential" language was inserted in the 1949 amendments to the FLSA to narrow the coverage of "fringe" production workers. Certain fringe workers are still covered under the FLSA. (For a more detailed discussion on this subject, see Chapter 2 under Fringe Employees.)

Although the EPA relies on the FLSA case law for coverage principles, there are significant differences. For example, the white-collar exemption under the FLSA for professional employees does not apply under the EPA. One federal court stated that the professional employees of a state university medical school are covered by the EPA, despite the FLSA exemption, because Title IX of the Education Amendments of 1972 makes the FLSA exemption inapplicable to equal pay claims. (*Friedman v. Weiner*)

Employers

An employer under the EPA is defined as "any person acting directly or indirectly in the interest of an employer in relation to an employee and includes a public agency." The Act specifically excludes "any labor organization (other than when acting as an employer), or any one acting in the capacity of officer or agent of such labor organization."

Subsequent to the passage of the EPA, the U.S. Supreme Court ruled in *National League of Cities v. Usery* that Congress lacked authority under the Commerce Clause to extend coverage of the FLSA to state and local governments. *National League of Cities* was decided in 1976, and following this decision, numerous circuit courts held that this decision did not affect Congress' extension of the EPA to a "public agency." (*Usery v. Dallas Indep. School Dist.; Usery v. John J. Kane Hosp.*)

In 1985, the U.S. Supreme Court ruled in *Garcia v. San Antonio Metropolitan Transit Authority* that the FLSA in fact did extend to state and local governments without violating the Tenth Amendment to the Constitution's protection of state sovereignty. This decision created a consistent, cohesive federal statutory scheme of wage-hour regulations over all sectors; federal, state, local, and private sector employers.

Under FLSA case law, employers are covered under two concepts; the enterprise coverage theory, and the establishment standard. Although these concepts were alluded to earlier in this chapter, they are discussed in detail below.

"Enterprise" Coverage

Under the 1961 FLSA amendments, Congress specifically acknowledged the necessity of the enterprise concept for FLSA coverage to reach subsidiary branches of an employer's operations. In the absence of the enterprise concept, these branches might otherwise be exempt from FLSA coverage, either based on the minimum-employee test or the dollar-volume standard. The Act extends coverage to employees, not specifically exempted otherwise, who are employed by certain enterprises engaged in interstate commerce or in the production of goods for commerce. The enterprise must:

- Have two or more employees engaged in interstate commerce or in the production of goods for commerce, including handling, selling, or otherwise working on goods that have moved in or were produced for commerce by any person; and
- Meet the appropriate dollar-volume test specified for the five types of enterprises and establishments falling under the enterprise test for coverage. Currently, the minimum dollar-volume test is $362,500 per annum for retail and service establishments not covered by the FLSA prior to December 31, 1981. There is a general $250,000 dollar-volume test for enterprises engaged in the laundry or drycleaning business, construction or reconstruction, the operation of hospitals, institutions or schools, or for public agencies. The dollar-volume test has been "grandfathered" with each revision in the minimum amount established, so that companies covered under a lower limit will not be deemed exempt under a higher limit.

"Establishment" Coverage

Prior to 1974, the FLSA covered certain retail or service stores in a chain based on an establishment test for coverage. The 1974 FLSA amendments phased out the establishment test incrementally, so that today, retail and service establishments are subject only to the general $362,500 dollar-volume test for businesses.

The establishment concept still applies, however, in EPA enforcement. The Act specifically prohibits discrimination on the basis of sex between employees "within any establishment in which such employees are employed." The employee bringing an EPA action has the burden to show that the allegedly unlawful wage disparity exists between employees within the same establishment. A federal district court illustrated the parameters of an establishment when it ruled that predominantly male pursers on an airline's international flights are not employed within the same establishment as the lower-paid and predominantly female cabin attendants on the airline's domestic flights. (*Maguire v. Trans World Airlines*)

EXCEPTIONS TO COVERAGE

As noted earlier, the EPA specifically excepts four categories of wage differentials, if they are:

- Based on a bona fide seniority system; or
- Based on a bona fide merit system; or
- Based on a system that measures earnings by quantity or quality of production; or
- Based on any factor other than sex.

According to the Wage-Hour Administrator, the first three bases are not limited to formal, written programs. If the criteria of a particular system or plan have been communicated to the employees, the employer may rely on that system or plan. However, a formal, written plan will serve both parties more effectively in an EPA dispute.

The fourth base, sex-based wage differentials, will be in violation of the Act according to the Wage-Hour Administrator. Regardless of the proffered basis for a wage differential, the Wage-Hour Division will examine the elements of any particular system or plan that allegedly discriminates on the basis of sex to determine whether the differential is sex-based or otherwise. As in FLSA enforcement, "titles" or labels will not determine the validity of a particular wage plan or system.

In examining the validity of wage differentials, courts have held:

- A hospital maintained an unlawful wage differential between janitors and maids, since all work was within the general cleaning function and there were only insubstantial or minor differences in the degree of effort, skill, or responsibility of the respective jobs; (*Brennan v. South Davis Community Hosp.*)
- An insurance company did not violate the Act by paying more to a male underwriter than to a female underwriter, since the differential was based on two different salary programs, neither of which had sex discrimination as its purpose or effect; (*EEOC v. Aetna Ins. Co.*) and
- An employer violated the Act when it paid a newly hired male employee $10,000 more than it paid a female worker, despite the employer's belief that it expected to gain greater profits from his work, since the employer failed to show that the male's work was actually more profitable. (*EEOC v. Hay Assocs.*)

Employers have come under scrutiny in the context of Equal Pay Act allegations for their job classification systems, "red circling" rates, merit-pay plans, and other wage and benefit programs.

The "factor other than sex" prong of the four statutory exceptions in the Act has provided a wide range of examples where employers have demonstrated that some sex-neutral element of the job warranted a wage differential. (The EPA creates this exception with the language "any other factor other than sex," the first "other" in the exception apparently resulting from a clerical error by the drafters.) Such sex-neutral elements as experience (*Trent v. Adria Laboratories, Inc.*), training programs (*Hodgson v. First Victoria Nat'l Bank*), and economic benefit to the employer (*Hodgson v. Anclote Manor Found.*) have been found to justify an employer's wage differential for certain work. On the other hand, the "market force" theory—that employers must pay more to acquire male workers in certain industries, and may pay less to female workers because this is what the "market will bear"—has been soundly rejected. (*Hodgson v. Brookhaven Gen. Hosp.*; *Brennan v. Victoria Bank & Trust Co.*)

The "factor other than sex" exception continues to be a fertile area for development of EPA law. For example, this exception has been applied in the following cases:

- A state statute requiring veterans service officers to be wartime veterans can be a legitimate factor other than sex that could justify the payment of a higher salary by the state Department of Veterans Affairs to employees in the all-male job of veterans service officer than to employees in the all-female job of veterans service officer associate. The court found eminently reasonable the state's belief that wartime veterans will have a "special camaraderie" with veterans needing the Department's help, enabling them to open up to a veterans service officer, when they otherwise might not do so. (*Fallon v. Illinois*)
- An employer that was opening a restaurant and hiring employees on an accelerated basis articulated a legitimate nondiscriminatory reason for paying female employees less than male employees doing substantially the same work, where it offered evidence that the decision on starting salaries was based on the strength of the employment application, the showing at the personal interview, past experience, and whether the current employee had personal knowledge of the applicant's abilities. (*Ebert v. Lamar Truck Plaza*)
- An employer failed to prove that its payment of a higher salary to a male employee than to a female employee was based on a factor other than sex, given the pure subjectivity of the process by which the employer set their salaries, the lack of testimony from the supervisor explaining his evaluations of their work, and the fact that the woman's sales goals were set as high or higher than the male's goals. (*Keziah v. W.M. Brown & Son*)

- A gender-neutral job classification system may qualify as a "factor-other-than-sex" defense, but only if the employer shows that the system is based on legitimate, job-related differences in work responsibilities and qualifications. (*Aldrich v. Randolph Cent. School Dist.*)

With regard to fringe benefits, the Wage-Hour Administrator has stated that unequal insurance benefits provided for male and female employees is lawful, if the premiums paid or costs incurred by the employer are equal. Similarly, unequal premiums paid or costs incurred by the employer are lawful, if the benefits provided are equal. (WH AdminOp, Oct. 14, 1965)

Similarly, a university's tuition remission program for faculty members who have children in college must treat male and female faculty members equally. The Wage-Hour Division has approved such a plan for married couples who are both on the university's faculty, where each received a one-half tuition payment for each child. The Division reasoned that the failure to pay this category of faculty members full tuition for each child does not appear to have an adverse impact on either sex. (WH AdminOp, Feb. 6, 1978)

The Act bars unions from causing or attempting to cause an employer to discriminate against an employee in a manner that would violate the equal pay standard. The union can be held liable in damages for such conduct. (*Hodgson v. Sagner, Inc.; Hodgson v. Clothing & Textile Workers, Baltimore Regional Joint Bd.*)

However, an employer that was found to have violated the Act may not obtain contributions from the union to alleviate some of its back-pay liability, where the union that negotiated the discriminatory contract clauses was not sued by the aggrieved employees who sued the employer. (*Northwest Airlines v. Transport Workers*)

PENALTIES

As an amendment to the FLSA, the Equal Pay Act carries the same penalties for violations as FLSA violations: a two-year limitations period for nonwillful violations; a three-year limitations period plus liquidated damages for willful violations; and prejudgment interest and costs, where appropriate. (*Hill v. J.C. Penney Co.*)

Each issuance of a paycheck to a civilian employee of the U.S. Army, who was at a lower classification than her male counterpart, constituted a new discriminatory action for purposes of the limitations period. The court rejected the Army's contention that each paycheck should not be considered a discriminatory event because the employee's original classification fixed her pay, which her supervisors were powerless to change. (*Nealon v. Stone*)

REMEDIES

The Equal Pay Act provides the same range of legal and equitable remedies as are available under the FLSA: back pay, liquidated damages, attorneys' fees, court costs, front pay, and injunctive relief (including reinstatement). Usually, when an employee establishes that the employer violated the Act, the employee will be awarded the remedies he or she sought. However, evidence of employee misconduct that an employer acquires after it discharges an employee may affect the remedies to which the employee would otherwise be entitled.

After the employee had been discharged, the employer discovered that the former employee had lied on her application form regarding a drug conviction. The appeals court ruled that this "after-acquired" evidence disqualified the former employee from the prospective remedies of reinstatement and front pay. (*Wallace v. Dunn Constr. Co.*)

5

WALSH-HEALEY PUBLIC CONTRACTS ACT

The Walsh-Healey Public Contracts Act (WHA) predates the Fair Labor Standards Act of 1938 by two years. As originally designed, the WHA established employment standards for contractors furnishing or manufacturing materials, articles, or equipment for the U.S. government. In tandem with the National Recovery Act, the WHA was intended to move the country out of the depths of the Great Depression by directly aiding the common man by regulating the wage rates that had to be observed when doing business with the federal government.

Although the National Recovery Act was eventually ruled unconstitutional, the WHA is alive and well, and was amended by Congress via the Department of Defense Authorization Act of 1986, which repealed the WHA's eight-hour day limit after which overtime rates had been mandatory.

Overtime under the WHA must be paid at a rate of one-and-one-half times the employee's "basic" rate of pay, instead of the "regular rate" as under the FLSA. The Department of Labor, however, has taken the position that the terms "regular rate" and "basic rate" are synonymous.

In applying this rule, the Department has consistently followed court decisions construing overtime obligations under the FLSA in deciding questions relating to overtime pay under the WHA. Thus, the basic rate of pay on which overtime pay is calculated is ordinarily determined by dividing the employee's total weekly pay, excluding any "overtime premiums," by the total number of hours worked by the employee during that week. Under the WHA, overtime is calculated on a weekly rather than a daily basis.

In addition to regulating hours of work and wages for work performed under government contract, the Act addresses child labor, convict labor, and hazardous working conditions.

REQUIREMENTS

Under the WHA, all contractors who agree to undertake performance contracts for the federal government for the manufacturing or furnishing of materials, supplies, articles, and equipment in any amount exceeding $10,000 must stipulate that:

- All employees on the project with certain exceptions, will be paid not less than the prevailing minimum rate determined by the Secretary of Labor for similar work in the locality;
- No employee will be permitted to work in excess of 40 hours in any week without the payment of overtime at a rate of time-and-one-half the employee's regular rate of pay for all hours in excess of 40 per week;
- No male worker under 16 years of age or female worker under 18 years of age will be employed on the contract;
- No convict laborer will be employed on the contract; and
- No part of the contract will be performed under working conditions that are unsanitary, hazardous, or dangerous to the health and safety of the employees.

The Secretary of Labor is authorized to permit an increase in the maximum hours of labor specified in the contracts executed under the Act, provided he establishes a rate of pay for overtime compensation that is not less than one-and-one-half times the basic hourly rate of pay received by any affected employee. The Secretary is also authorized to establish prevailing wage rates on an industrywide basis.

As administered by the Department of Labor's Wage-Hour Division, the WHA also applies to employees of manufacturers and "regular dealers" supplying the federal government with material, supplies, articles, or equipment on a contract whose value exceeds $10,000. Since the Act covers manufacturing and other public contract statutes cover "servicing" and "construction" and "alteration" and "repair," the courts have had to distinguish between these performances.

A typical dispute may involve large-scale repair of an engine; the issue becomes: "When does extensive 'repair' constitute wholesale 'manufacture'?" The Davis-Bacon Act (DBA), with the Contract Work Hours and Safety Standards Act, applies to mechanics and laborers engaged in the construction, alteration, or repair of public buildings or public works under contract with the federal government. Similarly, the McNamara-O'Hara Service Contract Act (Service Contract Act) governs service contracts performed for the federal government, and requires employers to pay employees the wages and fringe benefits prevailing in the locality, but in no event will the employees receive less than the minimum wage set under the Fair Labor Standards Act.

With this complex statutory scheme in mind, it becomes clear that some acts may be "cheaper" than others for the contractor performing under a government contract. This situation creates the incentive to operate, and ultimately to litigate, the extent of coverage of one federal contract act over another.

Where the government contract exceeds the $10,000 minimum amount, the WHA requires all primary and most secondary contractors (subcontractors or "subs") to comply with the standards unless their contracts are specifically exempt from the Act. The WHA, and certain regulations, have exempted such contracts as "open-market" agreements: contracts for the sale of perishables and other specified agricultural products, contracts for transport by common carrier, contracts for public utilities, and service contracts and rental agreements. (Contract exemptions will be discussed later in this chapter.)

All employees who actually work on the materials supplied under the government contract are covered by the WHA, including those engaged in manufacturing, fabricating, assembling, handling, supervising, or shipping. Employees who perform any preparatory work or other work necessary for the performance of the contract are also covered. If the contractor fails to segregate the work performed on the government contract from noncontract work, the WHA deems all employees as employed on the government contract and covered under the Act. As with the FLSA, all executive, administrative, and professional employees are exempt. Additionally, the WHA exempts all office and custodial workers from coverage. (Employee exemptions will be discussed in detail later in this chapter.)

COVERED CONTRACTS

Section 1 of the Act governs coverage over contracts and uses such phrases as "manufacturing," "furnishing," "fabrication," and "production." Such terms are inherently inartful, and changing needs and technology may make yesterdays' "manufacturing" become tomorrow's "repair."

In a series of Wage-Hour Administrative Opinions, the Wage-Hour Division has interpreted these phrases in a way that the Act was found to cover contracts:

- For the "construction" of sled-targets and position buoys. The Administrator rejected a plea that the items were exempt because they were not "manufactured," since they were in fact "produced," "fabricated," and "furnished" to the government; (*In re Anderson & Cristofani*)
- For the reconditioning of tools. Where the work requires a complete or substantial rebuilding, it is regarded as "manufacturing"; (WH AdminOp, Oct. 22, 1941)
- For the erecting or installing of articles or equipment after delivery, such as the installation of generators requiring a prepared foundation; (WH AdminOp, 1941) and

- For the maintenance, servicing, and repair of government vehicles, since such a contract assumes that the contractor will provide a substantial amount of parts and supplies. (WH AdminOp, Oct. 7, 1964)

The Act also applies to the "construction, alteration, furnishing, or equipping of any naval vessel."

The Act specifies a dollar-amount of $10,000, and administrative practice has established several rules for applying this standard to individual contracts. For example, the stated price of the contract controls, even if prompt payment may reduce the amount due on the contract to less than the statutory minimum. Similarly, a postexecution reduction in contract price, even where both parties mutually agree on the reduction, will not remove the contract from the Act's coverage. (*United States v. Ozmer*)

If the contract price exceeds the statutory minimum, individual component parts of the contract and separate manufacturers are all covered, even if each component would sell for less than $10,000. Not surprisingly, where several contracts, each less than the statutory minimum, are awarded simultaneously by the government's acceptance of a single bid, then each contract is covered as if it met the statutory minimum. (WH AdminOp, May 3, 1957)

Contracts for indefinite amounts are covered, if they *may exceed* the $10,000 figure. When a contract's price is undetermined because of exigent circumstances, most commonly the "needs of the government," these open-ended contracts also fall under the Act. (*In re Norris, Inc.; In re Pelham's*) Additionally, purchase-notice agreements, also known as "supply" contracts, are covered.

COVERED CONTRACTORS

The Act covers a manufacturer whose contract with the government exceeds $10,000. The Wage-Hour Administrator has interpreted this phrase to encompass a person, corporation, partnership, or other, that owns, operates, or maintains a factory or establishment that produces on its premises the materials, supplies, articles, or equipment that is the basis for the contract. A prime contractor may be held liable for the violations of his subcontractor. (*United States v. Davison Fuel & Dock Co.*)

The Act provides that a contractor must be a "regular dealer" of the materials, supplies, articles, or equipment to be supplied by performance of the contract. However, the Act does not define "regular dealer," but delegates to the Labor Secretary the responsibility for promulgating regulations to implement this term. The regulations define "regular dealer" as a person who owns, operates, or maintains a store, warehouse, or other establishment in which the materials, supplies, articles, or equipment of the general character described by the specifications and required under the contract are bought, kept in stock, and sold to the public in the usual course of business.

The regulations further establish six criteria that must be met in order for a particular contractor to qualify as a "regular dealer" under the Act:

- The bidder must have an establishment or leased or assigned space in which it regularly maintains a stock of goods in which it claims to be a dealer;
- The stock maintained must be a true inventory from which sales are made (the requirement is not satisfied by a stock of sample or display goods);
- The goods stocked must be of the same general character as the goods to be supplied under the contract;
- Sales must be made regularly from stock on a recurring basis;
- Sales must be made regularly in the usual course of business to the public, i.e., to purchasers other than federal, state, or local government agencies (this requirement is not satisfied if the contractor merely seeks to sell to the public but has not yet made such sales); and
- The business must be an established and ongoing concern.

A sole proprietorship applied to the General Services Administration (GSA) to be the federal government's provider of air-inflated mattresses. The GSA noted that the sole proprietorship did not maintain an inventory of mattresses or a permanent space to keep potential inventory. A federal district court upheld agency findings that the sole proprietorship did not buy products, did not have space where stock was maintained (other than on a "demand" basis), did not maintain a true inventory of stock from which sales were made, and did not sell to purchasers other than federal, state, or local governments. The court concluded that the sole proprietorship did not qualify as a "regular dealer" under the Walsh-Healey Act regulations. (*Levine v. United States*)

The Act also applies to a "regular dealer" in commodities, and the dealer's participation in a contract may expose a manufacturer who is not directly on the contract to liability under the contract. (*In re Negri*)

However, a regular dealer who contracts to furnish goods to the government may not be held liable for the failure of his manufacturing supplier to comply with the Act's wage and overtime provisions. (*United States v. New England Coal & Coke Co.*)

On the other hand, a substitute manufacturer, or successor contractor, who subcontracts part of the work he is obligated to perform may not be found liable for the violations of the "sub-substitute" manufacturer. (*In re Lyon & Borah, Inc.*)

PERSONAL LIABILITY

Section 2 of the Act provides that liability shall extend to the "party responsible." This provision has been used to impose personal liability on employer/contractor officials who would otherwise escape liability. The test for determining when personal liability should attach is whether the official *controlled* and *managed* the company during the relevant time in which the contract was performed. Under this test, employer officials were found liable, even though they did not sign the government contract, where they owned a majority of the stock and exercised exclusive control and supervision over the affairs of the contractor. (*In re A-AN-E Mfg. Corp.*)

On the other hand, a personnel director was found not to be personally liable, since he was not an officer of the contractor, had no property interest in it, and did not determine labor policy or control or manage the contractor's affairs.

However, financial interest of corporate officers, standing alone, is insufficient to bring these individuals within the meaning of "party responsible," such that personal liability would attach. (*United States v. Hudgins-Dize Co.*)

EXEMPTIONS

After it has been ascertained that an employer meets the Act's criteria for coverage (e.g., type of contract, dollar amount), the employer may attempt to fall within any of a number of exemptions contained both in the Act and in the regulations promulgated under the Act. There are three avenues for avoiding the Act's provisions: (*a*) subcontractor or successor employer exemptions; (*b*) employee exemptions; and (*c*) contract exemptions.

The Act specifically exempts open-market contracts (contracts that authorize the work to be done at rates currently available on the open market); contracts for the purchase of perishables, including dairy, livestock, and nursery products; agricultural or farm products processed for first sale by the original producers; contracts by the Secretary of Agriculture for the purchase of agricultural products; contracts for transportation by common carriers under published tariffs; and contracts with common carriers subject to the Federal Communications Act of 1934.

Under the regulations, the list of exempt contracts includes contracts for the construction of public works; rental of real or personal property; public utilities; delivery of newspapers, magazines, or periodicals by the publisher to sales agents or publisher representatives; and exclusive services.

The Secretary of Labor is authorized to exempt any contract that may impair the federal government's ability to conduct business, following a determination to that effect by the head of the federal agency involved in the contract. This authorization was used during World War II, but has fallen into disuse in recent years. (For further information, consult Walsh-Healey Rulings and Interpretations No. 3, issued in 1955 and last amended in 1963.)

Most of the confusion/litigation in this exemption scheme has involved the exemptions for specified employee classifications and for specified contracts. These will be examined in detail.

Subcontractor/Successor Exemption

Generally, the Act does not apply to work performed by a manufacturer other than the original contractor, unless that work would *normally* have been performed by the contractor itself. Thus, subcontractors who actually fill part or all of the government contract are not covered by the Act if it is the "regular practice" in the industry for the prime contractor to purchase such goods rather than to manufacture them.

Where, however, a contractor subcontracts part of the work to another manufacturer, the producer of the commodities not manufactured by the original contractor is a "substitute manufacturer" who is considered fully covered by the Act. A prime contractor is liable for damages arising from violations committed by its substitute manufacturer.

Employee Exemptions

The Act covers *all* employees under a government contract, except office, supervisory, custodial, and maintenance workers who do any work in preparation for or that is necessary for performance of the contract. The Wage-Hour Division maintains an extensive list of workers who are not "directly working in production" but who are nevertheless covered by the Act. The line of demarcation appears to be whether the employee is doing *any work connected with* the manufacture, fabrication, assembling, handling, supervision, or shipment of materials, supplies, or equipment required under a government contract under the Act. If there is no work done in connection with such a contract, the employee most likely will not be covered by the Act. Employees performing commercial work on a contract who are separated from employees performing work on a government contract, for example, will be treated as exempt, provided the contractor's records keep such employees separate from the employees on the government contract.

The list of employees who are exempt by virtue of their not being directly involved in production under a government contract covered by the Act includes employees who only perform office work and whose work is not connected with the production of goods under the contract; custodial employees whose work is directed to the maintenance of the plant or facility and who are not involved in any work necessary for the fulfillment of the government contract; executive, administrative, and professional employees, as defined by the Wage Hour Administrator under FLSA enforcement (exempt only from Walsh-Healey overtime provisions); foremen and instructors who do not operate machinery, perform manual work, or handle materials involved in a government contract; chief inspectors who are compensated on a salary basis and have a high degree of responsibility and authority; experimental workers who are not connected with the fulfillment of a government contract; requisition clerks who do nothing but prepare material orders and route orders through the plant; marine workers, if they are "seamen" under the FLSA; and convict laborers. However, paroled, pardoned, or discharged criminals, or prisoners participating in a work-release program are not deemed convict laborers for the purposes of this exemption.

Contract Exemptions

Several types of government contracts are exempt from the wage, hour, and child-labor provisions of the Act:

- Contracts for the construction of public works, which are covered by the Davis-Bacon and Contract Work Hours acts and the Anti-Kickback Law (Copeland Act);
- Contracts for agricultural or farm products processed for first sale by the original producer;

- Contracts made by the Secretary of Agriculture for the purchase of commodities or the products thereof;
- Contracts for the purchase of such materials, supplies, articles, or equipment "as may usually be bought in the open market" (the so-called open-market exemption). This exemption is construed by the Public Contracts Administrator as applying only to such purchases as the government *usually makes* in the open market, including purchases without ads for bids and purchases that the procurement agency is authorized to buy in the open market;
- Contracts for the "carriage of freight or personnel by vessel, airplane, bus, truck, express, or railway line where published tariff rates are in effect";
- Contracts exclusively for *personal* services;
- Contracts for the rental of real or personal property;
- Contracts for perishables, including dairy, livestock, and nursery products;
- Contracts for public utility services;
- Contracts for the furnishing of service by radio, telephone, telegraph, or cable companies subject to the Federal Communications Act of 1934; and
- Contracts to sales agents or publisher representatives for the delivery of newspapers, magazines, or periodicals by the publisher itself.

The Act also contains an exemption for "stockpiling" of goods, where the contractor "customarily" maintains a stockpile of material that cannot be identified as to the time work was done on any item in the pile.

RECORDKEEPING

The Act requires the contractor to maintain complete payroll records for each employee working on the government contract. These records must comply with FLSA requirements, and for purposes of Walsh-Healey compliance, must also contain injury-frequency rates, a record of the sex of each employee, and the number that identifies the contract on which each employee works.

ENFORCEMENT

The Secretary of Labor is authorized to investigate and decide cases involving alleged violations of the Act. This authority has been delegated to the Wage-Hour Administrator for daily enforcement purposes. Employers are liable for any underpayment of base wages or overtime and a penalty of $10 for each day an underage minor is employed.

The Defense Contract Management Command (formerly Defense Contract Administration Services) is responsible for conducting compliance reviews, pre-award reviews and complaint investigations for covered federal contractors performing defense work. (See Appendix J for list of regional offices.)

Once a contract has been awarded, the government will issue a "Notice to Proceed" with contract performance. Not infrequently, contract awards are followed by protests from unsuccessful bidders, challenging the awards. The standard for determining whether to proceed with contract performance in the presence of a protest is whether the contracting agency has a rational basis to find "urgent and compelling circumstances" that warrant awarding the contract.

A small, disadvantaged business protested the award of contracts to supply natural gas to the federal government, arguing that a regulatory exemption from the WHA relevant to public utilities was applicable to the contract solicitations. Applying this standard, the Defense Fuel Supply Center (DFSC), under the aegis of the Defense Contract Administration Services, denied the disadvantaged business' request that the DFSC suspend the contracts, pending the outcome of the challenges. Under the Competition in Contracting Act (CCA), a federal district court noted that the applicable regulations require (*a*) automatic suspension of contract performance until contract challenges are resolved, and (*b*) exemption from the automatic suspension requirement if the agency can show "urgent and compelling circumstances which significantly affect the interests of the United States." Based on DFSC's certification that "urgent and compelling circumstances" existed, the court ruled against the disadvantaged business. (*Commercial Energies, Inc. v. Cheney*)

Serious and willful violations of the Act may subject a contractor to the blacklist penalty, which bars the receipt of a government contract by that contractor for a period of three years.

Back-pay claims under the WHA, like those under the FLSA, are governed by the Portal-to-Portal Pay Act, including limitations periods and liquidated damages liability. (See Chapter 3 for more on this issue.)

The WHA may apply to both the "manufacture" of equipment and the "installation" of equipment on the job site. Where more than an incidental amount of installation work is required, however, the Davis-Bacon Act (DBA) may enter the picture. Whether the WHA or DBA should govern such installation work will be determined by the Solicitor of Labor, who has issued "interpretative guidelines" in the past.

Similarly, if a contractor manufacturers goods under a government contract and the goods are shipped across state lines, the contractor will be subject both to the WHA and the FLSA. (WH AdminOp, Oct. 11, 1941) The Supreme Court rejected a contractor's claim that the two laws could not apply concurrently, finding that the two laws are not mutually exclusive. (*Powell v. U.S. Cartridge Co.*)

SAFETY AND HEALTH STANDARDS

The WHA was the first of the federal laws regulating wages and hours to contain a provision requiring compliance with safety and health standards for the protection of workers. The Act provides that contracts entered into by any agency of the federal government calling for the manufacture or furnishing of materials, supplies, or equipment in any amount exceeding $10,000 must contain a stipulation that no part of such contract will be performed in any plant, factory, building, or surroundings or under working conditions that are unsanitary, hazardous, or dangerous to the health and safety of the employees engaged on contract work.

Failure to maintain proper safety and health standards in the performance of a contract subject to the Act constitutes a breach of that contract. This may provide the basis for the cancellation of the contract and make the party or parties responsible subject to the Act's blacklist penalty. Blacklisted persons are ineligible to receive federal contracts for a period of three years from the date the Secretary of Labor determines that the violation occurred.

To assist contractors in complying with these safety and health requirements, the Secretary of Labor has established specific safety and health standards in the regulations. These regulations set the *minimum* standards that will be applied in the enforcement of the law to determine whether particular contracts are being performed in compliance with the WHA's safety and health standards.

The regulations apply to all types of industrial plants and deal with such subjects as building and machine guarding, fire prevention and protection, sanitation, first aid facilities, ventilation, personal protective equipment, and the like.

6

McNamara-O'Hara Service Contract Act

The McNamara-O'Hara Service Contract Act of 1965 (Service Contract Act or SCA) covers contracts with the federal government for the provision of services to the government. This differs from the Walsh-Healey Act, which covers contracts for the furnishing or manufacturing of goods, materials, and equipment to the federal government; and from the Davis-Bacon Act, which covers contracts for the provision of construction or supplies for construction of public buildings or public works.

Service employees generally include persons engaged in a recognized trade or craft or in a manual labor occupation. Such employees working under an SCA-covered contract must be paid the wages and fringe benefits prevailing in the locality, as determined by the Secretary of Labor. The Act allows the contractor to provide the service employee with any equivalent combination of fringe benefits or to make differential payments in cash.

The Act authorizes the Secretary of Labor to withhold accrued payments due on any contract to the extent necessary to pay covered workers the difference between wages and benefits required by the contract and those actually paid. Other sanctions against a noncomplying contractor include contract termination and debarment.

The Secretary of Labor is authorized to maintain a lawsuit against the contractor for any underpayments to SCA-covered employees. The Secretary is also authorized to determine if "unusual circumstances" exist to warrant a lesser penalty than the three-year blacklist penalty under the debarment provision of the Act. The courts have ruled that only the Secretary is authorized to bring an action under the Act, while individual employees are restricted to administrative proceedings. (*Oji v. PSC Environmental Mgmt.*; and *Cimpi v. Dole*)

COVERAGE

The SCA covers all contracts with the federal government exceeding $2,500 in amount, whose primary purpose is the providing of *services* to the government. SCA regulations (29 C.F.R. Part 4.6) require the Secretary of Labor to include in SCA contracts language incorporating the Act's labor standards provisions for all government contracts in excess of the statutory minimum. Failure to include verbatim language from the Act formed the basis for a contractor's claim that it was thus not subject to the Act's minimum-wage and fringe-benefit provisions. The claim was unsuccessful. (*National Electro-Coatings v. Brock*)

Covered Contracts

The Act applies to contracts the "principal purpose" of which is the furnishing of services to the United States through the use of service employees. Unless specified otherwise, any contract with the government that is not for construction or supplies is a contract for services, according to the Wage-Hour Administrator. In a series of Administrative Opinions, the Division has determined that the SCA covers contracts for:

- Equipment or vehicle rental, including the equipment or vehicle operator;
- Surveying;
- Mapping;
- Spraying operations;
- Cafeteria and dormitory services;

- Car-washing, wheel-packing, chassis lubrication, vehicle maintenance, and storage;
- Office-equipment repair;
- Landscaping and grounds maintenance;
- Laundry services for the Armed Services;
- Subsurface exploration, involving drilling for soil samples and rock cores;
- Mail transportation;
- Shipping and storing of household goods;
- Printing and duplicating services, but only if the principal object of the contract is for services and the furnishing of printed or duplicated matter is secondary to the contract's main purpose;
- Computer maintenance and watch repair;
- Fire protection services;
- Engineering, design, programming, and testing;
- Furnishing hotel accommodations to military personnel;
- Inspection and maintenance services;
- Veterans' convalescent care in nursing homes; and
- Garbage removal.

This is only a partial list of covered contracts under the current $2,500 threshold. Suffice to say that, with a low threshold, few contracts for services for the government will ever be lower than the $2,500 minimum.

Section 7 of the Act concerns exemptions from SCA coverage. Where the Act is silent, and in line with the Administrator's pronouncements, certain operations may be regarded as covered in the absence of specific exclusions. These operations include:

- Galvanizing of steel products;
- Design functions;
- Motion-picture production; and
- Preparing title certificates for real property transactions.

Section 7 of the Act provides a list of exemptions from SCA coverage. This list includes:

- Contracts for constructing or repairing public works or public buildings;

- Contracts covered by the Walsh-Healey Act;
- Contracts for the carriage of freight or personnel where published tariffs are in effect;
- Contracts for the furnishing of services by radio, telephone, telegraph, or cable companies;
- Contracts for public utility services;
- Contracts for employment where an individual or individuals are to provide direct services to a federal agency; and
- Contracts with the U.S. Postal Service for the operation of a postal contract station.

The Wage-Hour Division, in determining which contracts are covered under the Act, has also established which contracts are not covered. The Division's list of exempt contracts includes contracts for:

- Medical services at a hospital under a Medicare program;
- Renting parking spaces;
- Creating topographic maps;
- Renting motor vehicles;
- Managing, operating, and maintaining research centers and a job corps center for women;
- Relocating persons under an agreement with a local redevelopment agency under the Federal Urban Renewal Program, even though the federal government pays all the expenses of moving an occupant displaced by urban renewal; and
- Tree trimming, tree removing, and landscaping functions that are part of an urban renewal project.

In many of these instances, the Division has treated a contract as exempt if the contract is not "entered into by the United States" as a contracting party. (WH AdminOp, Apr. 20, 1966)

Covered Employees

Under the Act, service contractors are required to pay the wages and fringe benefits prevailing in the locality to all "service employees" engaged in contract performance, including guards, watchmen, and any person in a recognized craft or trade, in a skilled mechanical craft, or in unskilled, semiskilled, or skilled manual labor occupations. The Act extends to foremen and supervisors whose jobs primarily require trade, craft, or laboring experience.

In addition to those employees who actually perform the service required under the contract, the Act covers workers whose duties are "necessary" to contract performance. Such employees include office workers who do clerical work in connection with the contract, for example. (WH AdminOp, May 16, 1966) Additionally, an individual who meets the definition of a service employee under the Act is also covered, regardless of the relationship existing between the individual and the contracting entity.

In 1976, Congress amended the Act by including in Section 8(b) a complete definition of "service employee":

> The term "service employee" means any person engaged in the performance of a contract entered into by the United States and not exempted under section 7, whether negotiated or advertised, the principal purpose of which is to furnish services in the United States (other than any person employed in a bona fide executive, administrative or professional capacity, as those terms are defined in part 541 of title 29, Code of Federal Regulations, as of July 30, 1976 and any subsequent revision of those regulations); and shall include all such persons regardless of any contractual relationship that may be alleged to exist between a contractor or subcontractor and such persons.

The language was intended to be all-inclusive. It obviates a series of Administrative Opinions issued by the Division that interpreted a publication by the Civil Service Commission (now the Office of Personnel Management, OPM) entitled "Handbook of Blue-Collar Occupational Families and Series." Under the present scheme, the OPM administers the Act. Whether a particular individual falls under the Act turns on whether he or she may be classified as a bona fide executive, administrative, or professional employee within the meaning of the FLSA.

PREVAILING WAGE STANDARD

The Act provides three bases for determining what rates will be paid to service employees:

- The wage rates for similar employment prevailing in the locality, as determined by the Secretary of Labor; or
- The rates established in a collective bargaining contract covering service employees including future wage increases; or
- The minimum wage rate under the FLSA, where no prevailing wage rate determination has been made.

The Act does not contain an overtime standard, but it states that all SCA contracts are covered by the Contract Work Hours and Safety Standards Act, which provides that in computing overtime compensation, the regular or basic rate of pay will be the same as that under the FLSA. The Secretary is required to establish prevailing wage rates for all contracts where five or more service employees are employed.

A primary element of an SCA prevailing wage case concerns the parameters of the locality that governs the wage rate determination. One federal court has held that "locality" should be given its ordinary and common meaning and that this phrase has a meaning under the SCA that is different from its meaning under the Walsh-Healey Act. Rejecting the Labor Secretary's claim that a nationwide locality was appropriate, the court advised that in 98 percent of cases, the Standard Metropolitan Statistical Area standard used by the EEOC was an adequate basis for establishing the locality. (*Southern Packaging & Storage Co. v. United States*)

Another court held that the prevailing rates should have been those for comparable employment in the area where the services were to be performed, rather than the location of the government installation that sought the contract. (*Descomp, Inc. v. Sampson*)

Finally, an administrative law judge determined that the locality was the county, not the federal enclave involved, where the appropriate criteria were:

- Comparability of similar employment in the surrounding area;
- The area in which the work force possessing similar skills resides; and
- An identifiable and related geographical area that may serve as a basis for making the required comparison. (*In re Applicability of Bargained Wages*)

SUCCESSORS

Section 4(c) of the Act binds successor contractors to the collective bargaining contract of the predecessor contractor, according to the Secretary of Labor. (*In re Eastern Serv. Mgmt. Co.*) However, successorship and seniority rights under the contract are not fringe benefits within the meaning of Section 4(c), and therefore a successor contractor did not violate the Act when he failed to hire some of the predecessor's employees and hired others at lower pay. (*Clark v. Unified Servs.*)

Nevertheless, a financing institution that purchased a contractor's accounts receivable cannot recover contract proceeds that had been withheld due to SCA violations, since the contractor had no right to the funds. (*United Cal. Discount Corp.*)

In addition, the Secretary of Labor does not have authority under the SCA to set aside the plain terms of a successor collective bargaining contract's wage and benefit provisions that are less than the Act's prevailing wage rates in the locality for similar work, even though the contract rates exceed the rates in the predecessor's contract. The Act requires only that the rates of the successor equal the rates of the predecessor and permits the Secretary to suspend the predecessor's rates only when wages are already higher than local rates for similar services. (*Holt Co. v. Electrical Workers (IBEW) Local 1340*)

In 1977, a successor contractor was awarded 10 contracts to provide security guard services to the Federal Aviation Administration and the General Services Administration for a five-year period. In the notice of award of contract, the FAA referred to the predecessor's bargaining agreement, but neither the agreement nor its supplemental version was attached to the notice. Instead, the predecessor's SCA contract included an erroneous minimum wage determination attachment, which listed the employees' pay rate at $2.45 per hour, rather than the collective bargaining agreement's rate of $3.20 per hour.

In 1981, the Labor Department charged the contractor with violating the wage, fringe benefit, and recordkeeping provisions of the Act. Relying on the FAA's failure to attach the bargaining agreement to the notice of award of contract, the contractor argued that the predecessor's SCA wage determination, rather than the predecessor's collective bargaining agreement rate, controlled. According to the First Circuit Court of Appeals, DOL regulations provide that a successor contractor shall not be relieved of its predecessor's bargaining agreement unless the Labor Secretary determines that the agreement was not entered into as a result of "arms-length" negotiations, and no such determination was made. Therefore, the appeals court ruled that the contractor was bound by the terms of the predecessor's collective bargaining agreement, since the contractor was aware of the existence of the bargaining agreement. (*Vigilantes, Inc. v. Wage & Hour Admin.*)

VARIANCE PROCEEDINGS

Section 4(c) also relieves a contractor from the obligation to comply with the contractually established wages and fringe benefits of the predecessor's contract, if the Labor Secretary finds that such wages and fringes are "substantially at variance with those which prevail for services of a character similar in the locality." (*In re Applicability of Bargained Wages*) The variance determination can therefore legally interfere with the collective bargaining process.

Where a contracting officer modified the prevailing wage rate on a construction project, a question was raised whether the federal government was bound by the modification based on the officer's erroneous interpretation of the regulation governing effective modifications. The court found that the contractor's request for an adjustment in the contract price was justified and that the government was bound to it since the officer's modification was not "palpably illegal" and there is nothing in writing saying that an officer is not authorized to make mistakes of law. (*Broad Ave. Laundry v. United States*)

WAGE PAYMENTS AND DEDUCTIONS

Noncompliance with the Act's wage provisions, either by nonpayment or underpayment, was found in the following rulings:

- Employees may not bargain away the payment of wages secured to them by the Act, and therefore, their signatures on erroneous time cards do not affect their entitlement;
- The contractor cannot attempt to comply with the Act by reallocating portions of payments made for other hours that are in excess of the specified minimum wage; and
- Payments to employees of amounts in excess of the minimum wages required in one workweek may not be credited toward amounts required to be paid in another workweek, since workweeks stand independent of one another. (*In re Roman*)

An employer was found to have violated the prevailing minimum wage requirements, as a result of certain deductions that lowered the employee's wages below the statutory minimum, in the following decisions:

- Where the employer deducted the cost of uniform laundering for food service employees; (*In re Quality Maintenance Co.*) and
- Where the employer required a prospective employee to pay for the cost of a uniform required to be worn on the job. (WH AdminOp, July 7, 1974, WH-274)

Finally, the Act requires the contractor to maintain adequate records of hours worked and wages paid to service employees. This requirement has led to a series of rulings on whether the employer has complied with the Act:

- Where an employee performs work on a covered contract and on nongovernment work in the same work week, the records must effectively segregate the types of work performed. If the records are inadequate, the employee must be paid according to the Act's requirements for all hours in any workweek if he works for any part of a day in that workweek on a covered contract; (WH AdminOp, Mar. 14, 1966)
- Where a maintenance worker spent part of his time on government work and part of his time on nongovernment work, the employer was not allowed to apply a pro rata system of wage payment, as an alternative to adequate recordkeeping, since this did not constitute compliance with the Act; (WH AdminOp, July 19, 1968) and
- Failure to maintain adequate records of segregated work only requires the government to show the amount and extent of work as a matter of "just and reasonable inference," even though the result is only approximate. (*In re Roman*)

FRINGE BENEFITS

The Act requires the contractor to furnish such fringe benefits as the Secretary determines to be prevailing for such employees in the locality. A contractor may satisfy its obligation to furnish specific fringe benefits by providing any equivalent combination of benefits or by making equivalent or differential payments in cash.

Since a contractor may discharge its fringe benefit obligation by paying the employee an equivalent amount in cash, the question has frequently arisen whether the cash value of the payment was in part equal to the fringe that would otherwise have been provided. For example, to find the hourly cash equivalent of a "one-week paid vacation," the employee's rate of pay is multiplied by the number of hours of vacation, using a standard 8-hour day and 40-hour week, unless otherwise specified. The total annual amount is divided by 2080, the number of regular working hours in a 52-week period, to arrive at the cash equivalent. (WH AdminOp, Aug. 15, 1966)

Vacation Pay

SCA regulations establish that eligibility for vacation benefits specified in a wage determination is based on completion of a standard period of past service. Where a determination contains the benefit of "one week's paid vacation after one year of service with a contractor or successor," the employee must receive this benefit if his or her total service on both governmental and commercial work equals one year or more. Work before and after a pertinent wage determination is issued must be counted in determining an employee's length of service.

A contractor had a one-year contract to provide guard services to the Navy, which authorized the government to extend the contract subject to labor rate adjustments required by the FLSA and the SCA. According to the Court of Appeals for the Federal Circuit, the contractor was entitled to a price adjustment for vacation pay to which its employees became entitled during the renewal option year. Vacation pay was due entirely to the wage rate determination applicable at the beginning of the renewal option period and had to be paid in accordance with a contract clause authorizing an adjustment for increased costs that resulted from a Labor Department determination of minimum prevailing wages and fringe benefits applicable at the beginning of the renewal options period. (*United States v. Service Ventures, Inc.*)

Where the determination lists the holidays for which payment is required under the Act, the contractor must furnish the holiday off with pay. The contractor may substitute another day off with pay if the substitution is done according to a plan that has been communicated to the affected employees. The contractor may pay the employee cash equivalents for specific holidays. (WH AdminOp, Jan. 28, 1970)

A contractor may meet the health and welfare benefits requirement by maintaining a self-insured plan, where the contractor has not refused to pay a claim or to provide an employee with a benefit required by the contract, and there has been no evidence of bad faith by the contractor. (*White Glove-Building Maintenance v. Hodgson*) The contractor's notice of its self-insured plan to all new employees satisfies the requirement that the substitution be made according to a plan that has been communicated to the affected employees.

Severance pay is a fringe benefit and must be included in the wage determination and the new government contract, unless after an administrative hearing, it is found to be inconsistent with the prevailing wages in the locality. (*Trinity Servs. v. Usery*)

FRINGE OFFSETS AND PAYMENTS

Under the Act a contractor may not:

- Obtain contributions toward fringe benefits from its employees to satisfy the fringe benefit standards set by the Secretary; (WH AdminOp, Apr. 7, 1966)
- Offset social security payments by decreasing its contribution to employee retirement funds; (WH AdminOp, Apr. 14, 1966) and
- Offset fringe benefit payments made for hours spent on nongovernment work against an employer's fringe obligation for work done on a government contract. (WH AdminOp, June 7, 1967)

Service employees of a contractor are entitled to receive fringe benefit payments for hours they do not work but for which they are paid even though such hours are holidays or vacation time. The Labor Department has ruled that the contractor does not have the prerogative to apply the wage determination in a manner that it considered reasonable. (*In re Emerald Maintenance, Inc.*)

Finally, as with the segregation of government and nongovernment work, the Act requires adequate recordkeeping of fringe benefit payments that are made as cash equivalents in lieu of fringes. (*In re Aarid Van Lines*)

ENFORCEMENT

Administrative Enforcement

On July 10, 1992, the Secretary of Labor issued Order No. 3-92, establishing the Board of Service Contract Appeals. The Board is authorized to decide appeals concerning questions of fact and law from final decisions of the Administrator, Wage and Hour Division, and administrative law judges arising under the SCA, and under the Contract Work Hours and Safety Standards Act (see Chapter 8), when the contract is also subject to the SCA.

The Board does not have jurisdiction to review the validity of DOL regulations or to review decisions to deny or grant exemptions, variations, and tolerances. The Board's members are the same as the Wage Appeals Board's members. (Decisions of both boards may be reviewed via an on-line data base, accessible to the public at no charge over the cost of the telephone call at 202-219-5286/5287 or 202-219-9039.) Since its inception, the SCA Board has made the following rulings:

- DOL acted reasonably in determining that benefits not provided to more than 50 percent of employees are not "prevailing" within the meaning of the Act;
- The SCA does not require the Labor Secretary to make any particular use of data concerning federal employees, but only to consider it and apply it where the Secretary deems it appropriate;
- DOL's policy regarding the timing of updates to fringe benefit determinations was presumptively valid, so long as it accurately reflects reality; and
- The Wage and Hour Division relied improperly on a 1986 study to determine health and welfare figures, since the number of establishments studied was statistically insignificant to support the Division's determinations. (*In re Service Employees Int'l Union*)

Court Enforcement

The Act may not be enforced through a private action, since the enforcement responsibilities are assigned exclusively to the Labor Secretary. (*Teamsters Local 427 v. Philco-Ford Corp.; Foster v. Parker Transfer Co.*) Although the Act limits the right to bring an action to the Secretary, it provides a range of mechanisms for obtaining compliance and/or imposing liabilities and penalties. The Act authorizes:

- The withholding of amounts due under a contract sufficient to pay employees the difference between the wages and the benefits required under the contract and those actually received;
- Court action against the contractor, subcontractor, or surety bond to recover any remaining amount of underpayments;
- Termination of the contract with the contractor liable for any resulting cost to the federal government; and
- Imposition of a debarment list (blacklist), banning a contractor from receiving a government contract for a period of three years, unless the Labor Secretary finds "unusual circumstances."

Where the Labor Secretary withholds sums due the contractor based on a finding of noncompliance with the wage and fringe benefit provisions of the Act, the amounts withheld are deposited in a special fund, and paid to the employees directly upon determinations of how much each is to receive.

The Labor Secretary deprived a contractor of its right to due process under the Fifth Amendment when the Secretary, who claimed that the contractor had violated the SCA, ordered the contracting agencies to withhold further payments. The court noted that the contractor received no due process hearing by a neutral decision maker prior to the suspension of payments due for work performed. (*Bailey v. Secretary of Labor*)

The Secretary is authorized to maintain an action for deficiencies where amounts withheld are insufficient to cover underpayments due employees. Any money not disbursed to employees is turned over to the U.S. Treasury. However, a contractor's bankruptcy proceeding does not affect a default proceeding under the SCA concerning the contractor's failure to respond to charges that it violated the Act's wage provisions. (*In re Beal*)

If the contractor violates any provision of the contract, the contracting agency may cancel the contract upon written notice to the contractor. The government may charge the original contractor with any added costs incurred in obtaining contract completion through a substitute contractor.

LIMITATIONS PERIOD

An important distinction between the SCA and other federal public contract acts is that the SCA contains its own statute of limitations rather than borrowing the two-year period from the FLSA.

The Portal-to-Portal Pay Act does not include the SCA within its coverage, and the Fourth Circuit reasoned that this omission by Congress was not inadvertent. Although this omission creates an inconsistency in enforcement of public contracts acts, the court ruled, the SCA limitations period is the six-year general statute of limitations under 28 U.S.C. Sec. 2415. (*United States v. Deluxe Cleaners & Laundry*)

Although the SCA does not follow FLSA limitations periods (through the Portal Act), it does adopt FLSA case law in appropriate circumstances. Approving the imposition of prejudgment interest on a noncomplying contractor, a federal district court held that silence on this issue within the SCA was not enough to defeat FLSA case law authorizing the grant of prejudgment interest in similar cases. (*United States v. Powers Bldg. Maintenance Co.*)

The SCA contains recordkeeping requirements similar to those in the Walsh-Healey Act, particularly with reference to the segregation of government and nongovernment work. These records must be made available for inspection by authorized representatives of the Wage-Hour and Public Contracts divisions.

BLACKLIST PENALTY

The Act requires that a noncomplying contractor be placed on the debarment list for a period of three years. The 1972 amendments to the SCA limited the Secretary's authority to deviate from this penalty, such that variance may only be granted upon a finding by the Secretary of "unusual circumstances." (*In re Dokken*)

The Act does not define "unusual circumstances," but certain elements should be present to justify such a finding. These include:

- Where the violation is clear and the contractor's conduct is culpable, willful, or aggravated, relief is not appropriate;
- Where there is a legitimate dispute as to a contract term leading to the violation, a contractor should not be penalized for electing to litigate an issue in doubt; and
- Where the contractor's conduct is not culpable, consideration should be given to the nature and gravity of the violation, its impact on the unpaid employees, and any good-faith conduct by the contractor to correct the violation and comply with the Act. (*In re Emerald Maintenance, Inc.*)

"Unusual circumstances" have been found in the following situations:

- Undercapitalization and poor bookkeeping; (*In re Glover*)
- No prior history of violations, a bona fide dispute, the contractor's position was not frivolous, and the amount in dispute was small; (*In re Taskpower Int'l*)
- Confusion concerning the number of years of experience necessary to qualify for accumulating vacation benefits and the contractor's reliance on statements of the contracting officer; (*In re Myers & Myers, Inc.*) and
- Action by the contracting agency that resulted in substantial monetary loss to the contractor. (*In re Quality Maintenance Co.*)

Contractors have been debarred based on a failure to demonstrate "unusual circumstances" in the following cases:

- Financial difficulties; (*In re Van Elk*)
- Ignorance of legal requirements and a nonchalant approach to ending violations; (*In re McLaughlin Storage*)
- Wage determination was at substantial variance with the prevailing rate in the locality but the contractor made no effort to have the determination corrected or modified; (*In re Electric City Linoleum*) and
- Simple negligent conduct. (*In re Dynamic Enters.*)

A federal district court refused to preliminarily enjoin enforcement of the debarment penalty against a contractor that violated the wage and fringe benefit provisions of the SCA, pending review of the Labor Department's final administrative action, even assuming the violations were *de minimis*. The court noted that the contractor failed to prove the existence of unusual circumstances, inasmuch as:

- The violations were deliberate and of an aggravated nature;
- The contractor did not show that it would suffer irreparable harm from the debarment penalty; and
- The harm to other interested parties and the public interest weigh against an injunction. (*Kirchdorfer v. McLaughlin*; see also *Vigilantes v. Wage & Hour Admin.*)

ATTORNEYS' FEES

The SCA is silent on the matter of attorneys' fees awards. However, Congress has provided for an award of reasonable attorneys' fees "to the prevailing party in any civil action brought by or against the United States . . . in any court having jurisdiction of such action." (Equal Access to Justice Act, 28 U.S.C. Sec. 2412(b))

The U.S. Court of Appeals for the Federal Circuit had an opportunity to address the application of the Equal Access to Justice Act (EAJA) in the context of a contractor that successfully protested an action of a federal contracting agency.

A public contractor was denied an upward price adjustment in the contract by a contracting officer. The Armed Services Board of Contract Appeals upheld the denial, even though it conceded that the officer's decision was based on her erroneous interpretation of an SCA regulation.

The contractor successfully appealed the Board's ruling to the U.S. Court of Claims, which granted the price adjustment but said nothing about the cost of the litigation. (*Broad Ave. Laundry v. United States*) The contractor then filed its request for fees under EAJA with the U.S. Court of Appeals for the Federal Circuit.

The EAJA provides that an agency or a court, in any "adversary adjudication" or "civil action . . . brought by or against the United States, shall award to a prevailing party other than the United States fees and other expenses, unless the position of the agency or the United States 'was substantially justified or that special circumstances make an award unjust.'"

The contractor was clearly a prevailing party as a result of the Claims Court's decision in favor of the price adjustment. The issue to be resolved by the appeals court was the meaning of the "position of the government" language in EAJA. The court rejected the claim that the Act was intended to cover the government's position at the administrative proceeding before the Board. It held, instead, that the "position of the government" meant the government's stance in litigation. The position of the government was therefore "substantially justified" in litigation, the court concluded, and no attorneys' fees were awarded.

A contractor that was relieved from the debarment penalty for its violations of the SCA and the CWHSSA was not entitled to attorneys' fees under EAJA, where:

- The regulations implementing EAJA exclude SCA and CWHSSA;
- The right to such fees arises under EAJA and not the labor standards acts; and
- EAJA authorizes fees only in "adversary adjudication," defined as proceedings required by law, and the SCA

authorizes but does not require the proceeding in the instant case. (*In re Verticare*)

Bankruptcy and the SCA

The Bankruptcy Code's automatic stay provisions do not apply to the Labor Secretary's distribution to former employees of wages withheld because of the employer's failure to pay prevailing wages under a SCA contract, since the amounts withheld are not property of the bankruptcy estate. (*In re Frank Mossa Trucking*)

The automatic stay provisions also do not apply to an administrative proceeding under the Act, since the proceeding falls within the Code's exception for a "governmental unit to enforce such governmental unit's police or regulatory powers." (*Eddleman v. U.S. Department of Labor*)

Finally, equitable considerations did not support a Bankruptcy Court's order requiring the Labor Department to return to a debtor's estate funds withheld from payments due bankrupt contractors who failed to pay employee benefits under the Act. The Ninth Circuit found that the equities weighed against withholding the payments from the contractors' employees, who had continued to work under the contract. Without their labor, the bankruptcy estate would have been depleted, the appeals court concluded. (*In re The Harris Mgmt. Co.*)

7
DAVIS-BACON ACT

The Davis-Bacon Act of 1931 (DBA), along with the Anti-Kickback Law (Copeland Act) and Contract Work Hours and Safety Standards Act, establishes employment standards for laborers and mechanics on public construction projects let under federal contracts for amounts in excess of $2,000. Since the $2,000 floor was established in 1935, Congress has considered, but not approved, many attempts to raise that floor.

The DBA requires covered contracts to specify prevailing minimum wage rates for various classes of mechanics and laborers employed on the project. Covered contracts include highway building, dredging, demolition, cleaning, and painting and decorating of public buildings. Covered employees include all mechanics and laborers employed directly on the site of the project, including subcontractor employees. Employees of "materialmen" (companies that supply material for the work away from the construction site and that maintain establishments where their goods are sold to the general public) are exempt if they do not spend more than 20 percent of their worktime at the construction site.

COVERAGE

In an early dispute concerning coverage of the Act, a conflict arose between the Comptroller General and the Attorney

General over the status of workers performing dredging operations. The Secretary of Labor had originally found that these workers were akin to mechanics and construction laborers, and therefore subject to the Act. The Attorney General held, to the contrary, that these workers are more like "seamen" and should be covered by the Maritime Workers Act rather than the DBA. The Comptroller General settled the dispute by siding with the Labor Secretary on the ground that the administration and enforcement responsibilities were delegated to the Labor Department and the Labor Secretary's position must control. (Comp Gen Dec. B-105067, Nov. 6, 1951)

This dispute illustrates the difficulty in establishing the parameters of the Act's coverage. The Act extends coverage based on the type of work called for in the contract, the type of contract involved, and the type of contractor involved.

The Act covers any lease-purchase agreement with the government for buildings or conversions, extensions, additions, or remodeling of existing structures. (Labor Solic Op, Dec. 1954) However, the Act does not apply to construction, alteration, or repair of buildings for occupancy by the federal government under any term-lease or lease-option agreement, since these types of contracts evidence a lack of a *firm commitment* by the government to acquire more than a leasehold interest in the property. (Comp Gen Dec. B-122382, July 18, 1962)

Demolition work as part of a contract for initial construction or demolition performed as part of "initial construction" (i.e., closely related or immediately incidental thereto) is covered by the labor standards provisions of the Act. (Asst. Labor Solic Op, June 20, 1961)

The Act has been interpreted to cover other contracts, including:

- The plugging of oil and gas wells and the removal of above-ground equipment in connection with the construction of a reservoir; (Solic Op, June 13, 1961)
- The spreading of oil on road surfaces during the construction of a highway, at the construction site; (Solic Ops, Oct. 8, 1962, and Nov. 6, 1962)

- The renting of equipment to a covered contractor, where the rental agreement calls for the employees of the rental company to operate the equipment on the construction project at the worksite; (*In re Griffith Co.*)
- The cleaning operations on public buildings or works performed by the process of steam or sandblast cleaning; (Solic Op, July 17, 1961)
- Contracts performed under the Area Redevelopment Act of 1961 must comply with the DBA's prevailing minimum wages (and overtime provisions of the Contract Work Hours and Safety Standards Act); and
- Contracts performed under the Federal-Aid Highway Act of 1956 (Sec. 115 of the Act).

In each of these agreements, it was determined that the work in question essentially constituted an "integral part" of the prime contractor's performance of its government contract. (*Sansone Co. v. California Dep't of Transp.*) Although not determinative, the "integral part" element is important in establishing the scope of the Act's coverage. The Act does not cover contracts for:

- The delivery of materials at a construction site, even if the drivers are employed by government contractors, since the drivers merely dropped off the material and did not engage in any work "integral" to the project; (*Building & Constr. Trades Dep't, AFL-CIO v. Labor Dep't (Midway Excavators)*)
- The delivery of standard materials (e.g., concrete aggregate, hot mix, and sand) to a construction site, performed independently of the contract; (*Zachry Co. v. United States*)
- The prefabrication of component roof panels for the contract, where the prefabrication work normally cannot be done at the construction site; (Solic Op, Aug. 2, 1961)
- The supplies, including installing or maintaining work that is only incidental to the furnishing of such supplies. However, the Act covers contracts for installation involving substantial construction, for transportation of

supplies to or from the building site by the contractor or subcontractor, such as window frames or millwork;
- Servicing or maintenance work in a building that is completed or substantially completed; the Act covers servicing or maintenance performed as part of the construction or repair of the public buildings or works;
- The complete dismantling or demolition of a construction site, where no construction is done by the dismantling or demolition company;
- Exploratory drilling;
- Construction work closely related to research and development, where the research work cannot be done separately, or where the construction work is the subject of the research;
- The construction or repair of vessels, aircraft, or other kinds of personal property; and
- Work outside the continental United States or a place not known or reasonably determinable at the time the contract is executed.

In addition, the Act does not cover preliminary survey work such as the preparation of metes and bounds prior to construction, especially if performed pursuant to a separate contract. Survey work done immediately prior to or during construction, performed as an aid to the crafts that are engaged in the actual construction project, is considered covered. (Solic Op, June 1960; Sec. Lab., Aug. 2, 1962)

Other work not regarded as Davis-Bacon work includes work performed off the construction site, whether done by contractors, subcontractors, or materialmen (Comp Gen Dec. B-148076, July 26, 1963) and certain types of installation work performed during the actual construction, that is only incidental to the actual construction. (Solic Op, Mar. 3, 1964)

The distinction between which contracts are covered and which are not is often characterized in terms of the work called for. Where the work brings the workers into close integration with ("integral part" of) the prime contractor's performance, the workers are classified as employees of a subcontractor covered under the Act. Where the workers do not perform work that is integral to the prime contractor's performance, they are classified as materialmen and not covered under the contract. But whether the examination focuses on the language in the contract or on the workers' classification, the determination turns on the actual nature of the work performed in relation to the prime contractor's performance.

Employees engaged in assembling major components of houses to be erected on nearby sites, for example, were deemed to be subcontractor employees, covered by the Act, even though they were employed in a mobile factory that could be located at a different site. The mobile factory operations are distinguishable from those of a factory producing prefabricated homes or components for a variety of customers, which may be regarded as a variant of the traditional materialman serving the construction industry. The employees performed work that was integrally related to the final assembly or conventional construction activities on the worksite, and thus constitute a part of the overall assembly or construction. (Solic Op, Aug. 27, 1969)

Site of Work

The DBA provides that every covered contract shall contain a stipulation that all mechanics and laborers "employed directly upon the site of work" shall be paid wage rates not less than those stated in the advertised specifications. Rulings on the meaning of "site of work" include the following:

- A contractor that agreed to construct modular housing units at a site in Alaska 3,000 miles from the site of the fabrication of the units in Oregon must pay prevailing wages under the Act for the work in Oregon of fabricating the units and assembling them on concrete slabs for transport to Alaska. The Wage Appeals Board ruled that the distance between the fabrication site and the assembly site was not too great for the fabrication site to be considered part of the "site of work." (*In re Atco Constr.*)
- Employees in Oregon who fabricated sections of a missile service tower, which were shipped to and erected at

a construction site in California, were not covered by the Act. The Wage Appeals Board ruled that the fabrication was 1,000 miles from the construction site. (*In re Titan IV Mobile Serv. Tower*)

- Work at a company's pit-and-batch plant was subject to the Act, since the facilities were dedicated exclusively or nearly so to the performance of the contractor or project, and they were so located in proximity to the actual construction location that it would be reasonable to include them. The district court upheld the Wage Appeals Board's ruling that there was no reason to abandon DOL's long-standing use of "functional" and "geographical" tests to determine whether a particular site was part of the "site of work." (*Ball, Ball & Brosamer v. Martin*)
- Mechanics and laborers employed off-site, such as suppliers, materialmen, and material delivery truck drivers, are not covered by the Act, regardless of their employer. (*Building & Constr. Trades Dep't, AFL-CIO v. Labor Dep't (Midway Excavators)*)

A variety of factors enters into the determination of whether a particular contract is covered by the Act, but the most decisive would appear to be the degree of integration or integral relations between the sub and prime contractors' performance.

In view of the variety of factors that can enter into the determination of whether a particular contract may be covered by the Act, it is advisable to contact the U.S. Labor Department, Davis-Bacon Office for clarification. (See Appendix J, Contract Standards Operations Division.)

CONFLICT WITH OTHER LAWS

When a contract calls for installation work, there may be some doubt as to whether the amount of installation work is substantial enough to justify coverage by the DBA, or whether the installation is merely incidental to the construction project, thus warranting Walsh-Healey Act coverage. A contract calling for the installation of Minuteman missile equipment at a construction site was determined to be only "incidental" to the construction project, since it involved a minimal amount of time. Therefore, the Act did not apply. (Solic Op, Apr. 16, 1962)

But where the construction costs were the major part of an installation contract, or where the installation was complex and substantial, the installation contract was deemed to be within the Act's coverage. (Solic Ops, Nov. 6, 1961, and Nov. 30, 1961)

An employer who was the subject of an FLSA action by employees loading and unloading government goods at an Army reservation was unsuccessful in establishing that the Davis-Bacon Act covered, and thus shielded it, from FLSA liability. The court declared that only laborers engaged in the construction or repair of public works, and not employees of a private firm working on a government reservation, were covered by the DBA. It added that the DBA and FLSA statutes are not necessarily incompatible. (*Ortiz v. San Juan Dock Co.; Walling v. Patton-Tulley Transp. Co.*)

PREVAILING WAGES

Unlike the Walsh-Healey Act, the Davis-Bacon Act authorizes the Labor Secretary to establish prevailing wage rates on a contract-by-contract basis. The Secretary is required to conduct a survey of the wage rates prevailing in the "locality" and to set DBA rates for the contract according to those rates. Area and regional differentials are thus recognized in the setting of rates under the DBA.

The Secretary is also required to establish a scale of rates for the various classifications of workers on a particular project, rather than establishing one minimum prevailing wage rate for the project or industry. The classifications range from "helpers" to apprentices to laborers to journeymen, and each rate takes into consideration the locality. Thus, the setting of such rates is a very complex and time-consuming process that has led to much litigation.

A good example of how complex and time consuming this process can be involves the Labor Department's effort to establish a "helper" regulation under the DBA. In 1982, the DOL issued rules permitting contractors to use semiskilled "helpers" on DBA projects. Among other things, the proposed rules would have established a maximum ratio of two helpers to every three journeymen on DBA projects. An alliance of union organizations sued to block issuance of the rules, and in 1987 the U.S. District Court for the District of Columbia eventually enjoined DOL from implementing the rules. In 1990, the district court vacated the injunction and DOL set a date in 1991, by which time the rules would become effective. However, in 1992, the U.S. Court of Appeals for the District of Columbia sustained all the union's challenges to the proposed rules, including the helper-to-journeyman ratio. Subsequently, DOL issued final "helper" rules that reflected the court of appeals' rulings as to the proposed rules. (*Building & Constr. Trades Dep't, AFL-CIO v. Martin*)

The constitutionality of the statutory mechanism for setting the prevailing wage rates for separate job classifications under the Act was contested and upheld in 1938. (*Gilioz v. Webb*) Similarly, the U.S. Supreme Court has declared that the Secretary's determination is not subject to judicial review. (*United States v. Binghamton Constr. Co.*) However, changes in the regulations implementing the process of setting the wage rates may be challenged, where the charging party demonstrates a substantial likelihood that it will prevail on the merits based on such things as improper promulgation of the regulations under the Administrative Procedure Act. (*Building & Constr. Trades v. Donovan*)

Because the Secretary's wage determinations are nonreviewable by a court, Congress established the Wage Appeals Board in 1964 to review:

- Wage determinations;
- Debarment cases;
- Controversies concerning payment of wages or proper classifications involving large sums of money or large groups of employees, or novel situations; and

- Adjustment of liquidated damages assessed under the Contract Work Hours and Safety Standards Act. Determinations of the Wage Appeals Board are reviewable on the grounds of lack of due process (*Framlau Corp. v. Dembling*) and fraud or gross error. (*Southwest Eng'g Corp. v. United States*)

Wage determination disputes usually arise at the time the rates are set, but do not get adjudicated until well after contract completion. Therefore, most disputes involve a contractor's attempt to gain reimbursement for what it regards as improperly high rates. In denying reimbursement, the U.S. Supreme Court has ruled that the rates established by the Secretary and included in the contract are not a representation or a warranty that such rates are prevailing in the local community. (*United States v. Binghamton Constr. Co.*)

In 1989, the Wage Appeals Board (WAB) ruled that the Davis-Bacon Act applied retroactively to privately funded construction of an outpatient clinic, built for exclusive lease by the Veterans Administration. The Labor Department's Wage-Hour Administrator had previously concluded that the VA solicitation resulted in a "contract to construct" within the meaning of the Act. The Administrator further determined that the clinic was a "public" building within the meaning of the Act, even though the federal government would not acquire title to the facility. (*In re Lease of Space for Outpatient Clinic, Crown Point, Ind.*)

The *Crown Point* decision affirmed a 1985 decision by the WAB, wherein the Board held that the Act should apply if more than an incidental amount of construction-type activity is involved in the execution of a government contract. (*Military Housing, Ft. Drum*)

Contractors have pursued reimbursement under three theories: (*a*) equitable adjustment, (*b*) mutual mistake of fact, and (*c*) redetermination of rates. The first two theories stem from basic contract law, and the third theory is the result of administrative practice by the Wage-Hour Division.

Under the equitable adjustment theory, a contractor was entitled to obtain $18,000 that a contracting officer had withheld following a downward redetermination of rates by the Labor Secretary. The rates had originally been set higher than what prevailed in the locality, and the contractor had originally submitted its bid based on the actual rates prevailing in the locality. The Court of Claims ruled that there was no equitable basis for the contracting agency to obtain the completed contract at a price less than that which it agreed to pay. The contractor was thus found equitably entitled to the reimbursement it sought. (*Burnett Constr. Co. v. United States*)

Under the "mutual mistake of fact" theory, the contractor obtained reimbursement based on the Labor Department's delay in adjusting the prevailing rates until after the contract was executed. The contractor incurred increased labor costs at the government's direction, and the court ruled that the parties had contracted under a mutual mistake of fact as to the maximum and minimum rates prevailing in the locality. The contract may be reformed to reflect the true intent of the parties. (*Poirier & McLane Corp. v. United States*)

However, another contractor was unsuccessful in using the "mutual mistake of fact" theory to avoid liability for unlawful underpayment of laborers on a roofing project. The U.S. Court of Appeals for the Federal Circuit ruled that the risk of loss was on the contractor, since the contractor acknowledged that it investigated and satisfied itself as to prevailing wages in the locality. (*Emerald Maintenance Inc. v. United States*)

Yet another "mistake" defense failed when the U.S. Court of Appeals for the Eleventh Circuit rejected a federal contractor's effort to take as a credit toward the DBA prevailing wage rates contributions the contractor made to an approved apprenticeship program that were greater than the plan required. (*Miree Constr. Corp. v. Dole;* see also *In re Tom Mistick & Sons*)

Under the redetermination of rates concept, a contractor was denied an adjustment, even though he incurred higher labor costs due to higher rates set after the contract was executed. The contract contained a clause for payment of wages to be determined by the Secretary *after* the contract was executed, and the Court of Claims stated that this clause was not against public policy, since it had been included for the benefit of the workers, rather than for the benefit of the contractor. (*Bushman Constr. Co. v. United States*)

However, a union unsuccessfully sought to compel a state transportation department to incorporate the appropriate prevailing wages in bid solicitations for a construction project pursuant to the Act. The Transportation Department had included in the original solicitation the wage rates erroneously published in the Federal Register, and two federal agencies had notified the department of this fact 11 days before the scheduled date of opening of the bids. The court noted that the union had obtained all the substantive relief it sought prior to the instant action, and the union was merely seeking to preserve its status as a "prevailing party" for purposes of an award of attorneys' fees. (*Operating Eng'rs Local 3 v. Bohn*)

States' prevailing wage laws are virtually always involved in state-funded construction projects. These state laws are often called "little Davis-Bacon Acts," since the purpose and language of the state laws generally follow closely their federal counterpart. However, the federal government has also taken note of the existence of these little Davis-Bacon Acts, and of the potential confusion created by a project covering more than one state boundary, especially where federal funds may be involved. To that end, the federal government has issued a rule to resolve such confusion. Federal prevailing wage rates determined under the federal Davis-Bacon Act preempt state prevailing wage rates for a given construction trade on public or Indian housing projects when the state prevailing wage is higher, according to a final regulation issued by the U.S. Department of Housing and Urban Development in 1988.

A final aspect of prevailing wage rate determinations involves Comptroller General rulings, such as:

- Obsolete rates may be adjusted by a change order; (Comp Gen Dec. B-106987, May 8, 1953)
- Issuance of a letter of inadvertence, acknowledging a mistake in the rate included in the contract, does not automatically authorize a change in the contract price; (Comp Gen Dec. B-129205, Nov. 15, 1957)

- Changed wage rates originally included in a contract to require payment of building instead of heavy-highway schedules represents a change in judgment, rather than a correction of inadvertent errors; (Comp Gen Dec. B-150293, Feb. 13, 1963)
- The Labor Secretary cannot restrict the use of spray painting work under a prevailing wage rate determination; (Comp Gen Dec. B-132044, June 10, 1957) and
- A Project Stabilization Agreement negotiated by construction industry employers and unions could be included in contracts for certain missile programs, in the interest of national defense, under the National Defense Contracts Act of 1958. The agreement covered all construction, fabrication, and related work covered by the Act at two military facilities, and called for the payment of fringe benefits and overtime pay. (Comp Gen Dec. B-148930, July 2, 1962)

A federal agency's failure to require that the Davis-Bacon Act's prevailing wage provisions be included in the contract can be remedied, even after performance of the construction work has been started under the contract. The Wage Appeals Board affirmed the Wage-Hour Administrator's order that the prevailing wage provisions be *retroactively* included in the agency's agreement with a private developer to construct a building for lease by the agency. A prior case with similar circumstances had resulted in a WAB ruling against such retroactive inclusion, where the contracting agency had concluded that the Act did not apply. This ruling prompted the Department of Labor to promulgate a regulation authorizing the Wage-Hour Administrator to issue a wage determination after the contract was awarded or after the beginning of construction, if the agency has failed to incorporate a wage determination in a contract required to contain prevailing wage provisions under the Act. (*In re Veterans Admin.*)

FRINGE BENEFITS

Contributions to fringe benefit funds may not be counted toward satisfying the minimum prevailing wage rates in the contract under the Act, unless the wage rate determination specifically indicates that the fringes are included in the rates. The Act was amended in 1965 to allow contractors to combine wage payments and fringe contributions, if they added up to the total in the wage-fringe determination. However, this does not permit the contract to apply this "mix" formula to wage-only determinations. The Labor Solicitor issued a memorandum in 1965 to clarify the crediting of fringe benefit contributions in meeting Act wage determinations. (Solic Memo, Oct. 15, 1965)

The Wage Appeals Board (WAB) has addressed the situation where a contractor made contributions to an apprenticeship benefit fund and attempted to claim fringe benefit credits under the Act. The contractor contributed a $500 tuition payment to an apprenticeship training plan on behalf of its sole apprentice and voluntarily contributed 25 cents per hour to an apprenticeship training fund for bricklayers, carpenters, and laborers on behalf of its employees who worked on five federally financed construction projects. The WAB ruled that:

- The contractor may not claim credits for these contributions under the "funded-plans" provisions of the DBA, since the Act provides that only *irrevocable* contributions made "pursuant to a fund, plan, or program" may be credited and these voluntary contributions are not irrevocable and were not made "pursuant" to a fund, plan, or program; and
- The contractor may claim credits under the Act's "unfunded-plans" provisions, but only as to actual costs necessary to provide training for apprentices registered in the plan. (*In re Miree Constr. Corp.*)

ENFORCEMENT

In view of the Act's purpose of protecting the wage standards of workers performing under government contracts, the Act and the regulations provide for a variety of methods for ensuring that workers receive the prevailing wages set in the contract.

For example, noncompliance by the contractor entitles the contracting agency to cancel the contract and to seek money from the contractor for the extra costs incurred in finding a substitute performer on the contract. Similarly, the Comptroller General may pay the workers directly and seek reimbursement from the contractor for any deficiencies. The government may also set off payments due the contractor under one contract for deficiencies under another contract where the contractor has failed to pay the prevailing wages. Finally, the workers themselves may bring an action to recover unpaid wages under Section 3(b) of the Act. If the contract does not contain prevailing wages, however, there is no private right of action under the Act.

Arbitration has recently been applied to resolve disputes arising under the DBA. For example, a state supreme court has ruled that:

- A collective bargaining contract containing an arbitration clause did not contemplate arbitration of disputes over a federal agency's determinations concerning what work the federal contractor was required to subcontract under the Act, where the agency has sole and absolute authority to make such determinations; and
- The union is entitled to an order requiring arbitration as to the federal contractor's duty under the collective bargaining agreement to use its "best efforts" to influence the federal agency's determinations concerning what work the contractor was required to subcontract under the Act, where the contractor officially participates in the agency's decision-making process, and the agency's determinations under the Act affect both the contractor and the union. (*Oil Workers Local 2-652 v. EG & G Idaho, Inc.*)

Fringe benefit payments are to be included in calculating overtime compensation, since the Act defines wages and prevailing wages as "basic hourly rate plus fringe benefits" and does not distinguish between overtime and nonovertime hours. (*Holloway Constr. v. Wage Appeals Bd.*)

As with the FLSA and the Walsh-Healey Act, Davis-Bacon Act lawsuits are governed by the Portal-to-Portal Pay Act, including limitations period determinations and imposition of liquidated damages liability. (See Chapter 3 for further information.)

However, a federal district court has upheld a ruling by the Wage Appeals Board that the Portal Act's limitations periods (two years for a violation or three years for a willful violation) do not apply to administrative proceedings initiated through the administrative law judge hearing procedures. (*In re Progressive Design & Build Inc.; Ball, Ball & Brosamer v. Martin*)

Employee Actions

The Act does not specifically confer on individual employees the right to bring an action for unpaid wages under a contract. On remand from the U.S. Supreme Court, however, the Court of Appeals for the Seventh Circuit made the definitive ruling on employee actions under the Act. It held:

- Laborers and mechanics are the "especial" beneficiaries of the Act, since the legislative history of the Act reveals that its fundamental purpose was to benefit laborers and mechanics by assuring they receive prevailing wages;
- The Act's grant of a right of action applies only to an action on a surety bond issued under the Miller Act, which requires the posting of a surety bond on most government contracts covered by the DBA;
- Employees have an implied right of action that effectuates congressional intent in passing the statute; and
- The right to recover unpaid portions of the prevailing wage is based on congressional policy, despite the fact that an action for breach of an employment contract is traditionally a state-court action. (*McDaniel v. University of Chicago*)

An important aspect of this particular case, which led to the recognition of a private right of action, albeit "inferred," was that the statutory remedies available under the Act were ineffective in remedying the employees' injury from underpayments:

- No funds had been withheld from the contractor, so no monies could be forwarded to the employees or set off against another contract;
- No bond had been required against which the government could move on behalf of the employees; and
- The government chose not to invoke the sanctions of contract termination or blacklisting. Had any of these circumstances not existed, the government would have had a means of using the statutory remedies to make "whole" the victims (employees) of the employer's noncompliance.

The existence of prevailing wages in the contract provides a basis for creating the inference of the private right of action. The absence of such wage rates destroys this inference, and allowing employees to sue under such circumstances would undercut the administrative mechanism created to assure consistency in the administration and enforcement of the Act. (*Universities Research Ass'n v. Coutu*)

Following *Universities Research Ass'n v. Coutu* in 1981, other courts have determined that a private right of action does exist under the DBA. (*Stampco Constr. Co. v. Guffey; Norling v. Valley Contracting & Pre-Mix*) However, one federal court has found that the Act does not create a private right of action, choosing to rely on a 1980 decision. (*Sorensen v. Holman Erection Co.*, relying on *United States v. Capeletti Bros., Inc.*)

Once it was established that a private right of action existed (albeit "inferred") under the DBA, it was not long before penumbral actions were recognized. For example, a union sought information concerning the names, addresses, and Social Security numbers of nonunion employees of a federal contractor, ostensibly to monitor the contractor's compliance with the Act, as well as the federal government's enforcement of the Act. The federal government resisted, and the union sued under the Freedom of Information Act (FOIA). The U.S. Court of Appeals for the Third Circuit ruled that the public interest in disclosure of the names and addresses of these nonunion workers was not barred, but that the workers' privacy interests barred disclosure of their Social Security numbers. (*Electrical Workers (IBEW) Local 5 v. Department of Housing & Urban Dev.*)

Another court ruled that the disclosure of identifying information in certified payroll records of DBA contractors was clearly unwarranted under the FOIA's exemption for agency records, the disclosure of which constitutes an invasion of personal privacy. There is little or no public interest in disclosure of the names, addresses, and wage information, according to the U.S. Court of Appeals for the Second Circuit, while there are significant personal privacy interests at stake. (*Hopkins v. Department of Housing & Urban Dev.*)

Actions Against U.S. Government

Several unions successfully sued to compel the government to enforce the Act, claiming that Labor Department officials had failed to examine payroll records and conduct investigations to assure compliance with the Act; to send notices and hold hearings on charges of willful violations; to debar contractors who willfully violated the Act; and to withhold underpayments due employees from willful violators. The Tenth Circuit ruled that such actions are nondiscretionary duties under the Act and the regulations, and that mandamus and injunctive relief are available where dereliction of duty is alleged. (*Painters Local 419 v. Brown*)

Where the Comptroller General withholds funds from a contractor on the ground of noncompliance with the prevailing wage provisions, employees seeking to obtain money from the government must show that they had made a demand for payment from the Comptroller General, that there had been a determination of their right to payment by the official, and that the official had refused payment, as a condition precedent to maintaining an action in court against the government. (*Veader v. Bay State Dredging & Contracting Co.*)

The Act requires a federal contractor to maintain payroll records with sufficient particularity so that the contractor, if necessary, may demonstrate that there has been compliance with the Act's wage provisions. The contractor may dispute computations of the Labor Department, but it must have its own records to support its contentions. (*In re Woodside Village*)

A contractor that had submitted false records under the Act was debarred for three years from government contracting. The contractor's claim that its officers went beyond the scope of their duties and that the debarment penalty was thus inappropriate was unavailing. (Comp Gen Dec. B-145606, Aug. 1, 1961)

Receipt from the Labor Secretary of a notice of intent to initiate administrative enforcement procedures does not support a contractor's request to enjoin the Secretary, where the regulations provide levels of administrative proceedings that apparently are adequate to protect the contractor's rights, and in any event, there is no present harm to the contractor and no certainty that there will be future harm. (*Home Improvement Corp. v. Brennan*)

DEBARMENT

The DBA authorizes debarment from future government contracts for up to three years, for violations of the wage provisions of the Act in the course of performing under a covered contract. The Act specifically states that "the Comptroller General of the United States is further authorized and is directed to distribute a list . . . of persons and firms whom he has found to have *disregarded their obligations* to employees and subcontractors." (Emphasis added.) (40 U.S.C. Section 276-2(a)) This basis for debarment has come to be known as the "disregard-of-obligations" standard.

In 1987, the Labor Department declared that the "disregard-of-obligations" standard for imposing the debarment penalty on a contractor for violating the wage provisions of the DBA requires some review of the contractor's intent, since there is no indication that the legislature intended debarment to be a strict liability offense. In that case, the Labor Department declined to debar a contractor that violated DBA wage provisions in six of seven government contracts that it had been awarded. The Department found that the contractor's violations were not willful or intentional, since lack of knowledge and inadvertent mistake do not amount to disregard of obligations. (*In re Jen-Beck Assocs., Inc.*)

However, the Wage Appeals Board has declared that a debarred contractor can request removal from the ineligible list after completing at least six months of the debarment period. (*In re A. Vento Constr.*)

In a case involving a federal contractor's earlier debarment by the U.S. Department of Housing and Urban Development (HUD) for mail fraud in connection with submitting false payroll records under the DBA, the U.S. Court of Appeals for the Third Circuit ruled that:

- The contractor may raise the HUD debarment as a preclusion defense in the Labor Department's debarment proceeding based on alleged DBA violations; and
- The Labor Department's administrative law judge *must* consider the preclusion defense, since the HUD debarment was both adjudicatory and final, and the HUD administrative law judge filed a detailed opinion. (*Facchiano v. Brock*)

The doctrines of collateral estoppel and res judicata did not preclude the Labor Department's government-wide debarment proceeding against the debarred contractor from participating in programs funded by HUD, according to the U.S. Court of Appeals for the Third Circuit, because of the mail fraud conviction of the contractor's officer. The appeals court concluded that individual corporate officers are also subject to debarment under federal regulations promulgated under the Act. (*Facchiano Constr. Co. v. Labor Dep't*)

8

CONTRACT WORK HOURS AND SAFETY STANDARDS ACT

The Contract Work Hours and Safety Standards Act of 1962 (CWHSSA) was enacted to supersede the collection of statutes that became law from 1892 to 1917, collectively entitled the Eight Hour Laws. Also called the Work-Hours Act, CWHSSA is intended to regulate the payment of overtime for all mechanics and laborers employed on any public works project under a government contract or a government-financed contract.

The CWHSSA, like the Eight Hour Laws, originally required payment of time-and-one-half for all hours worked in excess of eight in one day to laborers and mechanics on public works. CWHSSA extended this overtime requirement to a workweek maximum of 40 hours in any one week. Congress eliminated the eight-hour day limit, however, in an attempt to allow a more flexible work schedule for covered employees, by enacting the Department of Defense Authorization Act of 1986 (P.L. 99-145).

Although the eight-hour day maximum is no longer in effect, contractors are still required to comply with the Act's 40-hour per week overtime limit. Overtime is computed on the employee's "basic rate of pay," which is the equivalent of the FLSA's "regular rate" of pay. Consequently, weekly salaries and fluctuating workweek (Belo) plans may be applied in computing CWHSSA overtime pay. (See Chapter 2, FLSA, under Overtime for more information on Belo plans.)

The Act also provides that no covered employee shall be employed under working conditions that are "unsanitary, hazardous, or dangerous" to health and safety. Debarment, or the blacklist penalty, is available for willful or grossly negligent violations of the Act.

COVERAGE

Covered Contracts

The Act covers any contract that may require or involve laborers or mechanics on a public works project under a contract with the federal government or under a contract financed by the federal government. CWHSSA regulations (29 C.F.R. Part 4.6) require the Secretary of Labor to incorporate the Act's wage and fringe benefit provisions in all covered contracts. Failure to include verbatim language from the Act formed the basis for a contractor's claim that it was thus not subject to the Act's minimum-wage and fringe benefit provisions. The claim was unsuccessful. (*National Electro-Coatings, Inc. v. Brock*)

Section 103 specifies which contracts will be covered and provides a limitation on this coverage:

- A contract to which the United States or any agency or instrumentality thereof, any territory, or the District of Columbia, is a party;
- A contract that is made for or on behalf of the United States, any agency or instrumentality thereof, any territory, or the District of Columbia; and
- A contract for work financed in whole or in part by loans or grants from, or loans insured or guaranteed by, the United States or any agency or instrumentality thereof under any statute of the United States providing standards for such work. *Provided*, that the Act shall not apply to work where assistance from the United States or any agency or instrumentality is only in the nature of a "loan guarantee, or insurance."

The Act's legislative history indicates that this proviso was intended to exclude programs that involve only federal guarantees of private loans, such as home construction financed by the Federal Housing Authority or the Veterans Administration.

Under this proviso, municipal employees working on construction and beautification projects were found to be exempt from the Act. (WH AdminOp, Sept. 9, 1969)

Exempt Contracts

The Act specifically exempts contracts for transportation by land, air, or water; (*Martinez v. Phillips Petroleum Co.*) contracts for the transmission of intelligence; and contracts for the purchase of supplies or materials or articles ordinarily available in the open market ("Open market contracts"). The Act also states that it shall not apply to any contract covered by the Walsh-Healey Act.

Employee Coverage

The Act specifically covers all mechanics and laborers, including watchmen and guards, employed by any contractor or subcontractor in the performance of any part of the work contemplated by a covered contract. Workers performing services in connection with dredging or rock excavation in any river or harbor of the United States or any territory or of the District of Columbia are also covered. The Act exempts any employee working as a "seaman," however.

HEALTH AND SAFETY STANDARDS

The Act authorizes the Secretary of Labor to set reasonable limits and to make such rules and regulations allowing reasonable variations, tolerances, and exemptions to and from any or all provisions of the Act as he may find necessary and proper in the public interest to prevent injustice or undue hardship or to avoid serious impairment of the conduct of government business.

The Assistant Secretary of Labor for Occupational Safety and Health is responsible for promulgating and administering the regulations governing health and safety standards under CWHSSA.

The Act also authorizes the Secretary to promulgate regulations providing for health and safety standards that must be observed in the performance of any contract or subcontract let under the Act. To this end, the Secretary may make inspections, hold hearings, issue orders, and make decisions that are deemed necessary to gain compliance.

The Secretary may apply to the federal courts to enforce compliance with safety and health standards. Where the contract has been canceled or the contractor has been debarred due to noncompliance, the contractor may seek review in the appropriate circuit court.

ENFORCEMENT

Under CWHSSA, the contractor who violates the Act may be liable directly to its employees for unpaid overtime and to the federal government for liquidated damages. The Act also provides criminal sanctions for willful violations, including a fine of $1,000 or six months imprisonment, or both.

The major source of disagreement under the Act's predecessor, the Eight Hour Laws, involved whether employees working for a covered contractor or subcontractor had a private right to bring an action for recovery of unpaid wages. The courts rejected any notion of a private right to sue (*Filardo v. Foley Bros. Inc.; McDaniel v. Brown & Root, Inc.*)—some decisions rejected a theory based on an implied right to bring an action, and others rejected a theory based on third-party beneficiary of the contract.

However, CWHSSA specifically grants employees the right to bring an action for wages. The two major sources of litigation under the Act have involved disputes over the debarment or blacklist penalty and over the imposition of liquidated damages. Overtime rulings under CWHSSA include the following cases:

- Requiring employees to perform 15 to 20 minutes of extra work as part of a continuing work regimen was not a

de minimis violation of the Act; (*Cobra Constr. Co. v. United States*)
- The overtime exemption for preliminary and postliminary activities of traveling to and from the actual place of performance of the principal activity does not apply to 30 minutes per day that a private employer's guards spent before and after their shift in obtaining their weapons from and returning them to a federal building, since such pre- and post-shift activities are "integral" parts of the work that the guards were hired to perform; (*International Business Invs. Inc. v. United States; see also Whelan Sec. Co. v. United States*) and
- A contractor was liable for its subcontractor's failure to pay overtime to five employees who worked in excess of eight hours per day, even though (*a*) the Act had been amended to eliminate the eight-hour-day requirement, (*b*) employees chose to work 10-hour days, and (*c*) state law accepted the 40-hour threshold for overtime. The Wage Appeals Board ruled that federal law in effect during the performance on the contract required payment of overtime to employees who worked more than eight hours per day. (*In re Kos Kam, Inc.*)

In another case, the U.S. Claims Court found that it lacked jurisdiction and dismissed a subcontractor's claim to recover payments withheld by the Labor Department for CWHSSA violations. The U.S. Court of Appeals for the Federal Circuit declared that the Claims Court erred, where the subcontractor claimed that there was a contract barring the Labor Department from withholding funds until the dispute was resolved. Such a contract, according to the appeals court, would create jurisdiction in the Claims Court under the Tucker Act. (*Cooper General Contractor v. United States*)

LIQUIDATED DAMAGES

The Act provides that a noncomplying contractor will be assessed a penalty for liquidated damages in the amount of $10 per day for each calendar day on which a covered employee is permitted or required to work without receiving overtime pay for overtime work. The liquidated damages are withheld by and for the use of the federal government. The government withholds overtime pay on behalf of the employees, and the Comptroller General is authorized to pay these overtime wages directly to the employees.

If the amounts withheld under the contract are insufficient to reimburse the workers for their unpaid overtime, they are authorized to maintain private actions or interventions against the contractor and its sureties. The Act invalidates any agreement by the employees to accept less than the required wages or any voluntary refunds by them, as employer defenses to allegations of overtime violations.

A contractor who has had amounts withheld as liquidated damages may appeal this action to the head of the contracting agency, who has authority to issue a final order on the propriety of the withholding. The Secretary of Labor may accept or reject the contracting agency official's recommendation. The contractor has 60 days from the date of the Secretary's disposition of the case to appeal to the U.S. Court of Claims for review.

Most government contracts contain a standard Disputes Clause that establishes the time period within which a party to the contract must assert that a dispute has arisen. Most Dispute Clauses contain only a 30-day time period, even though the CWHSSA allows for 60 days to appeal. The 60-day period for appeal to the U.S. Court of Claims, however, is substantially shorter than the six-year limitations period characteristically allowed for ordinary contract disputes. The various boards of contract appeals have generally taken jurisdiction over such claims. (*In re Anaco Reproductions*)

A 1982 decision by the U.S. Court of Claims illustrates both the enforcement mechanisms for review of contracting agency determinations, and the application of the liquidated damages penalty. A contractor performing work under contracts covered by both the Service Contract Act and CWHSSA was assessed liquidated damages for underpayments under the latter statute. Following an investigation of the employer's recordkeeping and payroll practices, the Department of Labor recommended to the Secretary of the Army—the head of the contracting agency in this dispute—that the contractor be assessed liquidated damages. The Army Secretary imposed a penalty of $12,520 for the contractor's failure to exercise due care. The Court of Claims held that this finding by the Secretary was supported by substantial evidence. The court rejected the contractor's claim that its violations were "inadvertent notwithstanding exercise of due care." It concluded that the amount of damages was not so harsh as to constitute an "abuse of discretion" on the part of the Army Secretary. (*Inland Serv. Corp. v. United States*)

The Work-Hours Act, unlike the FLSA and the Walsh-Healey and Davis-Bacon acts, is *not* covered by the Portal-to-Portal Pay Act's "good-faith" defense. Under CWHSSA's predecessor, the Eight Hour Laws, a contractor's reliance on rulings of the War Department was not a defense in an action by an employee to recover overtime pay allegedly due under the Law. (*Finnan v. Elmhurst Contracting Co.*)

Although the Portal Act's "good-faith" defense is not available under CWHSSA, courts have declined to assess liquidated damages in the following situations:

- A prime contractor paid back wages in settlement of a charge that its subcontractor had violated the CWHSSA on the understanding that it was in full and complete settlement of all claims against the contractor (*In re Abernathy & Wood*); and
- Guards were not paid for 10 minutes per day spent obtaining and returning their weapons. This was found to be *de minimis* for purposes of avoiding liquidated damages liability, but failure to pay the guards for 30 minutes was considered more than a *de minimis* violation of the Act. (*International Business Invs., Inc. v. United States*)

DEBARMENT PENALTY

The CWHSSA does not specifically provide for the debarment (blacklist) penalty, but it does authorize the Labor Secretary to promulgate regulations to impose appropriate sanctions and measures to enforce the Act. Under the regulations (29 C.F.R. Sec. 5), the Secretary has prescribed this penalty for willful or aggravated violations of the Act. The Secretary's authority to impose debarment by promulgating a regulation, the propriety of inferring such a penalty where CWHSSA is silent and other statues specify it, and the appropriateness of imposing it in a particular case, were all upheld by the U.S. District Court for the District of Columbia in 1961. (*Copper Plumbing & Heating Co. v. Campbell*)

Acknowledging that CWHSSA does not specifically mention debarment as a sanction, the U.S. Court of Appeals for the Second Circuit nevertheless ruled that such action is necessary for enforcement of statutory labor standards. The Wage Appeals Board and a federal district court had both found the contractor to have willfully violated CWHSSA on two federally funded construction projects. Resisting the debarment penalty imposed by each, the contractor argued that debarment constituted a penalty and that penalties may not be imposed with out specific instruction from Congress. However, the appeals court reasoned that a sanction which serves to compel compliance with statutory goals should not be deemed a penalty, citing the U.S. Supreme Court in *Steuart & Bros. v. Bowles.* (*Janik Paving & Constr. v. Brock*)

Relief from the debarment penalty requires a showing of "unusual circumstances." (See also "Blacklist Penalty" in Chapter 6.) The Labor Department takes the position that financial problems do not constitute unusual circumstances for purposes of relieving a contractor of the debarment penalty. (*Labor Dep't v. Stafford's Might Maid*)

Attorneys' Fees

The CWHSSA is silent on the matter of attorneys' fees awards. However, Congress has provided for an award of reasonable attorneys' fees "to the prevailing party in any civil action brought by or against the United States . . . in any court having jurisdiction of such action." (Equal Access to Justice Act, 28 U.S.C. Sec. 2412(b))

A contractor that was relieved from the debarment penalty for its violations of the SCA and the CWHSSA was not entitled to attorneys' fees under EAJA, where:

- The regulations implementing EAJA exclude SCA and CWHSSA;
- The right to such fees arises under EAJA and not the labor standards acts; and
- EAJA authorizes fees only in "adversary adjudication," defined as proceedings required by law, and the SCA authorizes but does not require the proceeding in the instant case. (*In re Verticare*)

OTHER LAWS

CWHSSA specifically exempts contracts covered by the Walsh-Healey Act. Since Walsh-Healey does not cover contracts below $10,000 in amount, CWHSSA will likely cover these contracts without running afoul of Walsh-Healey coverage.

Walsh-Healey applies to an employee in any workweek in which the employee devotes *any time* to work covered by the Act. However, CWHSSA applies only where the employee works on a government contract for more than 40 hours in the workweek. (WH AdminOp, Oct. 7, 1964)

9

OTHER FEDERAL LAWS

In addition to the major statutes that govern wages, hours, recordkeeping, and safety-health standards that have been discussed in previous chapters, there is a plethora of minor statutes that affect these areas in one way or another. These statutes may only govern an area incidentally, rather than as a major intent of Congress, but employers must comply with them nevertheless.

ANTI-KICKBACK LAW (COPELAND ACT)

The Anti-Kickback Law (Copeland Act) of 1954 is designed to protect employees' wages from illegal "kickback" arrangements in government-financed public construction. It covers contracts governed by Davis-Bacon and Work Hours acts. The Copeland Act prohibits anyone from compelling employees to return wages "by force, intimidation, or threat of procuring dismissal from employment, or by any other manner whatsoever." The Act prescribes a penalty of a $5,000 fine, up to five years' imprisonment, or both.

TITLE III, CONSUMER CREDIT PROTECTION ACT

Title III of the Consumer Credit Protection Act of 1968 (CCPA) covers all employees, regardless of the size of the employer's business. Congress enacted this law under its authority to regulate commerce. The law is intended to create a uniform treatment under the bankruptcy law. Therefore, only a minimal involvement in interstate commerce is necessary for an employer to fall under the Act's coverage. The Act regulates and makes consistent employer practices regarding garnishments of employee wages. It defines "earnings," "disposable earnings," and "garnishment," and it establishes restrictions on the amount of wages that can be garnisheed.

The maximum amount that may be garnisheed is determined under a formula. Under this calculation, the amount of wages that is subject to garnishment may not exceed (*a*) 25 percent of the employee's disposable earnings for any workweek, or (*b*) the amount by which his disposable earnings are greater than 30 times the federal minimum hourly wage, whichever is less. However, these limits on amounts that may be garnisheed do not apply where:

- The wage deduction is based on a court order for support or on an order of a court of bankruptcy; and
- Wage deductions for any debt due on any state or federal tax.

The CCPA prohibits an employer from discharging an employee for having a "single" garnishment levied against his or her pay. Violation of this ban carries penalties of a $1,000 fine, one year imprisonment, or both. The Secretary of Labor is authorized to enforce the CCPA, and the courts have interpreted this statutory mandate to preclude discharged employees from filing private lawsuits. (*Le Vick v. Skaggs Co.*)

An employer violated the CCPA when it discharged an employee, allegedly because of poor performance and because of the employee's failure to give satisfactory answers when questioned about his performance. A notice of levy on the employee's wages was found to be the motivating factor in the discharge. The employee was entitled to damages in the amount of lost wages from the date of his next scheduled performance evaluation, but not to reinstatement. (*Martin v. Hawkeye Int'l Trucks, Inc.*)

Similarly, there is no implied private cause of action for damages for violations of the CCPA, and therefore, there can be no action under the Civil Rights Act of 1871 for those violations. (*Burris v. Mahaney*)

Because of the large number of state laws that regulate in this area, Congress added a section in the Act stating that the states are not precluded from applying their own garnishment laws, where the state laws prescribe higher or stricter standards restricting garnishment than the CCPA. The Act does not protect an employee who is discharged for having more than a single garnishment.

Long before Congress enacted federal legislation dealing with garnishment, the U.S. Supreme Court held unlawful state laws permitting a creditor to garnish an employee's wages without first giving him a hearing in court. Emphasizing that the state statute did not require the creditor to show that garnishment was necessary to collect the debt, the court ruled that a garnishment without notice or hearing amounts to a seizure of property without the procedural due process required under the Fourteenth Amendment to the U.S. Constitution. (*Sniadach v. Family Finance Corp.*)

Finally, any state may apply to the Secretary of Labor to have garnishments issued under state law exempted from CCPA restrictions, where the state law provides for restrictions that are substantially similar to the Act.

CHILD SUPPORT ENFORCEMENT ACT

The Child Support Enforcement Act of 1984 revises the Social Security Act and requires all states to have child support withholding laws in effect by January 1, 1986. Employers are required to withhold from an employee's wages any amounts determined to be due under support orders issued by a court or administrative body.

The Act prohibits employers from disciplining, discharging, or refusing to hire an individual because of a withholding order for support. Employees are entitled to advance notice and a hearing before any order becomes effective.

OCCUPATIONAL SAFETY AND HEALTH ACT

The Occupational Safety and Health Act of 1970 (OSHA; LRX 6201) covers all employers engaged in a business affecting commerce, but does not include the federal government or any state or political subdivision of a state. OSHA defines an employee as any individual employed in a business of the employer affecting commerce.

Although the Secretary of Labor has primary responsibility for enforcing OSHA, the Secretary of Health and Human Services and the Occupational Safety and Health Review Commission also have important duties under the Act. In addition, the states are free to conduct their own safety and health programs in areas where there are no federal standards.

The Act imposes on an employer the general duty to furnish each of its employees employment and a place of employment that are free from recognized hazards that are causing or are likely to cause death or serious physical harm to employees.

To constitute a violation of the employer's general duty, the hazard involved must be preventable by the employer and must therefore be foreseeable. The employer can satisfy this general duty by:

- Promulgating adequate safety rules;
- Enforcing such rules with reasonable sanctions adequate to deter violations;
- Providing adequate training and instruction to all employees involved in hazardous work;
- Providing adequate supervision to employees according to their experience and exposure to dangerous conditions; and
- Providing protective equipment and requiring use of such equipment, where necessary.

In establishing safety and health standards, Congress created the National Institute of Occupational Safety and Health (NIOSH). NIOSH is authorized to conduct research, develop innovative methods and techniques for identifying toxic substances, and set criteria for safe use.

The Act also authorizes "notice and comment" rulemaking, under the auspices of the Labor Secretary. Any person adversely affected by the standard may obtain review by the appropriate U.S. court of appeals.

The Labor Secretary is authorized to grant temporary variances, and variations, tolerances, and exemptions from any or all provisions of the Act due to national defense considerations. The Secretary is required to conduct investigations and to issue citations where appropriate.

For all violations, the Secretary must set a period of "abatement," by which time the employer must correct the infraction. However, the employer has several options:

- Challenging the determination and seeking to have the abatement order revoked or modified;
- Seeking to obtain a variance;
- Applying for a temporary variance, to gain time to comply with the abatement order; and
- Petitioning the Labor Secretary for revocation or modification of the order, on the ground that a good-faith attempt to comply has been unsuccessful because of factors beyond the employer's control.

Employers who violate the Act face a range of civil and/or criminal penalties that include fines of up to $10,000 and six months in jail for a first offense of willfully violating the Act, and a fine of up to $20,000 and one year imprisonment for each subsequent offense.

The Act encourages individual employees to contact the Occupational Health and Safety Administration when a violation is suspected. Employees are protected from retaliation for exercising their rights under the Act, such as filing complaints or testifying against their employer in a proceeding under the Act.

FAMILY AND MEDICAL LEAVE ACT

An important statute that regulates work hours and has an effect on FLSA exemptions is the Family and Medical Leave

Act of 1993. The Act contains provisions on employer coverage; employee eligibility for the Act's benefits; entitlement to leave, maintenance of health benefits during leave, and job restoration after leave; notice and certification of the need for FMLA leave; and protections for employees who request or take FMLA leave. The Act also requires employers to keep certain records of FMLA leave.

The FMLA requires covered employers to grant eligible employees requests for FMLA leave of up to 12 weeks of unpaid leave within a 12-month period for:

- The birth or placement of a child for adoption or foster care;
- The care of an immediate family member (spouse, child or parent, or someone who stands or stood in place of such immediate family member); or
- Medical leave when the employee is unable to work because of a "serious health condition." (See Appendix M.)

This leave may be used all at once, intermittently, or as part of a reduced work schedule. Where the leave is used intermittently or as part of a reduced work schedule, the employer is authorized to record FMLA leave to ensure that the 12 weeks of unpaid leave are available to the employee. Where the employee is also a FLSA-exempt employee whose "salary" is inviolate, the FMLA authorizes the employer to deduct from that employee's "salary" for partial day absences, where the employee takes unpaid leave, without losing the exemption.

Unlike most federal laws, the FMLA does not preempt state law that regulates in this area. As between the FMLA and differing state law leave provisions, the FMLA provides that employers are to observe the more generous leave provisions and to follow the least burdensome procedural provisions for allowing the leave. Where employers operate in more than one state, this federal/state scheme will require even greater scrutiny. For example, an employer that docks for partial day absences from the "salary" of a FLSA-exempt employee who is on FMLA leave could face unforeseen problems where the state law authorizes more than the FMLA maximum of 12 weeks of unpaid leave. Problems could arise where the employee continues to use FMLA-type leave under the state law. If the employer continues to dock from the employee's "salary" for unpaid leave after the docking authorization for the FLSA exemption has expired (at the conclusion of the FMLA 12-week period), it is possible that the exemption will be lost, not only for that employee but also for all employees in that exempt classification. The FMLA and its regulations are complex and require careful scrutiny. The Act is enforced by the Wage and Hour Division of the Employment Standards Administration, U.S. Labor Department. (See discussion on "Salary Basis Test" in Chapter 2 for more information on the FMLA leave provisions.)

MISCELLANEOUS STATUTES

A variety of laws contain "employee protection" provisions that relate to wages-hours and/or safety-health issues in the workplace, even though the underlying purpose of the law may be to regulate in some other area. These federal statutes include the Energy Reorganization Act, the Surface Transportation Assistance Act of 1982, the Rehabilitation Act of 1973, and the Americans with Disabilities Act of 1991.

Still other laws that touch on these areas of concern are the Employee Retirement Income Security Act of 1974, the Migrant and Seasonal Agricultural Worker Protection Act, the National Foundation on the Arts and Humanities Act, the Motor Carrier Act, the Mineral Land Act, the Area Redevelopment Act of 1961, the Merchant Marine Act, the Miller Act, and the Age Discrimination in Employment Act of 1967.

For example, the Tucker Act governs certain disputes that arise in federally funded construction projects. This statute has been involved in a dispute that would otherwise be enforced strictly under the Contract Work Hours and Safety Standards Act (CWHSSA; see Chapter 8 for more details). In that dispute, a subcontractor was found to have violated the CWHSSA's overtime provisions and the Labor Department withheld payments to the subcontractor. The subcontractor sued to recover the withheld payments and the dispute reached the U.S. Claims Court, which found that it lacked jurisdiction and dismissed the claim.

The U.S. Court of Appeals for the Federal Circuit declared that the Claims Court erred, where the subcontractor claimed that there was a *contract* barring the Labor Department from withholding funds until the dispute was resolved. Such a contract, according to the appeals court, would create jurisdiction in the Claims Court under the Tucker Act. (*Cooper General Contractor v. United States*)

Similarly, the Miller Act permits a person who has performed work on a government contract covered by the Miller Act to recover under the performance bond executed by the general contractor, if he or she has not been paid in full. Union trust funds sued a contractor under this provision of the Act for contributions for work performed by covered employees under collective bargaining agreements with the general contractor. However, because the trust funds had failed to comply with the Act's notice provisions, they were unsuccessful. (*Laborers' Pension Trust Fund v. Safeco Ins. Co. of Am.*)

In addition to these laws, many states have their own statutory scheme to regulate wages, hours of work, and other aspects of the employee's compensation scheme, such as the accrual and payment of sick or vacation leave, payment upon termination of employment, and other items. (State minimum wage requirements appear in Appendix E; state maximum hours and overtime requirements appear in Appendix G.)

Many states also have laws that establish prevailing wage rates for state-funded construction projects. These state laws are often called "little Davis-Bacon Acts," since the purpose and language of the state laws generally follow closely their federal counterpart. However, the federal government has also taken note of the existence of these little Davis-Bacon Acts, and the potential confusion created by a project covering more than one state boundary, especially where federal funds may be involved. To that end, the federal government has issued a rule to resolve such confusion. Federal prevailing wage rates determined under the federal Davis-Bacon Act preempt state prevailing wage rates for a given construction trade on public or Indian housing projects when the state prevailing wage is higher, according to a final regulation issued by the U.S. Department of Housing and Urban Development in 1988.

Last, but not least, employers may be obligated to pay certain wages and fringe benefits and scheduled increases under collective bargaining agreements or individual employment contracts.

Appendix A

Directory of U.S. Department of Labor Administrative and Regional Offices

U.S. DEPARTMENT OF LABOR
Administrative Offices

Address: 200 Constitution Avenue, N.W. Washington, D.C. 20210; Telephone: (202) 219-7316

OFFICE OF THE SECRETARY

Secretary: Robert B. Reich
Chief of Staff: Kitty Higgins

OFFICE OF THE DEPUTY SECRETARY

Deputy Secretary: Thomas P. Glynn III (*Designate*)
Associate Deputy Secretaries: Betty Bolden, Steve Rosenthal

INSPECTOR GENERAL

Inspector General: Charles C. Masten

ADMINISTRATIVE LAW JUDGES

Chief Judge: Nahum Litt
Deputy Chief Judge: John M. Vittone
Associate Chief Judges: G. Marvin Bober, James Guill

BENEFITS REVIEW BOARD

Chief Administrative Appeals Judge: Betty J. Stage
Administrative Appeals Judges: James F. Brown, Roy P. Smith, Nancy S. Dolder, Regina C. McGranery, Leonard Lawrence

EMPLOYEES' COMPENSATION APPEALS BOARD

Chairman: Michael J. Walsh
Members: David Gerson, George Rivers

WAGE APPEALS BOARD

Chairman: Charles E. Shearer, Jr.
Members: Ruth E. Peters, Anna Maria Farias

ASSISTANT SECRETARY FOR CONGRESSIONAL AND INTERGOVERNMENTAL AFFAIRS

Assistant Secretary: Geri D. Palast
Deputy Assistant Secretary: (*Vacant*)

ASSISTANT SECRETARY FOR PUBLIC AFFAIRS

Assistant Secretary: Anne Lewis (*Designate*)
Deputy Assistant Secretary: (*Vacant*)

ASSISTANT SECRETARY FOR ADMINISTRATION & MANAGEMENT

Assistant Secretary: Thomas C. Komarek
Deputy Assistant Secretary: Cecilia Bankins
Comptroller: William R. Reise

ASSISTANT SECRETARY FOR PENSION & WELFARE BENEFITS

Assistant Secretary: Olena Berg
Deputy Assistant Secretary, Policy: (*Vacant*)

ASSISTANT SECRETARY FOR POLICY

Assistant Secretary: John Donahue
Deputy Assistant Secretary, Program Economics & Research & Technical Support: (*Vacant*)
Deputy Assistant Secretary, Regulatory Economics & Economic Policy Analysis: Roland G. Droitsch

ASSISTANT SECRETARY FOR MINE SAFETY & HEALTH

Assistant Secretary: J. Davitt McAteer (*Designate*)
Deputy Assistant Secretary: Edward C. Hugler

ASSISTANT SECRETARY FOR EMPLOYMENT STANDARDS

Assistant Secretary: Bernard Anderson (*Designate*)
Deputy Assistant Secretary: (*Vacant*)

Administrator, Wage & Hour Division: Maria Echaveste

ASSISTANT SECRETARY FOR VETERANS' EMPLOYMENT & TRAINING

Acting Assistant Secretary: Jeffrey Crandall (*Acting*)
Deputy Assistant Secretary: (*Vacant*)

ASSISTANT SECRETARY FOR OCCUPATIONAL SAFETY & HEALTH

Assistant Secretary: Joseph Dear (*Designate*)
Deputy Assistant Secretary: Russell B. Swanson

ASSISTANT SECRETARY FOR EMPLOYMENT & TRAINING

Assistant Secretary: Douglas B. Ross
Deputy Assistant Secretaries: Carolyn M. Golding, Dave O. Williams

OFFICE OF THE AMERICAN WORKPLACE

Assistant Secretary: Martin Manley
Deputy Assistant Secretary; Office of Labor-Management Standards: (*Vacant*)
Deputy Assistant Secretary; Office of Work and Technology Policy: (*Vacant*)
Deputy Assistant Secretary; Office of Labor-Management Programs: Charles A. Richards

WOMEN'S BUREAU

Director: Karen Nussbaum

GLASS CEILING COMMISSION

Executive Director: Joyce Miller

BUREAU OF INTERNATIONAL LABOR AFFAIRS

Deputy Under Secretary: Joaquin F. Otero
Assoc. Deputy Under Secretary: (*Vacant*)
Director, Office of International Organizations: H. Charles Spring
Director, Office of Foreign Relations: John Ferch
Director, Office of International Economic Affairs: Jorge Perez-Lopez

U.S. National Administrative Office (NAFTA/NAALC)

Secretary: Jorge Perez-Lopez (*Acting, until Spring 1994*)

BUREAU OF LABOR STATISTICS

Commissioner: Katharine Abraham (*Designate*)

Office of Administration & Internal Operations

Deputy Commissioner: William G. Barron, Jr.

Office of Technology & Survey Processing

Assistant Commissioner: Carl J. Lowe

Office of Compensation & Working Conditions

Associate Commissioner: George L. Stelluto
Assistant Commissioner: Kathleen M. MacDonald

Office of Economic Growth & Employment Projections

Associate Commissioner: Ronald E. Kutscher

Office of Employment & Unemployment Statistics

Associate Commissioner: Thomas J. Plewes

Office of Field Operations
Associate Commissioner: Laura B. King

Office of Prices & Living Conditions
Associate Commissioner: Kenneth V. Dalton

Office of Productivity & Technology
Associate Commissioner: Edwin R. Dean

Office of Publications
Associate Commissioner: Deborah Klein

Office of Research & Evaluation
Associate Commissioner: Wesley L. Schaible

OFFICE OF THE SOLICITOR
Solicitor: Thomas S. Williamson, Jr. (*Designate*)
Deputy Solicitor, National Operations: David Fortney
Deputy Solicitor, Planning & Coordination: Judith E. Kramer
Deputy Solicitor, Regional Operations: Ronald G. Whiting

Appendix B
Chart of FLSA White-Collar Exemption Tests

Appendix B 171

White-Collar Exemption Chart

	"Streamlined" tests for employees with weekly salaries of at least $250*	Additional tests for lower-paid employees
EXECUTIVES	1) Primary duty is managing an enterprise of a customarily recognized department or subdivision. 2) Customarily and regularly direct the work of two or more employees.	3) Have a weekly salary of at least $155** exclusive of board, lodging, or other facilities. 4) Have the authority to hire and fire other employees or to recommend hiring, firing, promotion, or change of status of employees. 5) Customarily and regularly exercise discretionary powers. 6) Do not devote more than 20 percent of their worktime to activities that aren't directly and closely related to exempt work. (Exceptions include executives: a) in retail or service establishments, who may spend up to 40 percent of their worktime on unrelated activities; b) who own at least a 20-percent interest in the enterprise; or c) who are in charge of an independent establishment or physically separated branch establishment.)
ADMINISTRATIVE EMPLOYEES	1) Primary duty is performing office or nonmanual work directly related to management policies or general business operations of employer or its customers, administrative work in the academic field, or work relating to academic instruction. 2) Work requires the exercise of discretion and independent judgment.	3) Have a weekly salary of at least $155** exclusive of board, lodging, or other facilities. (In the academic field, employees must either meet this salary test or receive a salary at least equal to the starting salary for teachers in the same school system or academic institution.) 4) Regularly and directly assist a proprietor or a bona-fide executive or administrative employee; perform under only general supervision specialized or technical work requiring special experience, training, or knowledge; or work on special assignments or tasks under only general supervision. 5) Do not devote more than 20 percent of workweek to activities not closely related to work described in tests 1, 2, and 4. (Retail or service workers may spend up to 40 percent of their time in unrelated activities.)

White-Collar Exemption Chart — Contd.

	"Streamlined" tests for employees with weekly salaries of at least $250*	Additional tests for lower-paid employees
PROFESSIONALS	1) Primary duty is performing work that: (a) requires knowledge of advanced type in field of science or learning; (b) is original and creative in a recognized field of artistic endeavor; or (c) involves imparting knowledge as a certified or recognized teacher.	2) Have a weekly salary of at least $170** exclusive of board, lodging, or other facilities; or (a) have a valid license to practice and are practicing law or medicine; (b) have a medical degree and are in an internship or resident program; or (c) work as a teacher. 3) Work consistently requires discretion and judgment. 4) Work is predominantly intellectual and varied, and output or results cannot be standardized in relation to a given time period. 5) Time spent on unrelated activities is not more than 20 percent of the workweek.
OUTSIDE SALES EMPLOYEES	1) Customarily and regularly work away from the employer's premises in making sales or obtaining orders or contracts. This exempt work includes work incidental to and in conjunction with outside sales, such as incidental deliveries and collections. 2) Hours spent on other types of work do not exceed 20 percent of the workweek of the employer's nonexempt workers.	
COMPUTER-RELATED OCCUPATIONS	Highly-skilled computer-related workers who are paid less than 6.5 times the minimum wage but who qualify under other white-collar exemptions remain exempt as long as they meet the applicable duties and responsibilities tests. Those who are paid more than 6.5 times the minimum wage are exempt from overtime requirements, provided their primary job duties include: • The application of systems analysis techniques and procedures, to include consultations with users in order to determine hardware and software specifications; • The design of computer systems based on and related to user specifications; • The creation or modification of computer programs based on and related to system design specifications; • The creation or modification of computer programs related to machine operating systems; or • A combination of the above duties.	

* ($200 in Puerto Rico, Virgin Islands, American Samoa)
** ($150 in Puerto Rico, Virgin Islands, American Samoa)

Appendix C
Chart of FLSA Exemptions From Minimum Wage and Overtime

Appendix C

Exemption Chart

INDUSTRY OR OCCUPATION	OVERTIME EXEMPTION	MINIMUM-WAGE EXEMPTION
Airlines	Exemption except for employees engaged in activities not necessary to or related to air transportation.	None.
Amusement & recreational establishments	Exemption if (a) establishment doesn't operate more than 7 months during calendar year, or (b) its average receipts during any 6 months of prior calendar year don't exceed one third of its average receipts for the other 6 months of the year. 1977 amendments added organized camps or religious or non-profit educational conference centers as exempt establishments, but specifically deny exemption to concessioners in national parks, refuges, and forests, with exception of facilities operating in these areas that are directly relating to skiing.	Exemption under same terms as overtime exemption.
Apprentices (i.e., one who is at least age 16 and is hired to learn a skilled trade in conformity with established apprenticeship standards).	None.	Subminimum rates may be paid under special certificate.
Auto, farm implement, boat, aircraft dealers	Exemption for salesmen, partsmen, and mechanics primarily selling or servicing autos, trucks, or farm implements, if employed by non-manufacturer primarily selling to ultimate consumer. Exemption for salesmen primarily selling trailers, aircraft, or boats if employed by non-manufacturer primarily selling to ultimate consumer.	None.
Domestic Service Workers in Private Household	Exemption if not covered by the Social Security Act nor employed for more than 40 hours per week for one employer. Babysitters employed on a casual basis and persons employed to provide companion services are exempt. Live-in domestics are exempt from overtime.	Exemption if not covered by the Social Security Act nor employed for more than eight hours per week in the aggregate. Babysitters employed on a casual basis and persons employed to provide companion services are exempt.
Drivers and drivers' helpers	Exempt if making local deliveries and compensated on trip rate basis.	None.
Foreign employment	Exemption for services performed within a foreign country.	Exemption under same terms as overtime exemption.
Forestry or logging	Exemption if employer has 8 employees or less.	None.
Gasoline stations	Exemption for stations with annual sales of less than $250,000.	Exemption under same terms as overtime exemption.

INDUSTRY OR OCCUPATION	OVERTIME EXEMPTION	MINIMUM-WAGE EXEMPTION
Handicapped workers (i.e., one whose earning capacity has been impaired by age or physical or mental deficiency or injury).	None.	Subminimum rates may be paid under special certificate.
Holly-wreath manufacture	Exemption for homeworkers engaged in making of wreaths composed principally of natural evergreens.	Exemption under same terms as overtime exemption.
Hospitals and nursing homes	Hospital may use work period of 14 days, rather than 7 days, in computing overtime if employees agree in advance and 1½ times regular rate is paid for hours over 8 per day, and 80 in 14-day period. Otherwise, overtime rate applies after 40 hours per week.	None.
Hotels, motels, & restaurants (Other than those qualifying for retail-service exemptions)	Exemption for hotel, motel, and restaurant employees (other than hotel maids and custodial employees) provided they are paid 1½ times regular rate for hours over 44 per week effective January 1, 1976. Exemption was repealed effective January 1, 1979.	None.
Learners (i.e., a beginner at a skilled occupation).	None.	Subminim rates may be paid under special certificates.
Messengers	None.	Special certificates for employment at subminimum rates are authorized, but none has been issued.
Motion picture theaters	Exemption.	None.
Motor carriers	Exemption for employees whose hours of service are subject to regulation by Dept. of Transportation.	None.
Newsboys delivering newspapers to the consumer	Exemption.	Exemption.
Newpapers	Exemption for employees of paper with 4,000 or less circulation, major part of which is in county in which paper is published or in contiguous counties (paper may be printed elsewhere).	Exemption under same terms as overtime exemption.
Outside Salesman	Exempt.	Exempt.
Petroleum distributors	Exemption for any employee of independently owned & controlled local enterprise engaged in wholesale or bulk distribution of petroleum products, *provided* he is paid 1½ times the *statutory* minimum rate for work between 40 and 56 hours per week and 1½ times his *regular* rate for all work in excess of 12 hours per day and 56 per week.	None.

Appendix C

INDUSTRY OR OCCUPATION	OVERTIME EXEMPTION	MINIMUM-WAGE EXEMPTION
Professional, executive, and administrative personnel	Exempt if they meet regulatory tests.	Exemption under same terms as overtime exemption.
Radio & TV broadcasters	Exemptions for announcers, news editors, and chief engineers of radio or TV station whose major studio is located in (1) city of 100,000 or less that is not part of a metropolitan area of more than 100,000, or (2) city of 25,000 or less, even in such metropolitan area if it is located at least 40 airline miles from principal city in area.	None.
Railroad, steamship companies	Exemption for employees of employer subject to Part I of Interstate Commerce Act, i.e., common carriers engaged in (a) transporting passengers or property wholly by rail, or partly by rail and partly by water when both are used under common control, management, or arrangement for continuous carriage or shipment; or (b) transportation of oil or other commodities, except water and natural or artificial gas, by pipeline or partly by pipeline and partly by railroad or water.	None.
Retail-service establishments (other than a laundry-dry-cleaning establishment, hospital, nursing home, school for handicapped or gifted children, preschool, elementary, or secondary school, or college.	Exemption if (a) more than 50 percent of establishment's annual sales is intrastate, and (b) at least 75 percent of its annual dollar sales is not for resale and is recognized as retail in the industry. Under the 1977 amendments to the FLSA, the test for coverage of employees of enterprises composed of one or more retail or service establishments is raised to $362,500 in three steps as follows: • July 1, 1978 ....$275,000 • July 1, 1980 ....$325,000 • Dec. 31, 1981............................$362,500	Exemption under same terms as overtime exemption.
Retail commission salesmen	Exemption provided employee's regular rate (including salary and commissions) is more than 1½ times the statutory minimum, and more than half his compensation comes from commissions.	None.
Retail-manufacturing units (e.g., bakeries, ice-cream parlors, candy shops)	Exemptions for establishment if (a) it meets tests for retail-service establishments, (b) it is recognized in industry as retail establishment, (c) more than 85 percent of its dollar volume of annual sales is made intrastate, (d) the goods are made or processed and sold in the same establishment.	None.
Seamen	Exemption for all seamen, whether on U.S. or foreign vessels.	Exemption only for seamen on foreign vessels.

INDUSTRY OR OCCUPATION	OVERTIME EXEMPTION	MINIMUM-WAGE EXEMPTION
Students in agriculture	None.	Secretary of labor may permit employment of students part-time (20 hours a week or less) and full-time during vacations at 85 percent of statutory minimum.
Students in higher educational institutions	None.	Same as above.
Students in retailing	None	Secy. of labor may permit employment of students part-time (20 hours a week or less) and full-time during vacations at 85 percent of statutory minimum.
Substitute parents for institutionalized children	Exempt if employee and spouse are substitute parents for children residing in private non-profit educational institutions, receive jointly cash wages of $10,000 annually, and reside in the same facilities as the children receiving free room and board.	None.
Taxicab drivers	Exemption for drivers employed by taxicab company.	None.
Telephone exchanges	Exemption for employees of independently owned telephone company that has fewer than 750 stations.	Exemption under same terms as overtime exemption.

Appendix D

Directory of U.S. Department of Labor Employment Standards Administration, Administrative and Regional Offices

Appendix D

Employment Standards Administration
Administrative Offices

Address: U.S. Department of Labor Bldg.
200 Constitution Ave., N.W., Washington, D.C. 20210
Telephone: (202) 219-6191; 219-8743

ASSISTANT SECRETARY FOR EMPLOYMENT STANDARDS: (202-219-6191)

Assistant Secretary: Bernard Anderson (*Acting*)
Deputy Assistant: Donna Copson (*Acting*)
Executive Assistant: (*Vacant*)
Special Assistant: Don Wilson

EQUAL EMPLOYMENT OPPORTUNITY UNIT: (202-219-8741)

Coordinator: Carvin Cook

FEDERAL CONTRACT COMPLIANCE PROGRAMS: (219-9475)

Director: Leonard J. Biermann (A)
Deputy Director: Leonard J. Biermann
Chief, Program Policy Division: Annie Blackwell
Chief, Program Operations Division: Robert B. Greaux

MANAGEMENT, ADMINISTRATION, AND PLANNING: (202-219-6535)

Director (A): Donna Copson
Deputy Director: Eleanor Smith

POLICY, MANAGEMENT, AND ANALYSIS: (202-219-9575)

Director: Patrick Mowry

PROGRAM OPERATIONS: (202-219-8353)

Assistant Administrator: William W. Gross (A)
Deputy Assistant Administrator: William W. Gross

FAIR LABOR STANDARDS ACT OPERATIONS DIVISION: (202-219-7403)

Director: (*Vacant*)
Chief, Enforcement Branch: (*Vacant*)
Chief, Special Employment Branch: Howard B. Ostmann,

FARM LABOR, CHILD LABOR, AND POLYGRAPH STANDARDS DIVISION: (202-219-4670)

Director: Corlis L. Sellers
Chief, Child Labor and Polygraph Standards Branch: Nila J. Stovall
Chief, Farm Labor Progams Branch: Solomon Sugarman

WAGE DETERMINATIONS DIVISION: (202-219-7443)

Director: Alan Moss
Chief, Construction: Libby Hendrix

POLICY PLANNING AND REVIEW: (202-219-5409)

Assistant Administrator: Charles E. Pugh
Policy & Analysis Division
Director: J. Dean Speer
Planning & Review Division
Director: James W. Gantt

CONTRACT STANDARDS OPERATIONS DIVISION: (202-219-7541)

Director: Libby Hendrix (A)
Chief, Construction Contract Operations Branch: Libby Hendrix

PUBLIC AFFAIRS: (202-219-8743)

Director: Robert Cuccia

WAGE AND HOUR DIVISION: (202-219-8305)

Administrator: Maria Echaveste
Deputy Administrator: (*Vacant*)

WORKERS' COMPENSATION PROGRAMS: (202-219-7503)

Director: Lawrence W. Rogers Jr.
Deputy Director: Shelby Hallmark
Chief, Longshore & Harbor Workers' Compensation Division: Joseph Olimpio
Chief, Federal Employees' Compensation Division: Thomas Markey

Regional Offices (202-523-6535)

REGIONAL OFFICES SERVING VARIOUS STATES					
Region No.	State	Region No.	State	Region No.	State
4	Alabama	3	Maryland	1	Rhode Island
10	Alaska	1	Massachusetts	4	South Carolina
9	Arizona	5	Michigan	8	South Dakota
6	Arkansas	5	Minnesota	4	Tennessee
9	California	4	Mississippi	6	Texas
8	Colorado	7	Missouri	8	Utah
1	Connecticut	8	Montana	1	Vermont
3	Delaware	7	Nebraska	3	Virginia
3	District of Columbia	9	Nevada	10	Washington
4	Florida	1	New Hampshire	3	West Virginia
4	Georgia	2	New Jersey	5	Wisconsin
9	Hawaii	6	New Mexico	8	Wyoming
10	Idaho	2	New York		
5	Illinois	4	North Carolina	*Territories and*	
5	Indiana	8	North Dakota	*Possessions*	
7	Iowa	5	Ohio	1	Canal Zone
7	Kansas	6	Oklahoma	10	Guam
4	Kentucky	10	Oregon	2	Puerto Rico
6	Louisiana	3	Pennsylvania	2	Virgin Islands
1	Maine				

Region I

Regional Administrator: Walter P. Parker
Address: JFK Federal Bldg., Rm. 1612C, Boston MA 02203
Tel.: (617) 565-2066
Deputy Regional Administrator: Gerald A. Corrao
Address: Same
Tel.: (617) 565-2070

Wage-Hour District Offices

Boston
Address: J.W. McCormick Bldg., Rm. 806, P.O.C.H., Boston MA 02109
Tel.: (617) 424-4925

Hartford
Address: Federal Bldg., Rm. 310, 135 High St., Hartford CT 061031
Tel.: (203) 240-4160

Portland
Address: District Director, P.O. Box 211, Portland ME 04112
Tel.: (207) 780-3350

Providence
Address: District Director, 380 Westminster Mall, Rm. 346, Providence RI 02903
Tel.: (401) 528-4432

Region II

Regional Administrator: Doris D. Wooten
Address: 201 Varick St., Rm. 750, New York NY 10014
Tel.: (212) 337-2020
Assistant Regional Administrator: (*Vacant*)
Address: Same
Tel.: (212) 337-2020

Appendix D

Wage-Hour District Offices

Albany
Address: District Director, Leo W. O'Brien Federal Bldg., Rm. 822, Albany NY 12207
Tel.: (518) 472-3596

Bronx
Address: District Director, 1967 Turnbull Ave., Bronx NY 10473
Tel.: (212) 824-2158

Buffalo
Address: District Director, Harry J. Gray, Federal Bldg., Rm. 617, 111 West Huron St., Buffalo NY 14202
Tel.: (716) 846-4891

Hempstead L.I.
Address: District Director, 175 Fulton Ave., Rm. 315, Hempstead NY 11550
Tel.: (516) 227-3100

New York City
Address: District Director, 26 Federal Plaza, Rm. 3838, New York NY 10278
Tel.: (212) 264-8185

Newark
Address: District Director, 200 Sheffield St., Rm. 102, Mountainside NJ 07092
Tel.: (201) 645-2279

Trenton
Address: District Director, 3131 Princeton Pike, Bldg. 5, Rm. 216, Lawrenceville NJ 08648
Tel.: (609) 989-2247

Caribbean Office
Address: District Director, New San Juan Office Bldg., 159 Chardon St., Rm. 102, Hato Rey PR 00918
Tel.: (809) 766-5463

Region III
Regional Administrator: James W. Kight
Address: Gateway Bldg. Rm. 15230, 3535 Market St., Philadelphia PA 19104
Tel.: (215) 596-1185
Acting Assistant Regional Administrator: James E. Sykes
Address: Same

Tel.: (215) 596-1185

Wage-Hour District Offices

Baltimore
Address: District Director, Federal Office Bldg., Rm. 913, 31 Hopkins Plaza, Baltimore MD 21201
Tel.: (301) 962-2265

Charleston
Address: District Director, 2 Hale St., Rm. 301, Charleston WV 25301
Tel.: (304) 347-5206, Ext. 448

Harrisburg
Address: District Director, P.O. Box 1005, Federal Bldg., Rm. 774, 228 Walnut St., Harrisburg PA 17108
Tel.: (717) 782-4539

Hyattsville
Address: District Director, Al Morrone Presidential Bldg., 6525 Belcrest Rd., Suite 520, Hyattsville MD 20782
Tel.: (301) 436-6767

Philadelphia
Address: District Director, Second & Chestnut, Rm. 238, Philadelphia PA 19106
Tel.: (215) 597-4950

Pittsburgh
Address: District Director, Federal Bldg., Rm. 313, 1000 Liberty Ave., Pittsburgh PA 15222
Tel.: (412) 644-2996

Richmond
Address: District Director, Federal Bldg., Rm. 7000, 400 North Eighth St., Richmond VA 23240
Tel.: (804) 771-2995

Region IV
Regional Administrator: James L. Valin
Address: 1375 Peachtree St., NE, Rm. 662, Atlanta GA 30367
Tel.: (404) 347-4801
Deputy Regional Administrator: Alfred Perry
Address: Same
Tel.: (404) Same

Wage-Hour District Offices

Atlanta
Address: District Director, 1375 Peachtree St. NE, Rm. 668, Atlanta GA 30367
Tel.: (404) 347-4235

Birmingham
Address: District Director, 2015 Second Ave. N, Suite 301, Berry Bldg., Birmingham AL 35203
Tel.: (205) 731-1305

Charlotte
Address: District Director, 800 Briar Creek Road Suite CC-412, Charlotte NC 28205
Tel.: (704) 344-6302

Columbia SC
Address: District Director, Federal Bldg., Rm. 1072, 1835 Assembly St., Columbia SC 29201
Tel.: (803) 765-5981

Fort Lauderdale
Address: District Director, Federal Bldg., Rm. 409, 299 East Broward Blvd., Fort Lauderdale FL 33301
Tel.: (305) 356-7036, -7037

Jackson
Address: District Director, Federal Bldg., Suite 1020, 188 East Capitol St., Jackson MS 39201-2126
Tel.: (601) 965-4347

Jacksonville
Address: District Director, 3728 Phillips Highway Suite 219, Jacksonville FL 32207
Tel.: (904) 232-2489

Knoxville
Address: District Director, John Duncan Federal Bldg. Box 123, 710 Locust St., Knoxville TN 37902
Tel.: (615) 545-4619

Louisville
Address: District Director, 167 Federal Bldg., 600 Federal Place, Louisville KY 40202
Tel.: (502) 582-5226

Memphis
Address: District Director, Federal Office Bldg., Rm. 484, 167 North Main St., Memphis TN 38103
Tel.: (901) 544-3418

Miami
Address: District Director, Rm. 255, 10300 Sunset Dr., Miami FL 33173
Tel.: (305) 279-8393

Montgomery
Address: District Director, 474 South Court St., Rm. 130, Montgomery AL 36104-4158
Tel.: (205) 223-7450

Nashville
Address: District Director, 1321 Murfreesboro Rd. Suite 511, Nashville TN 37211
Tel.: (615) 781-5343, 7115

Orlando
Address: District Director, Federal Building, Rm. 128; 80 North Hughey St.; Orlando FL 32801
Tel.: (407) 648-6471

Raleigh
Address: District Director, 4407 Bland Rd., Suite 260, Raleigh NC 27609
Tel.: (919) 790-2741

Savannah
Address: District Director, Juliette Gordon Low Fed. Bldg. Complex, 124 Barnard St., Suite B210, Savannah GA 31401-3648
Tel.: (912) 652-4221

Tallahassee
Address: District Director, 227 North Bronough St., Rm. 5034; Tallahassee, FL 32301
Tel.: (904) 681-7160

Tampa
Address: District Director, Suite 300, Austin Laurel Bldg., 4905 W. Laurel Ave., Tampa FL 33607-3838
Tel.: (813) 228-2751, 2726

Appendix D

Region V

Regional Administrator: William Van Zanen
Address: 230 South Dearborn St., Chicago IL 60604
Tel.: (312) 353-7280
Assistant Regional Administrator: Richard A. McMahon, Jr.
Deputy Assistant Regional Administrator: Daniel New
Tel.: (312) 353-8845, 7250

Wage-Hour District Offices

Chicago
Address: District Director, Federal Building, Rm 412, 2305 Dearborn St., Chicago, IL 60604
Tel.: (312) 353-8145

Cincinnati
Address: District Director, Federal Office Bldg., Rm. 1523, 550 Main St., Cincinnati OH 45202
Tel.: (513) 684-2902

Cleveland
Address: District Director, Federal Office Bldg., Rm. 817, 1240 East 9th St., Cleveland OH 44199
Tel.: (216) 522-3892, 3893

Columbus
Address: District Director, 646 Federal Office Bldg., 200 N. High St., Columbus OH 43215
Tel.: (614) 469-5677

Detroit
Address: District Director, U.S. Courthouse and Federal Bldg., 231 Lafayette, Rm. 647, Detroit, MI 48226-2799
Tel.: (313) 226-7448

Grand Rapids
Address: District Director, Suite 100, 2920 Fuller NE, Grand Rapids MI 49503
Tel.: (616) 456-2183

Indianapolis
Address: District Director, Minton-CapeHart Bldg., Rm. 106, 575 N. Pennsylvania St., Indianapolis IN 46204
Tel.: (317) 226-6801

Madison
Address: District Director, Federal Center Bldg., Rm. 309, 212 E. Washington Ave., Madison WI 53703
Tel.: (608) 264-5221

Milwaukee
Address: District Director, Federal Bldg., Rm. 108, 517 E. Wisconsin Ave., Milwaukee WI 53202-4505
Tel.: (414) 297-3585

Minneapolis
Address: District Director, Bridge Place, Rm. 106, 220 South Second St., Minneapolis MN 55401-2401
Tel.: (612) 370-3371

South Bend
Address: District Director, 501 E. Monroe St., Rm. 160, South Bend IN 46601
Tel.: (219) 236-8331

Springfield
Address: District Director, 509 W. Capital, Suite 205, Springfield IL 62704
Tel.: (217) 492-4060

Region VI

Regional Administrator: Bill A. Belt
Address: Federal Bldg., 525 S. Griffin St., Dallas TX 75202-5007
Tel.: (214) 767-6894
Deputy Regional Administrator: Raymond Cordelli

Wage-Hour District Offices

Albuquerque
Address: District Director, 505 Marquette N.W., Albuquerque NM 87103
Tel.: (505) 840-8702

Baton Rouge
Address: District Director, 3535 Sherwood Forest Blvd., Suite 135, Baton Rouge LA 70816
Tel.: (504) 291-5132

Corpus Christi
Address: District Director, 400 Mann St., Rm. 307, Corpus Christi TX 78401
Tel.: (512) 888-3156

Dallas
Address: District Director, Rm. 507 Federal Bldg., 525 S. Griffin St., Dallas TX 75201-5007
Tel.: (214) 767-6294

Fort Worth
Address: District Director, 819 Taylor St., Rm. 7A12, Forth Worth TX 76102
Tel.: (817) 334-2678

Houston
Address: District Director, 2320 La-Branch, Rm. 2100, Houston TX 77004
Tel.: (713) 750-1682

Little Rock
Address: District Director, Suite 725, 425 W. Capitol Ave., Little Rock AR 72201
Tel.: (501) 324-5292

New Orleans
Address: District Director, 701 Loyola Ave., Rm. 13028, New Orleans LA 70113
Tel.: (504) 589-6171

San Antonio
Address: District Director, Ste 104, 10127 Morocco, San Antonio TX 78216
Tel.: (210) 229-4515,6126

Tulsa
Address: District Director, 5110 S. Yale, Robert S. Kerr Bldg., Rm. 208, 440 S. Houston, Tulsa OK 74135
Tel.: (918) 581-6791

Region VII
Regional Administrator: Everett P. Jennings
Address: Federal Office Bldg., Rm. 2000, 911 Walnut St., Kansas City MO 64106
Tel.: (816) 426-5381
Deputy Regional Administrator: Ronald N. Dean
Address: Same
Tel.: (816) 426-5386

Wage-Hour District Office

Des Moines
Address: District Director, Federal Bldg., Rm. 643, 210 Walnut St., Des Moines IA 50309
Tel.: (515) 284-4625

Kansas City MO
Address: District Director, Federal Office Bldg., Rm. 2900, 911 Walnut St., Kansas City MO 64106
Tel.: (816) 426-5721

Omaha
Address: District Director, 106 S. 15th St., Rm. 715, Omaha NE 68102
Tel.: (402) 221-4682

St. Louis
Address: District Director, 210 North Tucker Blvd., Rm. 563, St. Louis MO 63101
Tel.: (314) 425-4706

Region VIII
Regional Administrator: Everett Jennings (A)
Address: 1801 California St., Suite 930, Denver, CO 80202,
Tel.: (303) 391-6780
Assistant Regional Administrator: Richard Perkins
Address: Same
Tel.: Same

Wage-Hour District Offices

Denver
Address: District Director, 1961 Stout St., Drawer 3505, Denver CO 80294-9910
Tel.: (303) 536-7401

Salt Lake City
Address: District Director, 10 W. Broadway, Rm. 307, Salt Lake City UT 84101
Tel.: (801) 536-7401

Region IX
Regional Administrator: William C. Buhl
Address: 71 Stevenson St., Rm. 930, San Francisco CA 94105
Tel.: (415) 744-6625
Deputy Regional Administrator: (M.J. Villareal Jr.)
Address: Same
Tel.: Same

Appendix D

Wage-Hour District Offices

Glendale
Address: District Director, 300 S. Glendale Ave., Suite 400, Glendale CA 91205-1752
Tel: (213) 894-2685

Honolulu
Address: District Director, 300 Ala Moana Blvd., Rm. 7328, Honolulu, HI 96850
Tel.: (808) 541-1361

Los Angeles
Address: District Director, 3660 Wilshire Blvd., Suite 600, Los Angeles CA 90010
Tel.: (213) 252-7565

Phoenix
Address: District Director, 3221 N. 16th St., Suite 301, Phoenix AZ 85016
Tel.: (602) 640-2990

Sacramento
Address: District Director 2981 Fulton Ave., Sacramento CA 95821
Tel.: (916) 978-4233

San Diego
Address: District Director, 5675 Ruffin Rd., Suite 320, San Diego, CA 92123-5378
Tel.:(619) 557-5240

San Francisco
Address: District Director, Rm. 341, 211 Main St., San Francisco CA 94105
Tel.: (415) 744-6620

Santa Ana
Address: District Director, 34 Civic Center Plaza, Rm. 702, P.O. Box 12950, Santa Ana CA 92712
Tel.: (714) 836-2156

Region X

Regional Administrator: Wilbur J. Olson
Address: 1111 Third Ave., Rm. 600, Seattle WA 98101-3212
Tel.: (206) 553-1914

Wage-Hour District Offices

Portland
Address: District Director, 111 S.W. Columbia, Rm. 1010, Portland OR 97204
Tel.: (503) 326-3052

Seattle
Address: District Director, 1111 Third Ave., Rm. 755, Seattle, WA 98101-3212
Tel.: (206) 553-4482

Appendix E
Chart of State Minimum Wages

Appendix E

Comparison Chart — State Minimum Wage Rates

State	Minimum Wage Laws 1.30*	Minimum Wage Orders 2.030/2.30*	Notes
Alabama	—	—	
Alaska	$4.75	—	eff. 4/1/91 (Federal minimum + $0.50)
Arizona	—	—	
Arkansas	$4.15	—	eff. 8/1/93 ($4.25, eff. 7/1/94)
California	$4.25	(b) (e) (f) (g)	eff. 7/1/88
Colorado	$3.00	(b) (e) (g)	
Connecticut	$4.27	(b)	eff. 4/1/91 (Federal minimum + 0.5%)
Delaware	$4.25	—	eff. 4/1/91
District of Columbia	$5.25	(e) (g)	Eff. 10/1/93; rates reduced by $0.50 per hour if health benefits provided; other variations by industry
Florida	—	—	
Georgia	$3.25	—	
Hawaii	$5.25	—	eff. 1/1/93
Idaho	$4.25	—	eff. 4/1/91
Illinois	$4.25	—	eff. 4/1/91
Indiana	$3.35	—	eff. 7/1/90
Iowa	$4.65	—	eff. 1/1/92
Kansas	$2.65	—	eff. 7/1/88
Kentucky	$4.25	—	eff. 7/15/91
Louisiana	—	—	
Maine	$4.25	—	eff. 4/1/91
Maryland	$4.25	—	eff. 4/1/91
Massachusetts	$4.25	(e) (f) (g)	eff. 4/1/91
Michigan	$3.35	(a) (e)	
Minnesota	$4.25	(e) (f)	Employers grossing less than $362,500 pay $4.00; $2.07 for learners
Mississippi	—	—	

* Classification numbers in state-by-state digests found in Wages and Hours Binder ☆☆
(a) Price rates for agricultural products
(b) Provide exemptions to minimum wage laws
(c) State employees only
(d) Certain blind employees only
(e) By state wage board orders
(f) Different rates for apprentices, learners, minors
(g) Different rates for workers with handicaps

Comparison Chart — State Minimum Wage Rates, Contd.

State	Minimum Wage Laws 1.30*	Minimum Wage Orders 2.030/2.30*	Notes
Missouri	$4.25	—	eff. 4/1/91
Montana	$4.25	—	eff. 4/26/91; employers grossing less than $110,000 or less pay $4.00
Nebraska	$4.25	—	eff. 7/1/91
Nevada	$4.25	—	eff. 4/1/91; $3.61 for workers under 18
New Hampshire	$4.25	—	eff. 1/1/92
New Jersey	$5.05	(b)	eff. 4/1/92; $3.10 for certain occupations
New Mexico	$4.25	—	eff. 7/1/93
New York	$4.25	(b) (e)	eff. 4/1/91; farm workers: $4.25, eff. 1/1/92; other variations by industry
North Carolina	$4.25	—	eff. 1/1/93
North Dakota	$4.25	(b) (f)	eff. 8/1/91; State employees $350 monthly; also, lower rates for tipped employees
Ohio	$4.25	—	eff. 4/1/91; employers grossing less than $150,000 pay $2.80
Oklahoma	$4.25	—	eff. 4/1/91; employers grossing less than $100,000 and with 10 or fewer workers pay $2.00
Oregon	$4.75	—	eff. 1/1/91
Pennsylvania	$4.25	—	eff. 4/1/91
Puerto Rico	$0.24 to $6.50	(b) (e)	See p. 97:5501, Binder ☆
Rhode Island	$4.45	—	eff. 4/1/91
South Carolina	—	—	
South Dakota	$4.25	—	eff. 4/1/91
Tennessee	—	—	eff. 4/1/91
Texas	$3.35	—	eff. 9/1/87
Utah	$4.25	—	eff. 4/1/91
Vermont	$4.25	(b) (f) (g)	eff. 4/1/91
Virginia	$4.25	—	eff. 7/1/92
Washington	$4.90	(b) (e) (f) (g)	eff. 1/1/94; nursing homes under contract to state pay $5.15, eff. 1/1/89; other variations by industry
West Virginia	$4.25	—	eff. 4/1/92
Wisconsin	$4.25	$3.70-$4.25; (b)	eff. 3/1/92; agricultural employees $3.70-$4.05
Wyoming	$1.60	—	

Appendix F
Coefficient Table for Computing Overtime

Appendix F 195

FLSA Overtime Coefficient Table—Instructions

General. In determining the extra half-time that is due for overtime pay after 40 hours, the method of calculation commonly used is to divide the straight-time earnings by the total number of hours worked and multiply the result by the number of overtime hours divided by two. For instance, the Computation for 48 hours would be $\dfrac{\text{Earnings } 8}{48} \times \dfrac{8}{2}$—; for 50 hours, $\dfrac{\text{Earnings } 10}{50} \times \dfrac{10}{2}$—; for 47 ¾ hours,

$\dfrac{\text{Earnings } 7\,¾}{47\,¾} \times \dfrac{\text{O.T. Hours}}{2}$. The table on the reverse side contains the decimal equivalents of the fraction,

$\dfrac{\text{O.T. Hours}}{\text{Total Hr. X 2}}$.

For example, the decimal for 48 hours is $\dfrac{8}{48 \times 2} = \dfrac{1}{12} = .083$; for 50 hours it is $\dfrac{10}{50 \times 2} = \dfrac{1}{10} = .1$;

and for 47 ¾ hours $\dfrac{7\,¾}{47\,¾ \times 2} = \dfrac{7.75}{95.5} = .081$.

How to use: (a) Multiply the straight-time earnings for an overtime week by the applicable decimal and the result will be the extra half-time due. Thus, by using the decimals in the table (on the reverse side) the computations performed are, in effect, exactly the same as if the equivalent fractions were used, with the advantage of having eliminated the long division necessitated by the fractions. For example:

(1). A pieceworker earns varying wages each week. In a 43 9/10 hour week he earned $153.65 straight-time. The coefficient for 43 9/10 hours is .0444. .0444 X $153.65 = $6.82, additional half-time due. $153.65 + $6.82 = $160.47, the pieceworker's total pay for the week.

(2). Jones is paid a weekly salary of $180.25. He worked 51½ hours. The coefficient for 51½ hours is .112. .112 X $180.25 = $20.19. $180.25 + $20.19 = $200.44, Jones total pay for the week.

(b) The decimal table can also be used effectively when back wages are due because of additions to wages (such as a weekly bonus) that were not included in the regular rate in computing overtime. For example:

(1). An employee worked 48 hours and received a production bonus of $9.60 which was not included in the regular rate. Thus, $9.60 X .083 = $0.80, the additional half-time due on the bonus.

(2). Jones in the same week (example (a), (2) above) received a production bonus of $25.00. .112 X $25.00 = $2.80, the additional half-time due on the bonus. $180.25 + $20.19 + $25.00 + $2.80 = $228.24, Jones' total earnings. A further short-cut (combining (a), (2), and (b), (2)) would be: $180.25 + $25.00 = $205.25 X .112 = $22.99 + $205.25 = $228.24, Jones' total earnings.

(c) Short-cuts For Computing Back Wages. When both the overtime hours and the earnings vary, individual weekly computations must be made. However, if an employee is paid at a constant hourly rate, time can be saved by adding the unpaid overtime hours during the period and multiplying the total by one-half the hourly rate. When the weekly hours vary and the straight-time earnings are constant, add the decimals for the overtime weeks and multiply the total by the earnings for 1 week. When the weekly hours are constant but the earnings vary, add the earnings for the overtime weeks and multiply the total by the decimal for 1 week. For example:

VARYING HOURS—CONSTANT EARNINGS			CONSTANT HOURS—VARYING EARNINGS	
Hours	Decimal	Earnings	Hours	Earnings
42	0.024	$180.25	47	$164.50
43	.036	180.25	47	159.80
46	.064	180.25	47	162.15
	.124 x $180.25 = $22.35			$486.45 x .074 = $36.00

FLSA Overtime Coefficient Table

The following coefficient table (WH-134) and accompanying instructions were prepared by the Wage-Hour Division to help simplify the calculation of overtime pay. Ordinarily, the "extra half time" due employees for working overtime is figured by dividing straight-time earnings by the total number of hours worked and multiplying the result by the number of overtime hours divided by two. Calculating extra half-time pay is a comparatively simple task using the coefficient table; one merely selects the decimal coefficient corresponding to the number of hours worked and multiplies it by total straight-time earnings for the given workweek (see detailed instructions on the following page).

Hours	Even	1/4	1/2	3/4	1/10	2/10	3/10	4/10	6/10	7/10	8/10	9/10
40	—	0003	0006	0009	00012	0.0025	0.0037	0.0049	0.0074	0.0086	0.0098	0.0110
41	0.012	015	018	021	0134	0146	0157	0169	0192	0204	0215	0227
42	024	027	029	032	0249	0261	0272	0283	0305	0316	0327	0338
43	035	038	040	043	0360	0370	0381	0392	0413	0423	0434	0444
44	045	048	051	053	0465	0475	0485	0495	0516	0526	0536	0546
45	056	058	060	063	0565	0575	0585	0595	0614	0624	0633	0643
46	065	068	070	072	0662	0671	0680	0690	0708	0717	0726	0736
47	074	077	079	081	0754	0763	0772	0781	0798	0807	0816	0825
48	083	085	088	090	0842	0851	0859	0868	0885	0893	0902	0910
49	092	094	096	098	0927	0935	0943	0951	0968	0976	0984	0992
50	100	102	104	106	1008	1016	1024	1032	1047	1055	1063	1071
51	108	110	112	114	1086	1094	1101	1109	1124	1132	1139	1146
52	115	117	119	121	1161	1169	1176	1183	1198	1205	1212	1219
53	123	124	126	128	1234	1241	1248	1255	1269	1276	1283	1289
54	130	131	133	135	1303	1310	1317	1324	1337	1344	1350	1357
55	136	138	140	141	1370	1377	1383	1390	1403	1409	1416	1422
56	143	144	146	148	1435	1441	1448	1454	1466	1473	1479	1485
57	149	151	152	154	1497	1503	1510	1516	1528	1534	1540	1546
58	155	157	158	160	1558	1564	1569	1575	1587	1593	1599	1604
59	161	162	164	165	1616	1622	1627	1633	1644	1650	1656	1661
60	167	168	169	171	1672	1678	1683	1689	1700	1705	1711	1716
61	172	173	175	176	1727	1732	1737	1743	1753	1759	1764	1769
62	177	179	180	181	1779	1785	1790	1795	1805	1810	1815	1820
63	183	184	185	186	1830	1835	1840	1845	1855	1860	1865	1870
64	188	189	190	191	1880	1885	1890	1894	1904	1909	1914	1918
65	192	193	195	196	1928	1933	1937	1942	1951	1956	1960	1965
66	197	198	199	200	1974	1979	1983	1988	1997	2001	2006	2010
67	201	203	204	205	2019	2024	2028	2033	2041	2046	2050	2054
68	206	207	208	209	2063	2067	2072	2076	2085	2089	2093	2097
69	210	211	212	213	2106	2110	2114	2118	2126	2131	2135	2139
70	214	215	216	217	2147	2151	2155	2159	2167	2171	2175	2179
71	218	219	220	221	2187	2191	2195	2199	2207	2211	2214	2218
72	222	223	224	225	2226	2230	2234	2238	2245	2249	2253	2257
73	226	227	228	229	2264	2268	2271	2275	2283	2286	2290	2294
74	230	231	232	232	2301	2305	2308	2312	2319	2323	2326	2330
75	233	234	235	236	2337	2340	2344	2347	2354	2358	2361	2365
76	237	238	239	239	2372	2375	2379	2382	2389	2392	2396	2399
77	240	241	242	243	2406	2409	2413	2416	2423	2426	2429	2433
78	244	244	245	246	2439	2442	2446	2449	2455	2459	2462	2465
79	247	248	249	249	2472	2475	2478	2481	2487	2491	2494	2497
80	250	251	252	252	2503	2506	2509	2512	2519	2522	2525	2528
81	253	254	255	255	2534	2537	2540	2543	2549	2552	2555	2558
82	256	257	258	258	2564	2567	2570	2573	2579	2582	2585	2587
83	259	260	261	261	2593	2596	2599	2602	2608	2611	2613	2616
84	262	263	264	264	2622	2625	2628	2630	2636	2639	2642	2644
85	265	265	266	267	2650	2653	2655	2658	2664	2666	2669	2672

TO CONVERT INTO WEEKLY EQUIVALENT: Multiply SEMIMONTHLY salary by 0.4615; MONTHLY salary by 0.2308; ANNUAL salary by 0.01923.

TO CONVERT INTO STRAIGHT-TIME HOURLY EQUIVALENT FOR 40 HOURS: Multiply WEEKLY salary by 0.025; SEMIMONTHLY by 0.01154; MONTHLY salary by 0.00577; ANNUAL by 0.00048.

TO CONVERT INTO TIME AND ONE-HALF HOURLY RATE BASED ON 40 HOUR WEEK: Multiply WEEKLY salary by 0.0375; SEMIMONTHLY by 0.0173; MONTHLY salary by 0.00866; ANNUAL by 0.000721.

CAUTION: Be sure straight-time earnings are not below legal minimum.

Appendix G
Chart of State Maximum Hours-Overtime

Appendix G

State Maximum Hours and Overtime Laws — Comparison Chart

STATE	REQUIREMENTS AND PROVISIONS
Alabama	**Maximum Hours before Overtime** — No general provision. **Overtime Pay** — No general provision. **Employees Covered** — No general provision. **Special Occupations** — Truckdrivers: 10-hour day followed by 8-hour rest, plus certain provisions; special provisions apply in adverse weather. State Law Enforcement Officers: 1½ times regular pay or compensatory time for hours in excess of 8-hour day or 40-hour week. **Day of Rest** — No minor, apprentice, or servant may be required to perform any labor on Sunday, except customary domestic duties or works of charity; merchants, shopkeepers, druggists excepted, may not keep stores open on Sunday. Certain other specific operations exempted. **Meal and Rest Periods** — No general provision. **References** — Title 25, Alabama Code; Regulations of the Alabama Public Service Commission; §§13A-12-1, 36-21-4; regulations Section VII.
Alaska	**Maximum Hours before Overtime** — 8-hour day, 40-hour week; 10-hour day, 40-hour week for workers with flexible work hour plan if part of collective bargaining agreement or signed employer-employee agreement filed with state Department of Labor. **Overtime Pay** — 1½ times regular pay for hours in excess of maximum. **Employees Covered** — All employees, except: those of employer with fewer than 4 workers; those in executive, administrative, or professional capacity; outside salespersons, as defined; those employed in making dairy products and handling or preparing for market agricultural or horticultural products; agricultural employees; those employed in certain newspapers with circulation under 1,000; certain switchboard operators; taxicab employees whose compensation comes solely from customers and whose relationship to permit owners, operators, and dispatch companies is based solely on a contractual flat fee by driver; certain retail or service workers handling telegraphic, telephone or radio messages; seafarers; forestry and lumbering workers of firms with 12 or fewer workers; outside buyers of raw poultry or dairy products; casual employees, as defined; hospital workers; community health aides employed by local or regional health organizations. **Special Occupations** — Underground Mines: 8-hour day in all underground mines or workings, excluding days on which shifts are changed; emergencies; or meal periods. Mines with 12 or fewer workers may require 12-hour day, 56-hour week for up to 14 weeks during mining season, as defined. Line haul truck drivers employed for a trip that exceeds 100 miles one way are exempt, provided the compensation system under which the driver is paid includes overtime pay for work in excess of 40 hours per week or eight hours per day. **Day of Rest** — No general provision. **Meal and Rest Periods** — No general provision. Minors under age 18 must be given unpaid 30 minute break if scheduled to work six consecutive hours or more. Break may be scheduled at employer's convenience, but must occur after the first 1½ hours of work and before the beginning of the last hour of work. Minor under age 18 who works for five consecutive hours without a break is entitled to a break of at least 30 minutes before continuing to work. Provisions may be modified by collective bargaining agreement applicable to employment of minor under 18, or by mutual agreement between employer and employee. Failure to provide break periods on time creates a minimum wage liability for the break not received or received late. **References** — Alaska Statutes; Alaska Administrative Code; §§23.10.050, 23.10.055, 23.10.060, 43-2-2, 43-2-3.
Arizona	**Maximum Hours before Overtime** — No general provision. **Overtime Pay** — No general provision. **Employees Covered** — No general provision.

Comparison Chart — State Hours Laws — Contd.

STATE	REQUIREMENTS AND PROVISIONS
Arizona, contd.	**Special Occupations** — Law enforcement officers and security personnel in municipal correctional institution must receive 1½ times regular pay for hours in excess of 40 per week. Laundries: 8-hour day and 48-hour week, with certain exceptions. Mines: 8-hour day for workers in underground mines or workings; open cut or pit workings in connection with operation of smelters, reduction works, stamp mills, concentrating mills, chlorination processes, cyanide processes, cement works, rolling mills, rod mills, coke ovens, and blast furnaces (except in emergencies and during shift changes if not more than once in two weeks). Public Works Contractors: 8-hour day for manual or mechanical laborers, except in emergencies. Motor Transportation: 10-hour day (or 10-hour aggregate in any 24 hours, followed by 8 hours off) for truck and bus operators and their helpers, except for unforeseen delays and emergencies. Railroads: 16 hours followed by 9 hours rest, except for emergencies and actual necessity. **Day of Rest** — No general provision. **Meal and Rest Periods** — No general provision. **References** — Arizona Revised Statutes; §§23-282(A)-(E), 23-284(A), (B), and (D), 23-286, 23-287, 23-391, 23-392(A) and (B).
Arkansas	**Maximum Hours before Overtime** — 40-hour week; 44-hour week for employees of hotel, motel, restaurant, and tourist attraction with annual sales volume less than $500,000, eff. 7/1/91; 40-hour week eff. 7/1/92. **Overtime Pay** — 1½ times regular pay for hours in excess of maximum. **Employees Covered** — All employees of employer of four or more workers, except agricultural workers; bona fide executive, administrative, or professional employees; outside salespersons on commission; federal, state, or local government workers, except public school employees; students working for schools where they are enrolled; volunteers in educational, charitable, religious, nonprofit organizations; independent contractors; certain forestry and lumber workers. **Special Occupations** — Motor Transportation: 12 consecutive hours followed by 8 hours rest for drivers, except when wrecks or washouts occur. Highway Construction: 8-hour day. **Day of Rest** — On Sunday, unlawful for any person to sell, offer for sale, or employ others to sell certain specified goods. Law inapplicable to sale of goods for charitable or governmental purposes, or the advertising for sale of personal property. Person who conscientiously observes a day other than Sunday as a day of rest and abstains on that day from the sale of items prohibited also exempted. **Meal and Rest Periods** — No general provision. **References** — Arkansas Code Annotated; §§11-4-203(5), 11-4-211, 14-297-102 through 14-297-109, 23-13-101.
California	**Maximum Hours before Overtime** — 8-hour day unless contract specifies otherwise; for state employees, 8-hour day, 40-hour week, unless governor determines that 40 hours be performed in 4 days. **Overtime Pay** — 1½ times regular pay for hours in excess of maximum. Hospitals: Twice the regular pay for hospital workers, under certain conditions. Agriculture: Twice the regular rate for agricultural workers in excess of 8 hours on seventh day. manufacturing; personal service; canning, freezing, and preserving; professional, technical, clerical, mechanical, and similar occupations; laundry, linen supply, dry cleaning, and dyeing; mercantile occupations; farm products, after harvest; amusement and recreation; broadcasting; and preparing agricultural products for market, on the farm: 1½ times regular rate for hours in excess of 40 per week or eight per day; twice the regular pay for hours in excess of 12 hours a day and eight hours on seventh day. For alternative schedules, 1½ times regular pay for hours beyond schedule, up to twelve per day or 40 per week; twice the regular pay for hours in excess of twelve; for employees with 4-day week, 10-hour day agreement, 1½ times regular rate for first 8 hours of additional wo.'k-day, twice regular rate for additional hours. **Employees Covered** — All employees except those subject to specific hours, i.e., workers in a manufacturing establishment in operation 24 hours per day, 7 days per week; pharmacists; workers in motor vehicle or railroad transportation; apprentices; workers in the seasonal ski industry; employees of licensed hospitals; workers subject to wage board orders covering hours to be worked (see special occupations).

Comparison Chart — State Hours Laws — Contd.

STATE	REQUIREMENTS AND PROVISIONS
California, Contd.	**Special Occupations** — By Law: Manufacturing operations continuously working for 24 hour per day, 7 days per week: three 12-hour days per week, or two week period of three 12-hour days in first week and four 12-hour days in second. Mines: Not more than eight hours within any 24, unless collective bargaining agreement expressly provides for up to 12 hours within 24. Pharmacies: Nine-hour day or 108 hours/12 days within two consecutive weeks. Motor Vehicle Transportation: 10 consecutive hours, or 10 hours within 15 consecutive hours, if transporting people. Drivers of vehicles transporting merchandise, freight, materials, or other property may not work more than 12 of 15 consecutive hours. Thereafter, drivers must have eight consecutive hours off duty. The maximum driving time for operators of tank vehicles carrying more than 500 gallons of flammable liquid is 10 hours. Drivers for motor carriers may not work more than 80 hours in eight days. Drivers employed by agricultural carriers (including seasonal carriers) or by private carriers are not allowed to work more than 16 hours after eight consecutive hours off. They also are not permitted to drive for any period after working 112 hours in any consecutive eight-day period. When transporting from the field to first point of processsing or packing, or when tranpsorting livestock from pasture to pasture, such drivers may drive up to 12 hours of a 16-hour workday, as long as such driving time is during one period of up to 28 consecutive days or a combination of two periods totaling up to 28 days in a calendar year. Exceptions exist for employees of electrical, gas, or telephone corporation during the emergency restoration of public utility service; and for drivers assigned to fire suppression and prevention. Railroad Transportation: 12 consecutive hours off duty after 12 consecutive hours or work, or 8 hours off in 24. Persons directing trains in towers, offices, places, and stations operated continuously day and night, 9 hours within 24; 13 hours within 24 if operating only by day. Four additional hours on no more than three days in any week if emergency warrants. Seasonal ski industry: regularly established workweek of up to 56 hours, provided employees working more than 56 hours are paid 1½ times regular rate. Hospital employees: regular workweek of no more than three 12-hour days permitted, provided employer tries to find alternate employment for workers unable to work 12 consecutive hours. Apprentices: hours as prescribed by law for person of apprentice's age and sex. Hospitals: no more than three 12-hour days per week. By Order: common provisions: no more than 8-hour day, six-day week for minors, with 1½ times regular pay for hours over 40. 8-hour day, 40-hour week for: manufacturing; personal service; canning freezing, preserving industry; professional, technical, clerical, mechanical, and similar occupations; public housekeeping; laundry, linen supply, dry cleaning, and dyeing; mercantile occupations; transportation; amusement and recreation industry; broadcasting industry; motion picture industry; agricultural product preparation for market (on the farm). Ten-hour day, six-day week for agricultural employees age 18 and over; 8-hour day, six-day week for minors. At least 12 consecutive off-duty hours for live-in employee in household occupation. **Day of Rest** — All employees are entitled to one day's rest in seven, except: in emergencies; work performed in necessary care of animals, crops, or agricultural lands; work required to prevent loss of life or property; common carriers connected with movement of train; however, if nature of work requires seven or more consecutive days, days of rest may be accumulated and equivalent time off allowed during calendar month. Work on seventh day may be permitted if total hours of employment do not exceed six per day or 30 per week. **Meal and Rest Periods** — One-half hour between third and fifth hour of each day's shift for employees of plants or mills that process or manufacture any lumber or allied wood products. Thirty minute meal period after five consecutive hours, and 10 minute rest period for each four hours working time for employees in: manufacturing; personal service; canning, freezing, and preserving; professional, technical, clerical, mechanical, and similar occupations; laundry, linen supply, dry cleaning, and dyeing; mercantile occupations; farm products, after harvest; amusement and recreation; broadcasting; and preparing agricultural products for market, on the farm.

Comparison Chart — State Hours Laws — Contd.

STATE	REQUIREMENTS AND PROVISIONS
California, Contd.	**References** — California Labor Code, Part 4 of Division 2; WageOrders; §1182.6(d), Wage Orders 1-89, 2-80, 3-80, 4-89, 5-89, 6-80, 7-80, 8-80, 9-80, 10-89, 11-80, 12-80, 13-80, 14-80 (maximum before overtime, overtime pay); §1171, various Wage Orders (employees covered); §§602-607, 750, 750.5, 751, 751.5, 850, 852, 853, 854; Vehicle Code §§21702, 34501.2 (limits on hours worked by drivers); §554 (day of rest); Wage Orders: 3-80, 12-80, 13-80, Common Provisions (meal or rest period).
Colorado	**Maximum Hours before Overtime** — No general provision. **Overtime Pay** — 1½ times regular pay for hours in excess of 40 per workweek or 12 per day for employees in: laundry and dry cleaning; food and beverage services; beauty services; public housekeeping; medical profession (including office support personnel); janitorial services. 1½ times regular rate for hours in excess of 8 per day or 40 per week for minors. **Employees Covered** — By Order: employees in laundry and dry cleaning; retail trade; public housekeeping; beauty services; food and beverage services; medical profession (including office support personnel); janitorial services. **Special Occupations** — Cement and plaster factories: 8-hour day, except in emergencies; two periods of 8 hours each, separated by 8-hour rest period, not more than once per week during shift change. Municipal firefighters may not work more than aggregate of 12 hours per day, except in emergency; workers in underground mines may work more than 8 hours in 24 under agreement and with reasonable notice. Railroad employees who have worked 16 consecutive hours must have 10 hours rest before resuming work. Motor vehicle dealers may not stay open on Sundays. **Day of Rest** — No general provision; motor vehicle dealers forbidden to stay open on Sundays for purposes of selling vehicles. **Meal and Rest Periods** — At least 30 minute meal period after five hours of work (optional if workday is six hours or less) and 10 minute restperiod every four hours for employees in: laundry and dry cleaning; public housekeeping; beauty services; retail trade; food and beverage services; janitorial occupations; and medical profession, including office support. If nature of work requires it, meal may be eaten "on-the-job," in which case employee must be paid for meal time. **References** — Colorado Revised Statutes; Wage Orders — Common Provisions (maximum hours before overtime, overtime pay, and employees covered); §§8-13-102, 8-13-107, 8-13-108, 8-13-110 and 8-13-111, 40-32-101 and 40-32-102 (limits on hours worked); §§12-6-302 and 12-6-303 (day of rest); Wage Orders — Common Provisions (meal or rest period).
Connecticut	**Maximum Hours before Overtime** — Nine-hour day, 48-hour week in manufacturing/mechanical establishments for workers under 18 or over 66, handicapped persons, and disabled veterans. Ten-hour day, 55-hour week during emergencies or peak demand, with commissioner's permission, for limited period of time; for workweek of less than 5 days, daily hours may be extended provided weekly hours do not exceed limits. Nine-hour day (10 hours on one day per week), six-day, 48-hour week for employees under 18 or over 66, handicapped persons, and disabled veterans in: public restaurant, cafe, dining room, barber shop, hairdressing or manicuring establishment; amusement or recreational establishment; bowling alley; shoe shining establishment; billiard or pool room, or photographic gallery. Hotels exempt. Eight hour day, 48-hour, six-day week for workers under 18 or over 66, handicapped workers, and disabled veterans working in mercantile establishments. **Overtime Pay** — 1½ times regular pay for hours in excess of maximum.

Comparison Chart — State Hours Laws — Contd.

STATE	REQUIREMENTS AND PROVISIONS
Connecticut, Contd.	**Employees Covered** — All except: drivers or helpers with hours set by Interstate Commerce Commission; employees subject to Railroad Labor Act; seafarers; announcers, news editors, and chief engineers of TV/radio stations; bona fide executive, administrative, or professional employees; outside salespersons; inside salespersons working up to 54 hours/week whose regular pay exceeds two times the minimum wage or whose monthly compensation is more than half from commissions; taxicab drivers paid 40 percent or more of meter fares; milk and bakery route salespersons; automobile salespersons; agricultural employees; permanent municipal police and firefighters; firefighters employed by private non-profit firm under contract with municipality; beer delivery truck driver not paid on hourly basis; mechanics employed by sellers of motor vehicles or farm equipment provided the mechanics' actual pay exceeds the sum of regular pay for all hours worked plus ½ times regular rate for all hours in excess of 40. **Special Occupations** — Workweek limited to 40 hours for workers in: beauty shops; laundries; cleaning and dyeing; mercantile trade; 48-hour week for employees in hotel and restaurant services. **Day of Rest** — Employer may not compel employee engaged in commercial occupation or industrial process to work more than six days in calendar week. No person who conscientiously believes that a particular day of week ought to be observed as the Sabbath may be required by employer to work on such day. No person, firm, or corporation shall engage or employ others in work, labor, or business on Sunday except charitable, religious, or service organization; federal, state, municipal or local governmental agency; person, firm, or corporation performing acts necessary for public safety or health; or person who observes another day as the Sabbath. Inapplicable to certain specified business operations; the sale or furnishing of specified articles, if they are sold in ordinary course of business; or to isolated or occasional sales by persons not engaged in the sale, transfer, or exchange of property as a business. **Meal and Rest Periods** — At least 30 consecutive minutes for employee working 7½ or more consecutive hours; meal period must occur after the first two hours of work and before the last two hours. Exemptions may be granted by commission. **References** — Chapter 558, Connecticut General Statutes, Administrative Regulations; §§31-76c, 31-76(h) (maximum hours before overtime); §31-76b(1)(F) (overtime pay); §31-58(e), Wage Orders (employees covered); §§31-12, 31-13, 31-18 (limits on hours worked); §§53-302(a), 53-303(e) (day of rest); §1 (meal or rest period).
Delaware	**Maximum Hours before Overtime** —No general provision. **Overtime Pay** — No general provision. **Employees Covered** — No general provision. **Special Occupations** — No general provision. **Day of Rest** — No general provision. **Meal and Rest Periods** — Employer must allow unpaid meal break of at least 30 consecutive minutes if the employee works 7½ or more consecutive hours. Break must occur after first two hours of work and before last two hours. Does not apply to professional employees of school boards working directly with children, or if a collective bargaining agreement provides differently. Secretary of Labor may issue exemptions if: compliance would adversely affect public safety; only one employee can perform the duties; the employer has fewer than five employees on a shift (exemption applies only to that shift); continuous nature of employer's operations requires employees to respond to urgent or unusual conditions at all times, provided employees are compensated for the meal breaks. **References** — Title 19, Chapter 7, Delaware Code, §707(a)

Comparison Chart — State Hours Laws — Contd.

STATE	REQUIREMENTS AND PROVISIONS
District of Columbia	**Maximum Hours before Overtime** — 40-hour week for most employees. Automobile washers are exempt, if paid 1½ times their regular rate for hours in excess of 160 hours during any 4-week period. **Overtime Pay** — 1½ times regular pay for hours in excess of maximum. **Employees Covered** — All employees working in: private households; retail trade; laundry and dry cleaning establishments; beauty culture; manufacturing, wholesale trade, printing, and publishing; clerical and semi-technical occupations; building services; and miscellaneous occupations including machine trade, benchwork, and structural work occupations, parking and car wash attendants, guards, ushers, ticket takers, furniture movers, bus, truck, and cab drivers, lifeguards, and temporary help employees. Workers in bona fide executive, administrative, or professional capacity are exempt. **Special Occupations** — No provision. **Day of Rest** — No general provision. **Meal and Rest Periods** — No general provision. **References** — District of Columbia Code, Title 36, Chapter 2; §§36-202(5), 36-203(c), 36-204(a), (b); Wage Orders.
Florida	**Maximum Hours before Overtime** — No general provision. **Overtime Pay** — No general provision. **Employees Covered** — No general provision. **Special Occupations** — Manual Labor: 10-hour day; extra pay required for additional hours. Railway Employees: 8-hour rest after 13 consecutive hours, except when behind schedule or in emergencies. **Day of Rest** — No general provision. **Meal and Rest Periods** — No general provision. **References** — Florida Statutes; §§351.06, 448.01.
Georgia	**Maximum Hours before Overtime** — No general provision. **Overtime Pay** — No general provision. **Employees Covered** — No general provision. **Special Occupations** — Motor Carriers: 10-hour day followed by 10 hour rest for drivers of motor contract and common carriers, except in emergencies. Railroads: 13-hour day followed by 10 hour rest, except in case of casualty. Cotton or woolen manufacturer employees: 10-hour day, 60-hour week for all employees except engineers; firefighters; guards; mechanics; teamsters; yard employees; clericals; and repair employees. **Day of Rest** — Pursuit of business or work of ordinary calling forbidden on Lord's day, except works of necessity or charity. The operation of any business involved in sales, with some exceptions, on both the two consecutive days of Saturday and Sunday is a public nuisance and subject to penalty. Counties may exempt themselves by referendum. **Meal and Rest Periods** — No general provision. **References** — Title 34, Official Code of Georgia Annotated; §§18-106, 26-9908, 34-3-1, 68-522, 68-628.

Comparison Chart — State Hours Laws — Contd.

STATE	REQUIREMENTS AND PROVISIONS
Hawaii	**Maximum Hours before Overtime** — 40-hour week. **Overtime Pay** — 1½ times regular pay for hours in excess of maximum. **Employees Covered** — All employees except: those with guaranteed monthly salary of $1,250; agricultural work in any week when employer has fewer than 20 employees or engages in coffee harvesting; domestic workers; houseparents in charitable organizations; employer's relatives; bona fide executive, administrative, supervisory, or professional employees; outside salespersons or collectors; those in fish or aquatic farming industry prior to first processing; seafarers; on-call, fixed stand vehicle drivers; golf caddies; student employees of nonprofit school; seasonal employees of certain nonprofit youth camps; and automobile or truck salespersons for licensed dealer. **Special Occupations** — Employers in certain industries may select 20 workweeks per year during which they shall be exempt from the overtime compensation requirement, although they must pay 1½ times the regular rate for hours in excess of 48 per week. These industries are: agriculture; first processing of dairy products; processing of sugar cane molasses or sugar cane; first processing or canning or packing any agricultural or horticultural commodity; handling, slaughtering, or dressing poultry or livestock; agriculture and processing of agricultural products seasonally; or first processing or, canning or packing seasonal fresh fruits. **Day of Rest** — No general provision. **Meal and Rest Periods** — Lunch period of 45 minutes allowed all government employees. **References** — Hawaii Revised Statutes, Chapter 387; §§80-1, 94-2, 387-1, 387-2, 387-3.
Idaho	**Maximum Hours before Overtime** — 40 hours per seven-day week. **Overtime Pay** — 1½ times regular rate for hours in excess of maximum. **Employees Covered** — All whose employers are not exempted or excepted from the FLSA overtime provisions. **Special Occupations** — Mines: 8-hour day for workers in or upon underground mines and workings, and 10-hour day for workers in or upon surface mines and workings. Work over 10 hours per day in emergency only. Eight hour day, with extension to 10 hours permitted, in smelters, ore reduction works, stamp mills, concentrators, and other places where metalliferous ores are treated, except when life or property in imminent danger. Time worked in excess of 10 hours per day or 40 hours per week shall be paid at 1½ regular rate. **Day of Rest** — No general provision. **Meal and Rest Periods** — No general provision. **References** — Title 44, Chapter 15, Idaho Code; §§44-1104, 44-1105, 44-1502(3).

Comparison Chart — State Hours Laws — Contd.

STATE	REQUIREMENTS AND PROVISIONS
Illinois	**Maximum Hours before Overtime** — 40-hour week. **Overtime Pay** — 1½ times regular pay for hours in excess of maximum. **Employees Covered** — All employees, except: those working for employer with fewer than 4 employees; salespersons or mechanics in nonmanufacturing firm primarily selling or servicing automobiles, trucks, farm implements, boats, or aircraft; agricultural workers; government employees; those in bona fide executive, administrative, or professional capacity; commissioned employees, as defined by FLSA; domestic workers; outside salespersons; members of religious corporation or organization; certain camp counselors; employees working in another employee's stead as part of worktime exchange agreement; and employees of not-for-profit educational or residential child care institution if directly involved in educating or caring for children residing in institution and compensated at annual rate of at least $13,000 ($10,000 if board and lodging provided). **Special Occupations** — Motor Transportation: 10 hours followed by 8 hours off duty and 60 hours in seven days for operators unless emergency permission from Department of Law Enforcement, except for: public utility operators in emergency or temporary necessity, drivers connected with packing and preserving perishable fruits and vegetables, those hauling materials to and from construction site within 50-mile radius, and driver-salespersons within 50 miles of principal business. Municipal firefighters: 56 hours in any week of month for firefighters in towns over 10,000 in population. Residents and interns working in licensed hospitals subject to duty hour requirements established by the Accreditation Council for Graduate Medical Education. **Day of Rest** — At least 24 consecutive hours of rest in every calendar week in addition to regular period of rest allowed at the close of each working day. Inapplicable to part-time employees who work fewer than 20 hours per week; workers needed in case of breakdown of machinery or equipment, or other emergency requiring immediate services of experienced labor; agricultural and coal mining employees; watchmen or security guards; employees in bona fide executive, administrative, or professional capacity; outside salespersons; workers engaged for 20 or fewer weeks per calendar year in canning and processing of perishable products. Before operating on Sunday, employer must post in conspicuous place schedule containing list of employees required or allowed to work on Sunday, and designating day of rest for each. No employees shall be required to work on their designated day of rest. **Meal and Rest Periods** — At least 20 minutes for meal period beginning no later than five hours after the start of work period for employees working for 7½ continuous hours or longer. Inapplicable to employees for whom meal periods are established through collective bargaining. **References** — Illinois Revised Statutes; §§1004a(1) and (2) (maximum hours before overtime and overtime pay); §1003(d) and (g) (employees covered); §§10-3-3 and 11-1419 of Chapter 95½ (limits on hours worked); §8a and 8b (day of rest); §8c (meal or rest period).
Indiana	**Maximum Hours before Overtime** — No general provision. **Overtime Pay** — No general provision. **Employees Covered** — No general provision. **Special Occupations** — Railroads: 12-hour day followed by 10 hours off duty, or 12 hours aggregate in 24 hours followed by 8 hours off duty for employees engaged in movement of passenger or freight trains. Motor Transportation: Part 395 of federal Motor Carrier Safety Regulations adopted as Indiana law. **Day of Rest** — Common labor or pursuit of usual vocation on Sunday forbidden to persons age 14 and over, except for work of charity and necessity. Nothing shall be construed to affect those who observe conscientiously the Sabbath, those engaged in conveying travelers, toll bridge and gate keepers, ferry operators, newspaper employees, baseball and hockey players, after 1 p.m. and at least 1,000 feet from any established house of worship or public or private hospitals. **Meal and Rest Periods** — No general provision. **References** — Indiana Code; §§1-1-9-1(a) and (b), 8-2-7-43.5, 8-9-3-1.

Comparison Chart — State Hours Laws — Contd.

STATE	REQUIREMENTS AND PROVISIONS
Iowa	**Maximum Hours before Overtime** — No provision. **Overtime Pay** — No general provision. **Employees Covered** — No general provision. **Special Occupations** — Motor Transportation: 12 hours followed by 10 hours off duty, or 12 aggregate hours in 24 hours followed by 8 hours off duty. 12 hours in 24 hours for urban transit drivers; driver on split shift shall have at least 1 hour off between shifts. Railroads: 16 hours followed by 10 hours of rest, or 16 aggregate hours in 24 hours, for employees connected with movement of trains unless to protect life or property, except employees of sleeping car companies. **Day of Rest** — No general provision. **Meal and Rest Periods** — No general provision. **References** — Iowa Code; §§321.225, 321.226, 477.45 and 447.46.
Kansas	**Maximum Hours before Overtime** — 46-hour week. **Overtime Pay** — 1½ times regular pay for hours in excess of maximum. **Employees Covered** — All employees, except: employees primarily selling motor vehicles for nonmanufacturing retail firm; prisoners; those covered by FLSA; agricultural and domestic workers; those in bona fide executive, administrative, or professional capacity; outside salespersons on commission; federal employees; unpaid volunteers for nonprofit organization; part-time workers age 18 or under and age 60 or over; and students under 18 working between academic terms. **Special Occupations** — 258 hours in 28-day period (or equivalent hour/day ratio for periods from seven to 27 days) for firefighters, law enforcement personnel, and security personnel in correctional institution unless covered under FLSA. 8-hour day for employees in lead and zinc mines, except in emergencies. Grain inspection employees: regular hours are 7:00 a.m. to 4:30 p.m., Monday to Friday; however, samplers' hours may be adjusted to elevators' hours of operation, up to 8 per day. Work performed outside of regular hours is overtime. Railroads: 16 hours followed by 8 hours of rest, except in case of washout, wreck, or unavoidable blockade; inapplicable to train crews handling livestock or perishable freight; sleeping car, baggage, and express employees. Motor Transportation: Hours fixed by Public Utilities Commission. **Day of Rest** — Sunday labor prohibited except works of necessity or charity; not applicable to persons observing a different Sabbath. **Meal and Rest Periods** — No general provision. **References** — Kansas Statutes Annotated; §44-1204(a) (maximum hours before overtime, overtime pay); §§44-1202(e), 44-1204(a) and (b), 49-30-1 Rules and Regulations (employees covered); §§49-282, 66-1, 66-601, 66-602, 129(3) (limits on hours worked); §§21-952 through 21-956 (day of rest).

Comparison Chart — State Hours Laws — Contd.

STATE	REQUIREMENTS AND PROVISIONS
Kentucky	**Maximum Hours before Overtime** — 40-hour week. **Overtime Pay** — 1½ times regular pay for hours in excess of maximum. 1½ times regular pay for hours worked on seventh day of week. **Employees Covered** — All employees, except for: those whose primary duty is to direct or supervise; employees of telephone exchanges with less than 500 subscribers; stenographers; bookkeepers; technical assistants of licensed professions; employees subject to Federal Railway Labor Act; seafarers and those operating on navigable streams; those icing railroad cars; and employees of common carriers under supervision of bureau of vehicle regulation. **Special Occupations** — Motor Transportation: 12 hours followed by 8 hours off duty, or 16 hours in any 24 hours followed by 10 hours off duty, for motor vehicle drivers, except in emergencies or for those under collective bargaining agreement. **Day of Rest** — Fines will be levied on any person who works on Sunday or employs any other person in labor or other business, whether for profit or amusement, unless work or the employment of others is in the course of ordinary household duties, a necessity or charity, or required in the maintenance or operation of public service, utility, or system. Inapplicable to religious society which observes another day as Sabbath, certain specified operations, or employers using continuous work scheduling that permits at least one day of rest each calendar week for each employee. **Meal and Rest Periods** — Employers, except those subject to federal Railway Labor Act, shall grant employees a reasonable period for lunch, which shall be as close to the middle of the employee's scheduled shift as possible. Employee shall not be required to take lunch period sooner than three hours or later than five hours from commencement of shift; provision does not negate any provision of collective bargaining or mutual agreement between employer and employee. Rest period of 10 minutes during each four hours worked, except employees subject to FRLA. **References** — Kentucky Statutes Annotated; §337.285 (maximum hours before overtime); §§337.050, 337.285 (overtime pay); §337.010(2)(a) (employees covered); §281.730 (limits on hours worked); §436.160(1) to (4) (day of rest); §§337.355, 337.365, 337.991 (meal or rest period).
Louisiana	**Maximum Hours before Overtime** — No general provision. **Overtime Pay** — No general provision. **Employees Covered** — No general provision. **Special Occupations** — No provision. **Day of Rest** — No store or business opposed to being open on Sunday shall be required to open on Sunday, unless required by lease agreement. New or used car or truck dealers may not be open on Sunday. **Meal and Rest Periods** — No general provision. **References** — Louisiana Revised Statutes; Title 51, §§192 and 193.

Comparison Chart — State Hours Laws — Contd.

STATE	REQUIREMENTS AND PROVISIONS
Maine	**Maximum Hours before Overtime** — 40-hour week. **Overtime Pay** — 1½ times regular pay for hours in excess of maximum. **Employees Covered** — All employees, except: those processing, marketing, or storing agricultural products, meat, fish, and other perishable goods; seafarers; employees of hotel, motel, eating establishment, nursing home, or hospital; public employees except firefighters, who are covered; automobile mechanics or salespersons. **Special Occupations** — No provision. **Day of Rest** — No place of business shall be kept open on Sunday except for work of necessity, emergency, or charity; operation or maintenance of common contract or private carriers; taxicabs; airplanes; newspapers; radio and television stations; hotels, motels, rooming houses, tourist and trailer camps; restaurants; garages and auto service stations; retail monument dealers; automatic laundries; pharmacies; greenhouses; seasonal stands selling produce; public utilities; industries in continuous operation; agricultural processing plants; ship chandlers; marinas; establishments selling boats, sporting equipment, souvenirs, or novelties; motion picture theaters; sports and athletic events; musical concerts; lectures; scenic, historic, recreational, and amusement facilities; real estate brokers; salespersons; stores employing fewer than 5 persons; vending machines; bowling alleys; fireworks displays; mobile homes salespersons; public dancing. Isolated transactions by persons not engaged in sale, transfer, or exchange of property as a business are exempt. **Meal and Rest Periods** — In absence of collective bargaining or other agreement, worker may be employed or permitted to work for no more than six consecutive hours at one time without at least 30 consecutive minutes of rest time, except in cases of emergency in which there is danger to property, life, public safety, or health. Rest time may be used as meal time. Inapplicable to place of employment where fewer than three employees are on duty at one time, and nature of work allows employees frequent breaks during work day. **References** — Title 26, Maine Revised Statutes; §664 (maximum hours before overtime, overtime pay); §§663(3)(A) to (K), 664 (employees covered); Title 17, §3204 (day of rest); §§601 and 602 (meal or rest period).

Comparison Chart — State Hours Laws — Contd.

STATE	REQUIREMENTS AND PROVISIONS
Maryland	**Maximum Hours before Overtime** — 40-hour week; 48-hour week for employees in bowling establishments or resident employees in institution other than hospital engaged in care of sick, aged, or mentally ill; 60-hour week for farm workers exempt from overtime provisions of FLSA. **Overtime Pay** — 1½ times regular pay for hours in excess of maximum. **Employees Covered** — All employees, except: employees of amusement or recreational establishments operating less than seven months in calendar year and with average receipts for any six months are less than ⅓ of average receipts for other six months; computer systems analyst, computer programmer, software engineer, or other similarly skilled professional if paid more than 6½ times applicable minimum wage and performs specified duties; employees of interstate carriers covered by federal law; employees of hotel, motel, or restaurant; salespersons, partspersons, or mechanics primarily selling or servicing automobiles, trailers, trucks, or machinery in nonmanufacturing firm; gasoline service station employees; taxicab drivers; private country club employees; certain employees of nonprofit concert promoters, legitimate theaters, music festivals or pavilions, or theatrical shows; those working for nonprofit employer furnishing temporary at-home services for sick, aged, mentally ill, or handicapped. **Special Occupations** — Agricultural workers: 60-hour week. Railroads: 8-hour day for telephone and telegraph operators handling train movements under "block system," except when fewer than nine passenger or 20 freight trains each way in 24 hours. Cotton and Wool Manufacturing: 10-hour day for employees manufacturing cotton or woolen yarns, fabrics, or domestics, except during repairs, improvements, firing up, and readying machinery. Tobacco Warehouses (Baltimore only): hours from 7 a.m. to 12 noon and 1 p.m. to 6 p.m. for tobacco warehouse employees. **Day of Rest** — Retail establishment may operate on Sunday, provided that all employees other than managerial and professional employees are permitted to choose either Sunday or employee's Sabbath as day of rest. Outside Wicomico county, part-time employees (fewer than 25 hours per week) also must be given the option of choosing a day of rest. **Meal and Rest Periods** — No general provision. **References** — Maryland Annotated Code: Ch. 8, §3-415, 3-420 (maximum hours, overtime pay, employees covered); §3-704 (day of rest)
Massachusetts	**Maximum Hours before Overtime** — 40-hour week. **Overtime Pay** — 1½ times regular pay for hours in excess of maximum; commissions, drawing accounts, bonuses, or other incentive pay based on sales or production are excluded in computing regular rate and overtime pay. 1½ times regular rate for Sunday labor in retail establishments, except for employer with fewer than seven employees including proprietor, and workers in bona fide executive, administrative, or professional capacity earning over $200 a week. Employees in retail establishments required to work on the second Monday in October (Columbus Day) must be paid 1½ times their regular rate. **Employees Covered** — All employees, except: caretakers of residential property if furnished living quarters and paid at least $36 a week; golf caddies, news carriers, or child performers; those in bona fide executive, administrative, or professional capacity or training for such positions and earning more than $80 a week; outside salespersons and buyers; learners, apprentices, or handicapped, with special license; those catching or taking aquatic animal or vegetable life; public telephone switchboard operators; drivers and helpers under Interstate Commerce Commission or Railway Labor Act; those employed in business determined seasonal by Commissioner and existing not more than 120 days in any year; seafarers; employees of passenger motor carrier, as defined; hotel, motel, and restaurant employees; garage and gasoline station workers; those working in hospital, home for the aged, nonprofit school or summer camp; agricultural laborers; employees in amusement park operating not more than 150 days a year

Appendix G

Comparison Chart — State Hours Laws — Contd.

STATE	REQUIREMENTS AND PROVISIONS
Massachusetts, Contd.	**Special Occupations** — Railways: 9-hour day within 11 consecutive hours for employees of street, electric, or elevated railways. Motor Transportation: 12-hour day followed by 8 hours off duty, or 16 hours followed by 10 hours off duty, with 3 hours or more breaking continuity, for motor vehicle drivers. **Day of Rest** — For each seven consecutive days worked, employees must have 24 consecutive hours of rest, including unbroken period between 8 a.m. and 5 p.m., except in emergency for employees in workshop or manufacturing, mechanical, or mercantile establishments. Employees working on Sunday must be allowed 24 consecutive hours without work in the six days following, except employees in manufacture or distribution of gas, electricity, milk, or water; hotels, transportation, sale, or delivery of food by establishments other than restaurants; railroads or railways; janitors; employees whose only Sunday duties are: setting sponges in bakeries, caring for live animals, caring for machinery, maintaining fires, preparing, printing, publishing, or delivery of newspapers, farm or personal services, pharmacists in drug stores, or any labor called for by an emergency. Sunday labor prohibited, except works of necessity or charity, or employment specifically exempted. **Meal and Rest Periods** — No person shall be required to work for more than six hours a day without an interval of at least 30 minutes for a meal, with certain specified exceptions. **References** — Massachusetts General Laws; §13, Chapter 136, §1A, Chapter 151 (maximum hours before overtime, overtime pay); §§1A, 2, 9 of Chapter 151 (employees covered); §§13, 18 of Chapter 159, §103 of Chapter 161 (limits on hours worked); §6(50) of Chapter 136 (day of rest); §100 of Chapter 149 (meal or rest period).
Michigan	**Maximum Hours before Overtime** — 40-hour week. Ten hours a day in factories, workshops, salt blocks, saw-mills, logging or lumber camps, booms or drivers, mines or other places used for mechanical or manufacturing purposes. **Overtime Pay** — 1½ times regular pay for hours in excess of maximum. **Employees Covered** — All employees, except: those in bona fide executive, administrative, or professional capacity; elected and appointed government officials; workers in amusement or recreational establishment operating not more than seven months in calendar year; employees in all branches of agriculture; employees not subject to minimum hourly wage provisions. **Special Occupations** — 216 hours in 28 days (or equivalent hour/day ratio for periods from seven to 27 days) for public fire protection and law enforcement employees, including security personnel in correctional institution. Motor Transportation: 10 hours in any 15 consecutive hours followed by 8 hours off duty for drivers of motor trucks and truck tractors, except those operating government vehicles or operating within 50-mile radius of domicile, unless emergency, as defined. **Day of Rest** — Barber shops and pawn shops must be closed on Sunday. **Meal and Rest Periods** — No general provision. **References** — Michigan Annotated Statutes; §§408.384, 408.401, 408.402, 408.405 (maximum hours before overtime, overtime pay); §408.394 (employees covered); §§408, 480.11 to 480.17 (limits on hours worked); §§338.681, 446.217 (day of rest).

Comparison Chart — State Hours Laws — Contd.

STATE	REQUIREMENTS AND PROVISIONS
Minnesota	**Maximum Hours before Overtime** — 48-hour week. **Overtime Pay** — 1½ times regular pay for hours in excess of maximum. State and political subdivisions may grant time off at a rate of 1½ hours per hour worked in excess of 48 per week to public employees. Health care facility may agree with employees to accept work period of 14 days, with overtime pay due for workers who work more than 80 hours in 14 days or 8 hours in one day. **Employees Covered** — All employees, except: those subject to agreement under Sec. 7(b)(2) of FLSA; executive, administrative, professional employees; outside salespersons; elected officials; taxi drivers; seasonal camp or ski resort employees; sugar beet hand laborers on piece rate basis, when hourly pay exceeds minimum wage by 40 cents; salespersons, partspersons, and mechanics on commission or incentive basis for retail employer selling or servicing automobiles, trailers, trucks, or farm implements; those employed in farm silo construction or installing appurtenant equipment on unit or piece rate basis, when pay exceeds minimum wage; caretakers and other employees of residential building living on-site when available but not performing duties; companions of aged or infirm, under certain conditions. **Special Occupations** — Motor Transportation: 12 hours for truck drivers, unless transporting own products or fresh vegetables between farms, canneries, and viner stations. Railroads: 14 hours followed by 9 hours rest (less if worker requests). 16 hours out of 24, followed by 8 hours rest for those engaged in movement of trains, except in defined emergencies. **Day of Rest** — All trades, manufacturing, and mechanical employments are prohibited on Sunday, with certain specified exceptions. Violations are misdemeanors, but it is sufficient defense that another day of the week is kept uniformly as holy time and that the act complained of was done in such a manner as not to disturb others in observance of the Sabbath. **Meal and Rest Periods** — Adequate time within each four consecutive hours of work to visit nearest convenient restroom. Rest periods of less than 20 minutes may not be deducted from hours worked. Employee working 8 hours or more must have sufficient time to eat a meal; 30 minutes is considered bona fide meal period and meal time need not be paid. Meal periods of less than 20 minutes may not be deducted from hours worked. Employees on duty 24 hours or more may agree with employer on meal periods. **References** — Minnesota Statutes, Minnesota Rules; §§177.25(1), (2), and (3) (maximum hours before overtime, overtime pay); §§177.23(1) through (19), 177.25(1), (3), and (4) (employees covered); §§181.28, 181.29, 181.30, 221.02(13), and 221.32 (limits on hours worked); §§614.29, 614.30, 645.44(5) (day of rest); §§177.253(1) and (2), 177.254 (meal or rest period).
Mississippi	**Maximum Hours before Overtime** — No general provision. **Overtime Pay** — No general provision. **Employees Covered** — No general provision. **Special Occupations** — No provision. **Day of Rest** — Sunday work prohibited except for necessary household work; labor on railroads, steamboats, and common and contract motor vehicle carriers; telegraph or telephone lines; street railways; newspapers; livery stables; ice houses; garages and gasoline stations; meat markets; manufacturing operations which operate continuously; church or religious societies. In lieu of any one legal holiday, municipalities and counties may declare Mardi Gras Day a legal holiday. **Meal and Rest Period** — No general provision. **References** — Mississippi Code; §§97-23-63, 97-23-69; § 3-3-7(2) amended by H.B. 29, eff. 2/1/93.

Appendix G 213

Comparison Chart — State Hours Laws — Contd.

STATE	REQUIREMENTS AND PROVISIONS
Missouri	**Maximum Hours before Overtime** — 40 hours per week. **Overtime Pay** — 1½ times regular rate for hours in excess of maximum. **Employees Covered** — All except agricultural employers. **Special Occupations** — Mining: 8 hours within 24 for workers engaged in mining or crushing rocks, or in reducing, roasting, refining, or smelting minerals in ores for mechanical, chemical, manufacturing, or smelting company. Public Works: 8-hour day in 24 hours for laborers and mechanics on public works in second class city. Railroads: 9-hour day in 24 hours for employees operating interlocking tower. Amusement or recreation business employees (as defined in FLSA): 52-hour week before overtime. **Day of Rest** — It is unlawful to sell or expose for sale at retail on Sunday a number of specified articles. County with population over 400,000 may exempt itself by referendum; many counties and the City of St. Louis have done so. **Meal and Rest Periods** — No general provision. **References** — Revised Statutes of Missouri; §3 (maximum hours before overtime, overtime pay); §§1(3), 3(a) to (p), and 4 (employees covered); §§88.487, 88.490, 290.020, 389.960 (limits on hours worked); §578.100 (day of rest).
Montana	**Maximum Hours before Overtime** — 40 hours per week. 48-hour week for students employed by seasonal amusement or recreational area who are furnished with board, lodging, or other facilities. State constitution specifies 8 hours per day as regular workday, but has no overtime pay requirement. **Overtime Pay** — 1½ times regular pay for hours in excess of maximum. **Employees Covered** — All employees, except: farming and stock raising employees; those subject to U.S. Department of Transportation or Part I of Interstate Commerce Act; outside buyers of raw dairy and poultry products; outside salespersons selling advertising for newspaper or radio or television station on commission or contract basis; outside salespersons selling office supplies, computers, or other office equipment for an office equipment dealer on commission or contract basis; salespersons, partspersons, or mechanics on commission or contract selling or servicing automobiles, trucks, mobile homes, recreational vehicles, or farm implements for retail establishment; salespersons selling trailers, boats, or aircraft to ultimate purchaser; drivers and helpers making local deliveries and paid on delivery payment plan, with permit; agricultural workers; those engaged in supplying and storing water for agriculture; employees of country elevators with no more than five workers; taxicab drivers; spouses employed by nonprofit educational institution as resident children's parents and receiving board, lodging, and $10,000 a year; workers planting, tending, cruising, surveying, felling, or transporting trees or forestry products to mill, plant, or transportation terminal, if employed by employee with eight or fewer workers; municipal or county employees with collectively bargained workweek of 40 hours in 7-day period; public firefighters with collective bargaining agreement; police officers in third class city or police department employees in first or second class city working under chief's schedule; sheriff's or public safety employees working under established work period; students in distributive education program of accredited agency; domestic workers; caretakers of children directly employed by household head; hospital employees with work period of up to 80 hours in a 14-day period established by collective bargaining or mutual agreement; employer's relatives dependent on employer for at least half their support; volunteers in nonprofit organization; handicapped whose work is incidental to training or evaluation program or who are severely impaired and unable to compete; those in executive, administrative, or professional capacity; apprentices or learners for up to 30 days; learners under 18 employed as farm workers for up to 180 days; retired or semiretired persons performing part-time incident work as condition of residence on a farm or ranch; resident managers in lodging or personal care facilities who, under the terms of their employment, live in the facility; and federal employees.

Comparison Chart — State Hours Laws — Contd.

STATE	REQUIREMENTS AND PROVISIONS
Montana Contd.	**Special Occupations** — Mining: 8-hour day for workers in underground and strip mines or workings, except in emergencies. 8 hours in 24 hours for hoisting engineers, under certain conditions. Motor Transportation: 8-hour day followed by 12 hours rest in every 24 hours for drivers and attendants, except in emergencies. Railroads: 12 consecutive hours, or 16 aggregate hours in 24, followed by 8 hours off duty, except during emergencies. Public Amusements: 8 hour day, 48 hour week for persons employed or working in any carnival, circus, derby show, walkathon, marathon dance, race, or walk, or other endurance contest. Retail stores: 8-hour day and 48-hour week. Telephone operators: Nine hours in 24 hour period. State and Municipal Governments and School Districts: 8-hour day, except firefighters with work period established by collective bargaining agreement. 40-hour workweek of four consecutive 10-hour days for employees of road and bridge departments. 8-hour days for workers in cement plants, quarries, and hydroelectric dams, except in emergency. Sugar refineries: 8-hour day except in emergency. Restaurants: 8-hour day, 48-hour week. **Day of Rest** — No general provision. **Meal and Rest Periods** — No general provision. **References** — Montana Code Annotated; §39-3-405 (maximum hours before overtime, overtime pay); §§39-3-402(3), 39-3-406(1)(a) to (k) (employees covered); §§39-4-101, 39-4-102, 39-4-103, 39-4-105, 39-4-107 through 39-4-112, and Constitution Article VII, §2 (limits on hours worked).
Nebraska	**Maximum Hours before Overtime** — No general provision. **Overtime Pay** — No general provision. **Employees Covered** — No general provision. **Special Occupations** — Motor Transportation: 12 hours in 24 hours for motor carrier employees (passenger or freight), except taxicab drivers within city or village and in emergencies. Railroads: 16 consecutive hours followed by 10 continuous hours of rest, or 16 hours aggregate in 24-hour period followed by 8 hours of rest. 9-hour work period for employees in places operating day and night, and 13 hours in places operating during day only, except in certain emergencies allowing up to 4 more hours three times a week. **Day of Rest** — No general provision. **Meal and Rest Periods** — Employees in assembly plant, workshop, or mechanical establishments are required to have at least one-half hour lunch period between 12 noon and 1 p.m. without having to remain on premises, unless establishment operates in three 8-hour shifts each 24-hour period. **References** — Revised Statutes of Nebraska; §§60-1201 and 1202, 74-902 and 903 (limits on hours worked); §48-212 (meal or rest period).

Comparison Chart — State Hours Laws — Contd.

STATE	REQUIREMENTS AND PROVISIONS
Nevada	**Maximum Hours before Overtime** — 8-hour day, 40-hour week, unless mutually agreed 10-hour day, 4-day week. **Overtime Pay** — 1½ times regular pay for hours in excess of maximum. **Employees Covered** — All employees, except: those not covered by state minimum wage provisions; those paid not less than 1½ times the minimum wage; outside buyers; retail salespersons on commission if regular rate more than 1½ times the minimum rate and half of compensation comes from commissions; those in executive, administrative, or professional capacity; employees covered by collective bargaining agreement; motor carrier drivers, drivers' helpers, loaders, and mechanics subject to Motor Carrier Act; air carrier and railroad employees; drivers and helpers making local deliveries and paid on trip-rate or other delivery plan basis; taxicab and limousine drivers; agricultural workers; employees of businesses with annual gross sales less than $250,000; salespersons and mechanics primarily selling or servicing automobiles, trucks, or farm equipment. **Special Occupations** — Mining: 8 hours in 24-hour period for employees in underground and surface mines, except: in emergencies; when employee voluntarily agrees to more hours; when maintenance crew needs to complete work; or if no qualified worker available for relief. Smelting: 8-hour day in smelters and other places reducing or refining ore, except in emergencies or when employee voluntarily agrees to more hours. Cement: 8-hour day, except in emergencies. Railroads: 16 hours followed by 10 hours off duty, or 16 hours aggregate in 24 hours followed by 8 hours off duty. 8 hours, followed by 16 hours off duty, for employees handling orders for movement of trains. Motor Transportation: Maximum hours subject to order of public service commission. **Day of Rest** — No general provision. **Meal and Rest Periods** — At least one-half hour for meal for a continuous work period of eight hours. Rest periods of 10 minutes for every 4 hours worked. **References** — Nevada Revised Statutes; §608.018(1) (maximum hours before overtime, overtime pay); §§608.010(1), 608.018, 608.250 (employees covered); §§608.200, 608.210, 608.220, 608.230, 608.240, 705.210, 706.776 (limits on hours worked); §608.155 (meal or rest period).

Comparison Chart — State Hours Laws — Contd.

STATE	REQUIREMENTS AND PROVISIONS
New Hampshire	**Maximum Hours before Overtime** — 40-hour week. **Overtime Pay** — 1½ times regular pay for hours in excess of maximum. **Employees Covered** — All employees, except: those working in amusement, seasonal, or recreational establishment operating no more than seven months in calendar year or that received at least 75 percent of income during any six months of previous year; and employees covered by FLSA. **Special Occupations** — 10-hour day, 48-hour week for manual or mechanical labor in manufacturing. Regular employees in mercantile establishments during the seven-day period immediately preceding Christmas Day may work overtime, but weekly average for year may not exceed 54 hours. Laundry workers may be employed up to 10¼ hours per day, 60 hours per week, for up to three months of the year, with special license from commissioner. **Day of Rest** — Employers in manufacturing or mercantile establishments are required to give all employees a 24-hour rest period every 7 days. Employers in commercial, industrial, transportation, or communication establishments permitted to operate on Sunday are required to allow employees 24 hours' rest during the 6-day period thereafter, except for employers in manufacture or distribution of gas, electricity, milk, or water; hotels, restaurants, drug stores, livery stables, garages; transportation, sale, or delivery of food; janitors, guards, firefighters, or caretakers; employees whose Sunday duties include setting sponges in bakeries, caring for live animals, caring for machinery and plant equipment; preparation, printing, publication, sale, or delivery of newspapers; farm labor or personal services; labor due to emergency; theaters or motion picture houses, canning of perishable goods, telegraph and telephone offices. Employers may be exempt from Sunday provisions where mutual employer-employee agreements are reached, approval is given by the Commissioner, and it appears to be in the best interests of all concerned. **Meal and Rest Periods** — Employer may not require employee to work more than five consecutive hours without granting one-half hour lunch or eating period, unless it is feasible for employee to eat during performance of work and employer permits worker to do so. **References** — New Hampshire Revised Statutes Annotated; §279:21(VII) (maximum hours before overtime, overtime pay); §279:21(VII) and (VIII) (employees covered); §§275:13, 275:30 (limits on hours worked); §275:31-33 (day of rest); §275:30-a (meal or rest period).
New Jersey	**Maximum Hours before Overtime** — 40-hour week. **Overtime Pay** — 1½ times regular pay for hours in excess of maximum. **Employees Covered** — All employees, except: farm workers; hotel employees; those employed by passenger bus company; those raising or caring for livestock; employees in bona fide executive, administrative, or professional capacity; those working for nonprofit or religious summer camp, conference, or retreat. **Special Occupations** — Motor Transportation: 12 continuous hours (or 12 hours in aggregate of 16 hours) followed by 8 hours off duty. Street and Elevated Railways: 12 consecutive hours, except in emergencies. First Process of Farm Products: 1½ times regular rate for hours in excess of 48 per week, or 10 per day, for a period not to exceed 10 weeks; 1½ times regular rate for hours in excess of 50 per week or 10 per day for a period up to 10 weeks. **Day of Rest** — It is unlawful on Sunday for any person to engage in the business of selling, either at retail, wholesale, or by auction, certain specified articles except as works of necessity and charity or as isolated transactions not in the usual course of business. **Meal and Rest Periods** — No general provision. **References** — New Jersey Wage and Hour Law, New Jersey Annotated Code; §34:11-56a4, Wage Order No. 1 (maximum hours before overtime); §12:56-6.6 (overtime pay); §§12:56-7; 34:11-56a1(h), 34:11-56a4 (employees covered); §§34:19-3, 39:9-2 (limits on hours worked); §2A:171-5.8 to 5.18 (day of rest).

Comparison Chart — State Hours Laws — Contd.

STATE	REQUIREMENTS AND PROVISIONS
New Mexico	**Maximum Hours before Overtime** — For most employees, a 40-hour, 7-day week, eff. 7/1/93. For workers in hotels, restaurants, and eating houses, a 10-hour day, 70-hour, 7-day week. **Overtime Pay** — 1½ times regular pay for hours in excess of maximum. **Employees Covered** — All employees in hotels, restaurants, and eating houses, except: workers in interstate commerce, whose working hours are regulated by federal law; employees of hospitals or sanitariums, registered or practical nurses, midwives, domestic employees. **Special Occupations** — Motor Vehicle drivers: 10 hours, following 8 consecutive hours off duty; 60 hours in any seven consecutive days. Cotton Ginning Workers: exempt, if employed for 14 or fewer weeks of the year. Railroad Transportation: 10 consecutive hours rest following 16 consecutive hours work. 8 hours off after 16 hours aggregate work in 24 hours for workers in the movement of rolling stock, engines, or trains, except crews of wrecking or relief trains and sleeping car employees. **Day of Rest** — No general provision. **Meal and Rest Periods** — Not less than one-half hour excluded from working day. **References** — New Mexico Statutes Annotated; §50-4-13, 50-4-14, 50-4-22(D), 50-4-24, 50-4-30, 50-5-1, 50-5-2, 50-5-6, 50-5-7, 65-3-2.
New York	**Maximum Hours before Overtime** — 40-hour week for most employees; 44-hour week for resident employees. **Overtime Pay** — 1½ times regular pay for hours in excess of maximum. **Employees Covered** — All employees, except part-time babysitters and live-in companions; farmworkers; bona fide executives, administrators, and professionals; outside salespersons; taxi-cab drivers, volunteers for nonprofit organization; members of religious order; sextons; learners and trainees in nonprofit institution, under certain conditions; and counselors and employees in children's summer camp. **Special Occupations** — Motor Transportation: Driver may not drive more than 10 hours following 8 consecutive hours off-duty, nor for any period after having been on-duty 15 hours following 8 consecutive hours off-duty. Bus driver may not be on duty more than 60 hours in any 7 consecutive days if the employer does not operate every day; or more than 70 hours in any 8 consecutive days if the employer operates every day of the week. Pharmacies: No more than 70 hours per week, except 6 hours overtime may be worked if succeeding week is shortened so that aggregate hours for two weeks does not exceed 132; 54 hours per week, or two-week aggregate of 108 hours in cities over 1,000,000 population. Public Work Contractors: 8-hour day, 5-day week for laborers, workers, and mechanics, except in extraordinary emergency. Railroads: Employee operating trains may not exceed 16 hours, followed by 10 hours off duty, or aggregate of 16 hours in 24, with 8 hours off duty. Street or Elevated Railways: 10 consecutive hours in any day, including ½ hour for dinner. Brickyards: 10 hour day, no work prior to 7 a.m. Work in compressed air limited by board orders. Students: No more than four hours on any day preceding a school day, other than a Sunday or holiday, except that students enrolled in a cooperative work experience program approved by the department of education may be employed for no more than six hours on any day preceding a school day other than a Sunday or holiday.

Comparison Chart — State Hours Laws — Contd.

STATE	REQUIREMENTS AND PROVISIONS
New York, Contd.	**Day of Rest** — At least 24 consecutive hours of rest in each calendar week must be allowed employees by factory, mercantile establishments, hotel, restaurant, freight or passenger elevator in any building or place, including janitors, superintendents, supervisors, managers, and guards in warehouses, storage houses, offices, dwellings, apartments, lofts, and other buildings and structures; projectionists; firefighters; employees in places where legitimate stage productions are presented. Employers operating on Sunday must post notices listing employees scheduled to work and designating day of rest for each of them. All labor on Sunday is prohibited, except works of charity and necessity. All trades, manufacturing, agricultural, or mechanical employments on Sunday are prohibited, except when the same are works of necessity. All manner of public selling or offering for sale of any property is prohibited with certain specified exceptions; provision is inapplicable to those who uniformly keep another day of the week as holy time. One day a week may be set aside for rest and relaxation by owner of business or commercial enterprise. However, retail or merchant association or organization shall not have right to determine a day of rest and relaxation for its members. No provision of law shall be construed to prohibit any owner from doing business seven days a week where any other law, rule, or regulation does not specifically prohibit such activity. **Meal and Rest Periods** — Person employed in mercantile or other covered establishments and occupations shall be allowed at least 45 minutes and person employed in factories shall be allowed at least 60 minutes for a noon day meal. Employees on a shift starting before noon and continuing later than 7 p.m. allowed an additional meal period of at least 20 minutes between 5 p.m. and 7 p.m. Commissioner may grant permits for shorter meal periods. **References** — Article 19, Labor Law of the Consolidated Laws of New York, Codes, Rules, and Regulations; Wage Order, Administrative Regulations, Title 12, Parts 137 and 138 (maximum hours before overtime, overtime pay); §651(5), Title 12, Parts 138 and 142 (employees covered); Chapter 16, §1356, Chapter 31, §§163, 164, 165, 220 and Transportation Law §§210, 211, 213, 214 (limits on hours worked); McKinney's Consolidated Laws, General Business Law §§5,6,8,9 and Labor Law Chapter 31, §§17, 31 (day of rest); Chapter 31, §162 (meal or rest period).

Appendix G

Comparison Chart — State Hours Laws — Contd.

STATE	REQUIREMENTS AND PROVISIONS
North Carolina	**Maximum Hours before Overtime** — 45-hour week. 8-hour day and 80 hours in 14-day period for hospital and nursing home employees, if employees notified in advance. **Overtime Pay** — 1½ times regular pay for hours in excess of maximum. **Employees Covered** — All employees, except: those working for an employer with fewer than 3 employees; drivers, drivers' helpers, loaders, and mechanics, as defined by FLSA; taxicab drivers; seafarers; railroad and air carrier employees; salespersons and mechanics employed by automotive, truck, farm implement, trailer, boar, or aircraft dealer; child care or other live-in workers in home for dependent children; radio/TV announcers, performers, news editors, and chief engineers; agricultural and domestic workers; babysitters; pages in state legislature and governor's office; volunteers in medical, educational, religious, or nonprofit organization where no employer-employee relationship; those confined in public penal, correctional, or mental institution; employees of outdoor drama theaters except ushers, ticket takers, and parking attendants; those working in children's summer camp or seasonal religious or nonprofit educational conference center; employees in seafood industry through first sale; employer's spouse, child, parent, or qualified dependent under state tax laws; those in bona fide executive, administrative, professional, or outside sales capacity; employee of employer with two or fewer workers in any workweek; and public employees, including those in seasonal recreation program. **Special Occupations** — Railroads: 16 consecutive hours followed by 10 hours rest, or 16 aggregate hours in 24 hours followed by 8 hours rest. 9-hour day for employees handling movement of trains by telegraph or telephone in place operating day and night, and 13-hour day in place operating during day only, with 4 more hours a day not over three times a week in emergencies. State Institutions: 12 hours in any 24 hours or 84 hours in one week for employees of state correctional institution and Dorothea Dix, Broughton, and Cherry Hill Hospitals (unless emergency determined by superintendent), except for: state prison, institution controlled by Commissioner of Highways and Public Works, and hospital doctors and superintendents. Businesses are encouraged to provide employees with time to attend conferences with their children's teachers. **Day of Rest** — Board of county commissioners has power to regulate sale of merchandise on Sundays in certain designated counties. **Meal and Rest Periods** — No general provision. **References** — North Carolina General Statutes, Chapter 95 of the Wage and Hour Act; §§95-25.4(a) and (b) (maximum hours before overtime, overtime pay); §§95-25.14, 95-25.2(4) (employees covered); §§62-230, 95-28 (limits on hours worked); §153-9 (day of rest).

Comparison Chart — State Hours Laws — Contd.

STATE	REQUIREMENTS AND PROVISIONS
North Dakota	**Maximum Hours before Overtime** — 40 hours per week. Hospitals and residential care establishments may adopt, with employee agreement, fourteen-day overtime period if employees are paid at least 1½ times regular rate for all hours in excess of eight per day or eighty per fourteen-day work period, whichever produces a greater number of overtime hours. Maximum is 50 hours per week for individuals employed by taxicab companies as drivers. **Overtime Pay** — 1½ times regular pay for hours in excess of maximum. **Employees Covered** — All employees except those employed in bona fide executive, administrative, or professional capacities; live-in domestic employees; technical and clerical employees, earning $250 or more per week, and spending more than 50 percent of worktime supervising two or more employees; agricultural employees; employees of shelters and similar establishments who primarily provide temporary shelter, crisis intervention, prevention, education, and fellowship; retail automobile, trailer, boat, aircraft, truck, or farm implement dealership salespersons compensated by straight commission, unless the salesperson is required to be on the premises for more than 40 hours in a week. **Special Occupations** — Railroads: 12 hours, followed by 10 hours of rest. **Day of Rest** — Effective 2/6/91, employers may not require employees to work seven consecutive days in a business that sells merchandise at retail. Employee must have at least one period of 24 consecutive hours of time for rest or worship in each seven day period. This time off is in addition to the regular time off allowed during each work day. Employers must accommodate their employee's religious beliefs and practices unless such accommodation would cause an undue hardship. It is a misdemeanor to conduct business or labor for profit as usual or to operate a business open to the public, or to cause, direct, or authorize employee or agent to do so, with some exceptions, between the hours of 12 midnight and 12 noon on Sunday. Not applicable to person who in good faith observes day other than Sunday as the Sabbath, provided that individual refrains from engaging in or conducting business or labor for profit and closes the place of business to the public between the hours of 12 midnight and 12 noon on the day observed as the Sabbath. **Meal and Rest Periods** — 30 minute uninterrupted meal time in each shift exceeding five hours when there are two or more employees on duty. Employees not allowed to leave the premises during the break must be compensated at their regular rate of pay or provided with in-kind compensation, such as a meal, of a value equal to or greater than the minimum wage. Collectively bargained agreements will prevail over this provision. **References** — North Dakota Century Code, §§12.1-30-01(1), 31-01-08 and 09, 34-06-11 and 12, 49-13-9 and 49-13-18, General Wage Order (note: the state attorney general has declared the General Wage Order invalid until it takes the form of an administrative rule — Attorney General Opinion, September 6, 1989).
Ohio	**Maximum Hours before Overtime** — 40-hour week. 8-hour day in mechanical, manufacturing, and mining businesses, unless contract otherwise specifies. **Overtime Pay** — 1½ times regular pay in excess of maximum. **Employees Covered** — All employees, except: agricultural workers; individual working for employer with annual gross sales of less than $150,000; federal employees; babysitters and companions; outside salespersons; newspaper deliverers; and employees exempt under FLSA. **Special Occupations** — Motor Transportation: 14 consecutive hours (or 14 aggregate hours in 24 hours) followed by 8 hours off duty. Railroads and Railways: 15 hours, followed by 8 hours of rest (regulated so that employee has 8 consecutive hours off in each 24 hours). **Day of Rest** — No general provision. **Meal and Rest Periods** — No general provision. **References** — Ohio Revised Statutes; §4111.03(A) (maximum hours before overtime, overtime pay); §4111.03(D) and (E) (employees covered); §§4113.01, 4921.300, 4923.16, 4973.11 (limits on hours worked).

Comparison Chart — State Hours Laws — Contd.

STATE	REQUIREMENTS AND PROVISIONS
Oklahoma	**Maximum Hours before Overtime** — No general provision. **Overtime Pay** — No general provision. **Employees Covered** — No general provision. **Special Occupations** — No provision. **Day of Rest** — It is unlawful to do any servile work or to work at any trade, manufacturing, or mechanical employment on Sunday, except for works of charity or necessity and other specified exemptions. **Meal and Rest Periods** — No general provision. **References** — Oklahoma Statutes; Title 21, §908.
Oregon	**Maximum Hours before Overtime** — 10-hour day and 40-hour week. Waiting and on-call time may be considered hours worked. Employees may not be allowed or permitted to work more than 13 hours in 24-hour period. Hospitals and residential care establishments may adopt, with employee agreement before work begins, a 14-day overtime period if employees are paid at least 1½ the regular rate for all hours in excess of eight hours per day or 80 hours per 14-day work period. Minors may not work more than 44 hours per week (except minors employed in organized youth camps or agriculture), unless the employer is issued a Special Emergency Overtime Permit from the Wage and Hour Commission. **Overtime Pay** — 1½ times regular pay, or 1½ times regular price for piece work, for hours in excess of maximum. Regular rate must be computed without benefit of commissions, overrides spiffs, bonuses, tips, or similar benefits, including discretionary bonuses, gifts, profit sharing, thrift and savings programs, trusts, reimbursement for expenses, holiday or vacation pay. **Employees Covered** — Employees in mill, factory, or manufacturing establishment, except: members of logging train crew; watch personnel; those whose primary duty is operation/cleaning of boilers; those whose regular duty involves transportation of other employees to and from work; repair personnel; those engaged in emergency work when life or property is threatened; those whose primary work is cleaning, guarding, repairing and caring for living quarters of other employees; those whose primary duty is caring for livestock; messhall employees; supervisors, managers, and foremen/women, permanent or temporary; those whose primary duty is loading and removal of finished forest products; those engaged in catching, taking, harvesting, or farming of aquatic animal or vegetable life; those engaged in the first processing, canning, or packing of marine products at sea in conjunction with fishing operations; employees of nonprofit amusement or recreational establishments; those subject to collective bargaining agreement where employer and labor organization have agreed on hours and overtime, unless a strike or lockout is in progress. Employees who perform both exempt and nonexempt work are exempt only when exempt work takes more than 50 percent of working time. Employees of sawmills, shingle mills, planing mills, or logging camps are not covered unless Washington, Idaho, and California enact similar legislation. **Special Occupations** — Lumber: 8-hour day and 48-hour week for workers in saw, planing, and shingle mills and logging camps with 3 hours overtime permitted, except for: logging train crews; watch personnel; those engaged in necessary repairs, emergencies, or transporting workers; and certain other personnel. Mining: 8 consecutive hours for those working in underground metal mines, excluding those in first stage of mine development. Minors employed in canneries may not work more than 10 hours per day, unless administrator issues Special Emergency Overtime Permit. **Day of Rest** — No general provision.

Comparison Chart — State Hours Laws — Contd.

STATE	REQUIREMENTS AND PROVISIONS
Oregon, contd.	**Meal and Rest Periods** — Employees shall receive meal period of not less than 30 minutes for each work period of not less than six nor more than eight hours for a meal to be take between the second and fifth hour worked (if work period is seven hours or less) or between the third and sixth hour worked (if work period is more than seven hours). Where employees cannot be relieved of all duties, a period in which to eat while continuing to work is permitted, provided time is not deducted from employees' hours. A meal period of 20 minutes is permitted if employer can show that industry practice or custom has established such a meal period. Employer may apply for exemption. On 3/2/94, the U.S. Court of Appeals for the Ninth Circuit struck down provisions in the state law that excluded employees covered by collective bargaining agreements from mandated rest periods of at least 10 minutes per four hours worked. For workers employed 24 hours or more at a time, meal and sleeping time may be excluded by agreement. Minor employees must be provided 30 minutes for rest and meal period within the first 5 hours and 1 minute of work reporting for work; if nature of work does not permit minor to be relieved of all work, and minor is 16 years of age or older, a 30 minute meal period while continuing to perform duties is required and may not be deducted from hours worked. In addition to meal periods, minors must be given periods of rest of at least 15 minutes for every four hours or major part worked in one work period. Rest period shall be, as far as feasible, approximately in the middle of each work period. **References** — Oregon Revised Statutes and Wage and Hour Rules; §653.265 (maximum hours before overtime, overtime pay); §652.020(1) - (4) (employees covered); §§652.020, 652.040, 652.990 (limits on hours worked); Wage and Hour Rule 893-21-022, McCollum v. Roberts, CA 9, No. 91-35977, 3/2/94 (meal and rest period).
Pennsylvania	**Maximum Hours before Overtime** — 40-hour week. 10-hour day, 48-hour, 6-day week for seasonal farm workers. **Overtime Pay** — 1½ times regular pay for hours in excess of maximum. **Employees Covered** — All employees, except: students in seasonal occupations excluded by regulation; seafarers; salespersons, partspersons, and mechanics primarily selling or servicing automobiles, trailers, trucks, farm implements, or aircraft for retail dealer; taxicab drivers; certain radio/TV station employees; nonseasonal farm labor; domestic workers; newspaper deliverers; executive, administrative, professional employees; outside salespersons; golf caddies; employees processing maple sap; movie theater employees; employees of motor carriers with respect to whom the Federal Secretary of Transportation has power to establish qualifications and maximum hours of service. **Special Occupations** — Agriculture: 10-hour day, 48-hour, 6-day week for seasonal farm workers, regardless of number of employers. Mining: 8 hours within 24 hours for hoisting engineers in anthracite mines. Railway Transportation: 12-hour day. Bakeries: 6-day week (between 6 p.m. Sunday and 6 p.m. Saturday) for bakery and confectionery workers. Compressed Air: Certain hours, as defined. **Day of Rest** — Worldly employment or business on Sunday is prohibited, except for works of necessity and charity and wholesome recreation. Special provisions for particular types of selling activity, sports, etc. Motion picture places must allow each employee one calendar day of 24 consecutive hours of rest in each calendar week. **Meal and Rest Periods** — No seasonal farm worker shall be permitted to work more than five hours continuously without meal or rest period of at least 30 minutes, which shall not be considered part of labor hours. No period of less than 30 minutes shall be deemed to interrupt a continuous work period. **References** — Pennsylvania Minimum Wage Act, Title 43; §333.104(c) (maximum hours before overtime, overtime pay); §§333.103, 333.105(b) (employees covered); §§207(a) and (b), 361, 450, Title 52 §474, Title 67 §311 (limits on hours worked); Title 43, §481; Title 18 §7361 (day of rest); §107, 207(c) (meal or rest period).

Comparison Chart — State Hours Laws — Contd.

STATE	REQUIREMENTS AND PROVISIONS
Puerto Rico	**Maximum Hours before Overtime** — 8-hour day, 40-hour week. **Overtime Pay** — Twice the regular pay for hours in excess of maximum, except: 1½ times the regular pay for employees covered by FLSA. Board order or collective bargaining agreement may fix other working or compensation standards. **Employees Covered** — All employees, except: those in executive, administrative, or professional capacity; traveling agents and mobile salespersons; labor union officers and organizers, when acting as such; domestic workers (who are entitled to one day of rest a week); government employees, except those engaged in proprietary endeavors; workers in continuous operation commercial establishments, if exempted by Secretary of Labor; and drivers and chauffeurs on commission. For temporary employees, the mandatory decree applicable to the temporary employment company applies for vacations and sick leave, while the mandatory decree applicable to the client company applies for all other working conditions. **Special Occupations** — No provision. **Day of Rest** — No general provision. **Meal and Rest Periods** — At least one hour must be allowed for meals unless shorter period is fixed for convenience of employee, stipulated by employee and employer and approved by Secretary of Labor. Meal period must begin after third hour of work ends and before sixth hour begins. Meal period outside regular workday may be waived if employee has not worked more than 2 hours after regular workday. Employee who works during mealtime shall receive double-time. **References** — Title 29, Laws of Puerto Rico; §Mandatory Decrees, §§273, 274, 275; (maximum hours before overtime, overtime pay); §§285, 288 (employees covered); Title 33, §§4, 5 (day of rest); §§283, 467 (meal or rest period).
Rhode Island	**Maximum Hours before Overtime** — 40-hour week. **Overtime Pay** — 1½ times regular pay for hours in excess of maximum and for Sunday or holiday work. **Employees Covered** — All employees except: those working in summer camp open no more than six months a year; state employees on "non-standard" work schedule; municipal police and firefighters; executive, administrative, or professional employees; salaried employees of nonprofit national voluntary health agency who elect to take time off for hours worked in excess of 40 hours; agricultural workers; domestic employees; drivers, drivers' helpers, loaders, and mechanics of motor carrier under hour regulation of U.S. Department of Transportation. **Special Occupations** — Motor Transportation: 12 hours followed by 8 hours off duty, or 16 aggregate hours in 24 hours followed by 10 hours off duty, except in emergencies. Street Railways: 12 consecutive hours followed by 10 hours off duty during 24 hours for conductors and motormen, except for emergencies or holidays when extra compensation must be paid. **Day of Rest** — No person may engage in gainful activities in any store, mill, or factory; in commercial occupations; in work of transportation or communication; or in industrial processes on Sundays, except work of necessity and charity and in licensed athletic meets and contests. Unlawful for employer to require or permit employee to work on Sunday or holiday except work of absolute necessity. "Employee" does not include individuals employed in certain specified trades. Town councils may grant licenses for certain retail sales on Sundays and holidays; certain other retail and service businesses may be carried on without a license. Retail employees who work on Sunday or a holiday must be paid time and one-half and must be guaranteed at least four hours of employment, except for retail establishments that prepare or sell bakery products and pharmacies. No license shall be issued for sales on December 25 or on Thanksgiving, except to pharmacies; food retailers employing fewer than 6 employees per shift; video cassette rental stores; and retailers of baked goods. Director may exempt by regulation any class of employers due to nature or size of operations.

Comparison Chart — State Hours Laws — Contd.

STATE	REQUIREMENTS AND PROVISIONS
Rhode Island, contd.	**Meal and Rest Periods** — At least 20 minutes must be allowed for meals after 6 consecutive hours of work, except telephone operators who are not required to operate switchboard continuously but are able to sleep during considerable part of the night. Work period of 6½ hours allowed if employment ends no later than 1 p.m. and worker is dismissed for the day. Work period of 7½ hours allowed if employment ends no later than 2 p.m. and worker has sufficient opportunity to eat on the job. **References** — General Laws of Rhode Island, Title 25; §§28-12-4.1, 28-12-4.2, Administrative Regulations (maximum hours before overtime, employees covered); §§28-11-2, 28-11-4, 31-27-5, 31-27-8 (limits on hours worked); §§5-23-2 and 6, 11-40-1 and 2, 25-1-6 (Sunday and holiday work, day of rest); §28-3-14 (meal or rest period).
South Carolina	**Maximum Hours before Overtime** — No general provision. **Overtime Pay** — No general provision. **Employees Covered** — No general provision. **Special Occupations** — No provision. **Day of Rest** — It is unlawful to employ others to work on Sunday except certain works of necessity or charity and in certain specified businesses and services; sale of certain specified items also prohibited. Not applicable to any business or service that was lawful prior to April 7, 1962. Moving pictures, athletic sports, and musical concerts lawful after 2 p.m. on Sunday, but not between 7 p.m. and 9 p.m. Sunday work exemptions granted to manufacture and finishing of textile products and operation of machine shops provided no person is required to work who is conscientiously opposed to Sunday work. Sunday work prohibited in manufacturing or mercantile establishments, except cafeterias and restaurants, with certain exceptions. **Meal and Rest Periods** — No general provision. **References** — Code of Laws of South Carolina; §§53-1-40, 53-1-50.
South Dakota	**Maximum Hours before Overtime** — 8 hours per day for adult employees in manufacturing or mechanical establishment, unless agreement to contrary. 10 hours per day for all employees, unless agreement to contrary. **Overtime Pay** — No general provision. **Employees Covered** — No general provision. **Special Occupations** — 10-hour day unless express agreement to contrary. 8-hour day for employees in manufacturing or mechanical establishment unless express agreement to contrary, except those employed by week, month, or year. Railroads: 16 hours followed by 10 hours off duty, or 16 aggregate hours in 24 hours followed by 8 hours off duty. Municipal firefighters: 212 hours in 28-day period or 204 hours during 27 day work period, as agreed. **Day of Rest** — No general provision. **Meal and Rest Periods** — No general provision. **References** — South Dakota Compiled Laws; §§3-6-17, 49-24-5 and 6, 60-11-1.
Tennessee	**Meal and Rest Periods** — Employees must have a 30-minute unpaid rest break or meal period if scheduled to work six consecutive hours. An exception is made for workplaces that, due to the nature of their business, provide ample opportunity for employees to rest or take the required break. **References** — Tennessee Code Annotated, §50-2-103 (meal and rest periods).

Comparison Chart — State Hours Laws — Contd.

STATE	REQUIREMENTS AND PROVISIONS
Texas	**Maximum Hours before Overtime** — No general provision. **Overtime Pay** — No general provision. **Employees Covered** — No general provision. **Special Occupations** — Railroads: 16 hours, followed by 10 hours of rest. **Day of Rest** — Employer may not require employee to work seven consecutive days in retail establishment and may not deny employee at least 24 consecutive hours off for rest or worship in seven-day period. Employer must accommodate employee's religious practices unless it can be shown that to do so would constitute undue business hardship, and may not require employee to work during period employee requests to be off to attend one regular worship service a week of employee's religion. No employer may compel employee to sell or offer for sale motor vehicle on both consecutive Saturday and Sunday. **Meal and Rest Periods** — No general provision. **References** — Texas Statutes Annotated; §§1 and 4 of Article 5165.4, Articles 6390 and 6391; §142.0017, Local Government Code.
Utah	**Maximum Hours before Overtime** — No general provision. **Overtime Pay** — No general provision. **Employees Covered** — No general provision. **Special Occupations** — Mining: 8-hour day for underground miners and those reducing or refining ores or metals, except in emergencies or with written certificate from industrial commission. 8½-hour day for hoisters and pumpers on underground pumps in continuous operation. Public Works: 40 hour workweek for state, county, or municipal works. 1½ times regular rate for all hours over 40 per week. **Day of Rest** — No general provision. **Meal and Rest Periods** — No general provision. Minors must be given opportunity for a meal period of at least 30 minutes no later than five hours after beginning of workday. If minor is not permitted to leave work station, and completely relieved of all duties, meal period must be paid as time worked. Minors also must have at least 10-minute paid rest period for each four hours or fraction thereof; however, no minor shall be required to work more than three consecutive hours without 10-minute rest period. **References** — Utah Code Annotated; §§34-21-2(1) - (3), 34-30-8, 34-30-9.

Comparison Chart — State Hours Laws — Contd.

STATE	REQUIREMENTS AND PROVISIONS
Vermont	**Maximum Hours before Overtime** — 40-hour week. **Overtime Pay** — 1½ times regular pay for hours in excess of maximum. **Employees Covered** — All employees of employers with two or more workers, except: those in amusement or recreation industry not operating more than seven months in calendar year, or whose average receipts for any six months in preceding year not more than 1/3 of average receipts for other six months; employees of hotel, motel, restaurant; hospital, public health center, nursing and maternity home, therapeutic community residence, and community care home workers, provided employer pays biweekly, employee elects to be covered, and employee receives 1½ times regular rate for work in excess of 8 hours per day or 80 hours per biweekly period; transportation employees covered by FLSA; state employees. **Special Occupations** — No provision. **Day of Rest** — No general provision. **Meal and Rest Periods** — No general provision. **References** — Vermont Statutes Annotated; §384(b) (maximum hours before overtime, overtime pay); §§382, 383(2) and (3) (employees covered).
Virginia	**Maximum Hours before Overtime** — No state provision. **Overtime Pay** — No provision. **Employees Covered** — No provision. **Special Occupations** — No provision. **Day of Rest** — No person shall engage in work, labor, or business or employ others to engage in same on Sunday, with certain exceptions; inapplicable to works of charity conducted solely for charitable purposes by any person or nonprofit organization. Except in emergency, employer shall allow employee at least 24 consecutive hours of rest in each calendar week in addition to regular rest periods normally allowed or legally required in each work day. Nonmanagerial employee upon written notice is entitled to choose Sunday as a day of rest; however, nonmanagerial employee who conscientiously believes that the seventh day of the week ought to be observed as a Sabbath and actually refrains from all secular business and labor on that day shall be entitled to choose the seventh day of the week as a day of rest. Provision not applicable to persons engaged in certain specified industries or businesses. **Meal and Rest Periods** — No general provision. **References** — Virginia Minimum Wage Act; §§18.2-341, 40.1-28.1, 40.1-28.2.

Comparison Chart — State Hours Laws — Contd.

STATE	REQUIREMENTS AND PROVISIONS
Washington	**Maximum Hours before Overtime** — 40-hour week. **Overtime Pay** — 1½ times regular pay, or 1½ times regular piece work rate (unless specifically exempted), for hours in excess of maximum. **Employees Covered** — All employees, except: casual labor about private home; bona fide executives, administrators, professionals, or outside salespersons; services for educational, charitable, religious, state or local governmental or nonprofit organization performed by non-employees; newspaper vendors or carriers; truck or bus drivers subject to Federal Motor Carrier Act; employees in forest protection and fire prevention activities; charitable child care workers; resident, inmate, or patient of public correctional or rehabilitation institution; elected or appointed public officials; seafarers; workers requesting time off in lieu of overtime pay; seasonal workers at concessions and recreational establishments at agricultural fair employed not more than 14 days; agricultural workers; motion picture projectionists covered by union contract; workers in industry covered by federal law providing for different hours, even if the specific employer/employee is not subject to federal jurisdiction. **Special Occupations** — Firefighters and Law Enforcement Personnel: 240 hours in 28 consecutive days, or tours of duty in period of more than seven but less than 28 days which bear the same ratio to number of consecutive days in work period as 240 hours bears to 28 days. Mining: 8-hour day for coal miners working underground; 10-hour day for mining engineers, rope-riders, motormen, cagers, and others transporting miners in and out of mines, except in emergencies or weekly change of shift. Railroads: 12-hour day followed by 10 hours of rest, or 12 aggregate hours in 24 hours followed by 8 hours of rest, for those connected with movement of trains, except in emergencies. Domestic and Household Employees: 60-hour week, including hours on call, except in emergencies. Motor Carriers subject to rules of utilities and transportation commission. Commissioned salespeople primarily selling automobiles and trucks to consumers: must be paid at least minimum wage for first 40 hours per week and 1½ times the hourly rate for hours over 40 in a week; or be paid straight commission, salary plus commission, or a salary plus bonus applied to gross salary. Minors under the age of 16 may work in agriculture up to 3 hours per day on school days, up to 8 hours per day on nonschool days, up to 21 hours per week during weeks when school is in session and up to 40 hours per week when school is not in session. Minors who are 16 or 17 years old may work in agriculture up to 28 hours per week, up to 4 hours per day on school days and up to 8 hours per day on nonschool days in weeks when school is in session. When school is not in session, these minors may work up to 10 hours per day and up to 50 hours per week when school is not in session, except they may work up to 60 hours per week in mechanical harvest of certain crops when school is not in session. Emancipated minors are not subject to hours limitations. **Day of Rest** — No general provision. **Meal and Rest Periods** — 30 minute meal period beginning no less than two nor more than 5 hours from beginning of shift; additional 30 minute meal period prior to or during overtime period of three or more hours following normal workday, for all employees except volunteers, bona fide executives, administrators, professionals, or outside salespersons; or independent contractors. Rest periods of at least 10 minutes per four hours working time, applicable to same employees as meal periods. **References** — Washington Revised Code; §§49.46.130(1) and (2) (maximum hours before overtime, overtime pay); §§49.12.005(4), 49.46.130(2) (employees covered); §§49.28.80, 78.34.010 - 78.34.030, 81.40.040, 81.80.211 (limits on hours worked); 49.30.030 (meal or rest period).

Comparison Chart — State Hours Laws — Contd.

STATE	REQUIREMENTS AND PROVISIONS
West Virginia	**Maximum Hours before Overtime** — 40-hour week. **Overtime Pay** — 1½ times regular pay for hours in excess of maximum. **Employees Covered** — All employees except: salespersons, partspersons, or mechanics primarily engaged in selling or servicing automobiles, trailers, trucks, farm implements, or aircraft; employees exempt from the state minimum wage law. **Special Occupations** — Railroads: 8-hour day in any 24 consecutive hours for telephone or telegraph operators spacing or blocking trains, handling train orders, or interlocking switches, except in cases of emergency, when operators may work 13 hours in 24, but for no longer than 2 days; operators may agree to work between 8 and 12 hours. **Day of Rest** — Sunday work prohibited except in household or other work of necessity or charity; work of necessity or charity does not include selling at retail, wholesale, or auction but lengthy list of permitted Sunday activities exists. Exception also made for those who conscientiously observe Saturday as Sabbath as long as they do not compel others to work on Sunday. **Meal and Rest Periods** — Where employee is required to be on duty 24 hours or more, employer and employee may agree on bona fide meal and sleeping periods; if no expressed or implied agreement is made, eight hours' sleeping time and lunch periods shall constitute hours worked. **References** — Labor Laws of West Virginia; §§21-5C-1(f)(16), 21-5C-3(a) (maximum hours before overtime, overtime pay); §§21-5C-1(f)(16), 21-5C-3(b)(1) to (7), 21-5C-3(a) and (d) (employees covered); §24-1-1 (limits on hours worked); §25-29 (day of rest); Administrative Regulations 400-11 (meal or rest period).
Wisconsin	**Maximum Hours before Overtime** — 40-hour week; 44-hour week for restaurant employees. **Overtime Pay** — 1½ times regular pay for hours in excess of maximum. **Employees Covered** — Employees in manufacturing, mechanical, or mercantile establishment; beauty parlor; laundry; restaurant; confectionery store; telegraph or telephone office or exchange, or express or transportation company; and hotel. Exceptions: persons employed in farming, as defined; domestic household employees; employees in primarily executive, administrative, or professional capacity; outside salespersons, as defined; commission employees of retail and service establishments if 50 percent of earnings is in commissions, and 1½ times the minimum wage is received for all hours worked; drivers, drivers' helpers, loaders, or mechanics; common rail and air carrier employees; taxicab drivers; automobile, truck, farm implement, trailer, boat, motorcycle, snowmobile, recreational vehicle, or aircraft salespersons, partspersons, or mechanics; employees of recreational or amusement establishments operating seven months or less per year; employees of independent contractors in specified industries; movie theater employees; resident hospital and institution employees under agreement with employer; funeral establishment employees.

Comparison Chart — State Hours Laws — Contd.

STATE	REQUIREMENTS AND PROVISIONS
Wisconsin Contd.	**Special Occupations** — Railroads: 16 hours followed by 10 hours of rest, or 16 aggregate hours in 24 hours followed by 8 hours of rest, except in specified emergencies. Motor Transportation: Motor Vehicle Department prescribes rules. **Day of Rest** — Employees in factory or mercantile establishments are entitled to at least 24 consecutive hours of rest every seven consecutive days, with certain specified exceptions. Work on seventh day permitted in case of breakdown of machinery or equipment requiring immediate services of experienced and competent labor to prevent serious injury to person, damage to property, or suspension of essential operation. **Meal and Rest Periods** — Employees must receive at least 30 minutes for each meal period reasonably close to usual meal period time or near middle of a shift. Employee must be completely relieved from duty during the meal period; if worker must remain at work station during meal time, time is compensable. Shifts of more than six consecutive hours without a meal period should be avoided; requirements mandatory for minors under 18. Rest periods of short duration (less than 30 minutes) are considered hours worked, and may not be offset against other working time such as waiting or on-call time. Employees required to be on duty 24 or more consecutive hours may have up to 8 hours sleeping time deducted per 24 hour period. If employee is called to work during sleeping time, time worked must be compensated. If sleeping time is interrupted to such an extent that employee cannot get "reasonable night's sleep," entire period must be paid. **References** — Wisconsin Statutes, Wisconsin Administrative Code; WAC §Ind. 74.03 (maximum hours before overtime, overtime pay), WAC §Ind. 74.04(1)–(13) (employees covered); WS §§192.24, 192.38 (limits on hours worked); WS §103.85 (day of rest); WAC §Ind. 72.12 (meal or rest period).
Wyoming	**Maximum Hours before Overtime** — No general provision. **Overtime Pay** — No general provision. **Employees Covered** — No general provision. **Special Occupations** — Mining: 8-hour day in all underground mines and workings, except when employer-employee agreement for longer period not to exceed 16 hours in 24 hours. **Day of Rest** — No general provision. **Meal and Rest Periods** — No general provision. **References** — Wyoming Statutes Annotated; §§27-5-102, 27-5-108, 27-5-110.

APPENDIX H

CHART OF OVERTIME COMPENSATION RULES FOR STATE AND LOCAL GOVERNMENT EMPLOYEES*

*Source: 29 C.F.R. §§553.230–553.233.

Appendix H

Following is the text of Overtime Compensation Rules for police personnel and firefighters of state and local governments.

Overtime Compensation Rules

§ 553.230 Maximum hours standards for work periods of 7 to 28 days—section 7(k).

(a) For those employees engaged in fire protection activities who have a work period of at least 7 but less than 28 consecutive days, no overtime compensation is required under section 7(k) until the number of hours worked exceeds the number of hours which bears the same relationship to 212 as the number of days in the work period bears to 28.

(b) For those employees engaged in law enforcement activities (including security personnel in correctional institutions) who have a work period of at least 7 but less than 28 consecutive days, no overtime compensation is required under section 7(k) until the number of hours worked exceeds the number of hours which bears the same relationship to 171 as the number of days in the work period bears to 28.

(c) The ratio of 212 hours to 28 days for employees engaged in fire protection activities is 7.57 hours per day (rounded) and the ratio of 171 hours to 28 days for employees engaged in law enforcement activities is 6.11 hours per day (rounded). Accordingly, overtime compensation (in premium pay or compensatory time) is required for all hours worked in excess of the following maximum hours standards (rounded to the nearest whole hour):

Work period (days)	Maximum hours standards	
	Fire Protection	Law enforcement
28	212	171
27	204	165
26	197	159
25	189	153
24	182	147
23	174	141
22	167	134
21	159	128
20	151	122
19	144	116
18	136	110
17	129	104
16	121	98
15	114	92
14	106	86
13	98	79
12	91	73
11	83	67
10	76	61
9	68	55
8	61	49
7	53	43

§ 553.231 Compensatory time off.

(a) Law enforcement and fire protection employees who are subject to the section 7(k) exemption may receive compensatory time off in lieu of overtime pay for hours worked in excess of the maximum for their work period as set forth in §553.230. The rules for compensatory time off are set forth in §§553.20 through 553.28.

(b) Section 7(k) permits public agencies to balance the hours of work over an entire work period for law enforcement and fire protection employees. For example, if a firefighter's work period is 28 consecutive days and he or she works 80 hours in each of the first two weeks, but only 52 hours in the third week, and does not work in the fourth week, no overtime compensation (in cash wages or compensatory time) would be required since the total hours worked do not exceed 212 for the work period. If the same firefighter had a work period of only 14 days, overtime compensation or compensatory time off would be due for 54 hours (160 minus 106 hours) in the first 14-day work period.

§ 553.232 Overtime pay requirements.

If a public agency pays employees subject to section 7(k) for overtime hours worked in cash wages rather than compensatory time off, such wages must be paid at one and one-half times the employees' regular rates of pay. In addition, employees who have accrued the maximum 480 hours of compensatory time must be paid cash wages of time and one-half their regular rates of pay for overtime hours in excess of the maximum for the work period set forth in § 553.230.

§ 553.233 "Regular rate" defined.

The rules for computing an employee's "regular rate," for purposes of the Act's overtime pay requirements, are set forth in 29 CFR Part 778. These rules are applicable to employees for whom the section 7(k) exemption is claimed when overtime compensation is provided in cash wages. However, whenever the word "workweek" is used in Part 778, the words "work period" should be substituted.

Appendix I

Directory of U.S. Equal Employment Opportunity Commission Administrative and District Area Offices

Equal Employment Opportunity Commission Administrative Offices

Address: 1801 L Street, N.W., Washington, D.C. 20507

Filing a Charge
1-800-669-4000

This number will put the caller in contact with the EEOC field office that has jurisdiction in the caller's area.

Written Information
1-800-669-3362

This number will put the caller in contact with the Publication Distribution Center and should be used to obtain written materials on the laws enforced by EEOC.

Public Affairs & Employee Locator
202-663-4900

This number will put the caller in contact with the employee locator for the headquarters in Washington and also should be used to contact public affairs and media specialists.

Office of General Counsel
202-663-4702

Deputy General Counsel
James R. Neely

CHAIRMAN AND COMMISSIONERS

OFFICE OF THE CHAIRMAN (CH)

Chairman
Tony E. Gallegos,
663-4001

COMMISSIONERS

Commissioner
Joyce E. Tucker
663-4081

OFFICE OF THE VICE CHAIRMAN (VCH)

Vice Chairman
R. Gaull Silberman (VCH),
663-4026

FIELD ORGANIZATION SECTION

Albuquerque Area Office/(Phoenix District)
505 Marquette, N.W., Suite 900
Albuquerque, New Mexico 87102-2189
(Hours — 9:30 a.m. — 6:30 p.m. EST)

(Hours — 7:30 a.m. — 4:30 p.m. MST)
(505) 766-2061, TDD (505) 766-1831

Director
Andrew Lopez — 766-5973

Atlanta District Office
75 Piedmont Avenue, N.E., Suite 1100
Atlanta, Georgia 30335
(Hours — 8:30 a.m. — 5:00 p.m. EST)
(404) 331-0604, TDD (404) 331-6091
Director
  Chris Roggerson — 331-6093
Deputy Director
  Bernice Kimbrough — 331-4781
Regional Attorney
  William Snapp — 331-6092
Administrative Officer
  Thomas Edwards — 331-4817
Personnel Management Specialist
  Thomas Edwards — 331-4817
Management Information Specialist
  Polly M. Kimber — 331-6619

Baltimore District Office
10 S. Howard Street, 3rd Floor
Baltimore, Maryland 21201
(Hours — 8:30 a.m. — 5:00 p.m. EST)
(410) 962-3932, TDD (410) 962-6065
Director
  Issie L. Jenkins — 962-5634
Deputy Director
  Haywood L. Perry — 962-0894
Regional Attorney
  Gerald S. Kiel — 962-3872
Administrative Officer
  Bernard S. Tinsley — 962-4194
Personnel Management Specialist
  Pamela Lichtenberg — 962-4070
Management Information Specialist
  Deborah Szymanik — 962-4179

Birmingham District Office
1900 3rd Avenue, North, Suite 101
Birmingham, Alabama 35203-2397
(Hours — 9:00 a.m. — 5:30 p.m. EST)
(Hours — 8:00 a.m. — 4:30 p.m. CST)
(205) 731-0082, TDD (205) 731-0095
Director
  Warren A. Bullock — 731-1182
Deputy Director
  Thomas McPherson, Jr. — 731-0793
Regional Attorney
  Jerome C. Rose — 731-2067
Administrative Officer
  Fannie Thomas — 731-0516
Personnel Management Specialist
  Fannie Thomas — 731-0516

Management Information Specialist
  Iris Elom — 731-0834

Boston Area Office/(New York District)
1 Congress Street, 10th Floor
Boston, Massachusetts 02114
(Hours — 8:30 a.m. — 5:00 p.m. EST)
(617) 565-3200, TDD (617) 565-3204
Director
  Vacant — 565-3190

Buffalo Local Office/(New York District)
6 Fountain Plaza, Ste. 350
Buffalo, New York 14203
(Hours — 8:45 a.m. — 5:15 p.m. EST)
(716) 846-4441, TDD (716) 846-5923
Director
  Jon Patterson — 846-4443

Charlotte District Office
5500 Central Avenue
Charlotte, North Carolina 28212-2708
(Hours — 8:30 a.m. — 5:30 p.m. EST)
(704) 567-7100, TDD (704) 567-7174
Director
  Marsha Drane — 567-7103
Deputy Director
  Lawrence E. Koziarz — 567-7111
Regional Attorney
  Ronald Arrington — 567-7101
Administrative Officer
  Annie C. Clay — 567-7106
Personnel Management Specialist
  Annie Clay — 567-7106
Management Information Specialist
  Alcinda J. Clay — 567-7187

Chicago District Office
500 W. Madison Street, Suite 2800
Chicago, Illinois 60661
(Hours — 9:30 a.m. — 6:00 p.m. EST)
(Hours —8:30 a.m. — 5:00 p.m. (CST)
(312) 353-7213, TDD (312) 353-2421
Director
  John P. Rowe — 353-8550
Deputy Director
  Cynthia G. Pierre — 353-8995
Regional Attorney
  John C. Hendrickson —353-8551
Administrative Officer
  Rita B. Coffey — 353-7233

Personnel Management Specialist
  Garfield Freeman — 353-8562
Management Information Specialist
  Frank Keller — 886-2396

Cincinnati Area Office/(Cleveland District)
525 Vine Street, Suite 810
Cincinnati, Ohio 45202-3122
(Hours — 8:15 a.m. — 5:00 p.m. EST)
(513) 684-2851, TDD (513) 684-6698
Full Talk TDD: (513) 684-2074
Director
  Earl Haley — 684-2379

Cleveland District Office
1660 W. Second Street, Suite 850
Cleveland, Ohio 44113-1454
(Hours — 8:15 a.m. — 5:00 p.m. EST)
(216) 522-2001, TDD (216) 522-7296
Full Talk TDD: (216) 522-8441
Director
  Susan L. McDuffie — 522-4784
Deputy Director
  Hollis H. Larkins — 522-7410
Regional Attorney (Acting)
  C. Larry Watson — 522-7455
Administrative Officer
  Donna M. Nichols — 522-7659
Personnel Management Specialist
  Louise Stowe — 522-4808
Management Information Specialist
  Terrence Taylor — 522-4835

Dallas District Office
207 S. Houston Street, 3rd Floor
Dallas, Texas 75202-4726
(Hours — 9:30 a.m. — 6:00 p.m. EST)
(Hours — 8:30 a.m. — 5:00 p.m. CST)
(214) 655-3355, TDD (214) 655-3363
Director
  Jacqueline R. Bradley — 655-3300
Deputy Director
  Brian B. McGovern — 655-3302
Regional Attorney
  Jeffrey C. Bannon — 655-3325
Administrative Officer
  Barbara Triggs — 655-3311
Personnel Management Specialist
  Virginia S. Adams — 655-3312
Management Information Specialist
  William P. Luckett — 655-3313

Denver District Office
1845 Sherman Street, 2nd Floor
Denver, Colorado 80203
(Hours — 10:00 a.m. — 7:00 p.m. EST)
(Hours — 8:00 a.m. — 5:00 p.m. MST)
(303) 866-1300, TDD (303) 866-1950
Director
  Francisco J. Flores — 866-1369
Deputy Director
  Carlos Villescas — 866-1300
Regional Attorney
  William J. Martinez — 866-1370
Administrative Officer
  Jerry Mabry — 866-1307
Personnel Management Specialist
  Nina Taylor Else — 866-1383
Management Information Specialist
  David Williams — 866-1350

Detroit District Office
477 Michigan Ave., Room 1540
Detroit, Michigan 48226-9704
(Hours — 8:30 a.m. — 5:00 p.m. EST)
(313) 226-7636, TDD (313) 226-7599
Director
  A. William Schukar — 226-7639
Deputy Director
  Andrew J. Sheppard — 226-3828
Regional Attorney
  Adele Rapport — 226-6701
Administrative Officer
  Jesse A. Vidaurri — 226-7635
Personnel Management Specialist
  Marie Canty — 226-5675
Management Information Specialist
  Richard Wagner — 226-7840

El Paso Area Office/(San Antonio District Office)
The Commons, Bldg. C., Suite 100
4171 N. Mesa Street
El Paso, Texas 79902
(Hours — 9:30 a.m. — 6:00 p.m. EST)
(Hours — 8:30 a.m. — 5:00 p.m. CST)
(915) 534-6550, TDD (915) 534-6545
Director
  Eliazar Salinas — 534-6540

Fresno Local Office/(San Francisco District)
1265 W. Shaw Ave., Ste. 103
Fresno, California 93711

(Hours — 11:00 a.m. — 7:30 p.m. EST)
(Hours — 8:00 a.m. — 4:30 p.m. PST)
(209) 487-5793, TDD (209) 487-5837
Director
David Rodriguez — 487-5793

Greensboro Local Office/(Charlotte District)

801 Summit Ave
Greensboro, North Carolina 27045-7813
(Hours — 8:30 a.m. — 5:00 p.m. EST)
(919) 333-5174, TDD (919) 333-5542
Director
Daisy Crenshaw — 333-5174

Greenville Local Office/(Charlotte District)

SCN Building, Suite 530
15 South Main Street
Greenville, South Carolina 29601
(Hours — 8:30 a.m. — 5:00 p.m. EST)
(803) 241-4400, TDD (803) 241-4403
Director
Sherald Carter — 241-4410

Honolulu Local Office/(San Francisco District)

677 Ala Moana Blvd., Suite 404
P. O. Box 50082
Honolulu, Hawaii 96813
(Hours — 8:00 a.m. — 4:30 p.m. HAT*)
*Time is Hawaiian Aleutian and is 6 hours behind EST
(808) 541-3120, TDD (808) 541-3131
Director
Rodolfo Martinez — 541-3120

Houston District Office

1919 Smith Street, 7th Floor
Houston, Texas 77002
(Hours — 9:00 a.m. — 6:00 p.m. EST)
(Hours — 8:00 a.m. — 5:00 p.m. CST)
(713) 653-3377, TDD (713) 653-3367
Director
Harriet J. Ehrlich — 653-3379
Regional Attorney
Jim Sacher — 653-3398
Administrative Officer
Marie S. Stovall — 653-3382
Personnel Management Specialist
Deborah Foster — 653-3422

Management Information Specialist
Rocky R. Ruiz — 653-3385

Indianapolis District Office

101 W. Ohio St., Ste. 1900
Indianapolis, Indiana 46204-4203
(Hours — 8:00 a.m. — 4:30 p.m. EST)
(317) 226-7212, TDD (317) 226-5162
Director
Thomas P. Hadfield — 226-7215
Deputy Director
Danny G. Harter — 226-6736
Regional Attorney
Laurie A. Young — 226-7208
Administrative Officer
Terry W. Crum — 226-7952
Personnel Management Specialist
Robert F. Feagan — 226-7227
Management Information Specialist
John P. Pierce — 226-6380

Jackson Area Office/(Birmingham District)

207 West Amite Street
Jackson, Mississippi 39201
(Hours — 9:00 a.m. — 5:30 p.m. EST)
(Hours — 8:00 a.m. — 4:30 p.m. CST)
(601) 965-4537, TDD (601) 965-4915
Director
Henrene P. Matthews — 965-4537

Kansas City Area Office/(St. Louis District)

911 Walnut, 10th Floor
Kansas City, Missouri 64106
(Hours — 9:00 a.m. — 5:30 p.m. EST)
(Hours — 8:00 a.m. — 4:30 p.m. CST)
(816) 426-5773, TDD (816) 426-5775
Director
Joseph P. Doherty — 426-5773

Little Rock Area Office/(Memphis District)

320 W. Capitol Ave., 6th floor
Little Rock, Arkansas 72201
(Hours — 9:00 a.m. — 5:30 p.m. EST)
(Hours — 8:00 a.m. — 4:30 p.m. CST)
(501) 324-5060, TDD (501) 324-5481
Director
W.P. Brown — 324-5060

Los Angeles District Office

255 E. Temple, 4th Floor
Los Angeles, California 90012
(Hours — 11:30 a.m. — 8:00 p.m. EST
(Hours — 8:30 a.m. — 5:00 p.m. PST)
(213) 894-1000, TDD (213) 894-1121
Director
Dorothy J. Porter — 894-1112
Deputy Director
Donald P. Burris — 894-1111
Regional Attorney
Pamela Thomason — 894-1083
Administrative Officer
Vacant — 894-1108
Personnel Management Specialist
Ann Tatnall — 894-1106
Management Information Specialist
Pat Franco — 894-1103

Louisville Area Office/(Indianapolis District)

600 Martin Luther King Jr. Place, Ste. 268
Louisville, Kentucky 40202
(Hours — 8:00 a.m. — 4:30 p.m. EST)
(502) 582-6082, TDD (502) 582-6285
Director
Clifford J. Johnson — 582-6744

Memphis District Office

1407 Union Avenue, Suite 621
Memphis, Tennessee 38104
(Hours — 9:00 a.m. — 5:30 p.m. EST)
(Hours — 8:00 a.m. — 4:30 p.m. CST)
(901) 722-2617, TDD (901) 722-2604
Director
Walter S. Grabon — 722-2608
Deputy Director
Martha Jordon — 722-2753
Regional Attorney
Joseph Ray Terry Jr. — 722-2804
Administrative Officer
Minnie Hilliard-Taylor — 722-2519
Personnel Management Specialist
Minnie Hilliard-Taylor — 722-2519
Management Information Specialist
Joan Ward — 722-2537

Miami District Office

1 Northeast First Street, 6th Floor
Miami, Florida 33132-2491
(Hours — 8:00 a.m. — 4:30 p.m. EST)
(305) 536-4491, TDD (305) 536-5721
Director
Federico Costales — 530-6060
Deputy Director
Thelma Houston Taylor — 536-4306
Regional Attorney
Stanley Kiszkiel — 530-6000
Administrative Office
Frank R. Dial — 530-6033
Personnel Management Specialist
Mercedes Brando — 536-4458
Management Information Specialist
Larry N. Ignash — 536-6022

Milwaukee District Office

310 West Wisconsin Avenue, Suite 800
Milwaukee, Wisconsin 53203-2292
(Hours — 9:00 a.m. — 5:30 p.m. EST)
(Hours — 8:00 a.m. — 4:30 p.m. CST)
(414) 297-1111, TDD (414) 297-1115
Director
Chester V. Bailey — 297-1265
Deputy Director
Eugene R. Koepp — 297-1121
Regional Attorney
Reuben Daniels — 297-1856
Administrative Officer
Barbara A. Rebernick — 297-3145
Personnel Management Specialist
Paul J. Cooke — 297-3483
Management Information Specialist
Heidi A. Mays — 297-3407

Minneapolis Local Office/(Milwaukee District)

330 South Second Avenue, Suite 430
Minneapolis, Minnesota 55401-2224
(Hours — 9:00 a.m. — 5:30 p.m. EST)
(Hours — 8:00 a.m. — 4:30 p.m. CST)
(612) 335-4040, TDD (612) 405-4045
Director
Michael J. Bloyer — 335-4040

Nashville Area Office/(Memphis District)

50 Vantage Way, Suite 202
Nashville, Tennessee 37228
(Hours — 9:00 a.m. — 5:30 p.m. EST)

(Hours — 8:00 a.m. — 4:30 p.m. CST)
(615) 736-5820, TDD (615)736-5870
Director
Allen Pahmeyer — 736-5823

Newark Area Office/(Philadelphia District)

1 Newark Center, 21st Floor
Newark, New Jersey 07102-5233
(Hours — 8:00 a.m. — 4:30 p.m. EST)
(201) 645-6383, TDD (201) 645-3004
Director
Corrado Gigante — 645-5978

New Orleans District Office

701 Loyola Avenue, Suite 600
New Orleans, Louisiana 70113-9936
(Hours — 9:00 a.m. — 5:30 p.m. EST)
(Hours — 8:00 a.m. — 4:30 p.m. CST)
(504) 589-2329, TDD (504) 589-2958
Director
Patricia F. Bivins — 589-3842
Deputy Director
Michael B. McReynolds — 589-6819
Regional Attorney
Keith Hill — 589-3844
Administrative Officer
Beverly A. Poole — 589-2994
Personnel Management Specialist
Zaida Moncoduit — 589-2995
Management Information Specialist
DeEtra Branch — 589-4269

New York District Office

7 World Trade Center, 18th Floor
New York, New York 10048-0948
(Hours — 8:45 a.m. — 5:15 p.m. EST)
(212) 748-8500, TDD (212) 748-8399
Director
Spencer H. Lewis Jr. — 748-8400
Deputy Director
Richard B. Alpert — 748-8405
Regional Attorney
James L. Lee — 748-8512
Administrative Officer
Louise Council — 748-8484
Personnel Management Specialist
Wilma Buckle — 748-8489
Management Information Specialist
Gordon Lung — 748-8459

Norfolk Area Office/(Baltimore District)

252 Monticello Avenue, 1st Floor
Norfolk, Virginia 23510
(Hours — 8:30 a.m. — 5:00 p.m. EST)
(804) 441-3470, TDD (804) 441-3578
Director
Kathryne E. Stokes — 441-6669

Oakland Local Office/(San Francisco District)

1301 Clay Street, Suite 1170-N
Oakland, California 94612
(Hours — 11:00 a.m. — 7:30 p.m. EST)
(Hours — 8:00 a.m. — 4:30 p.m. PST)
(501) 637-3230, TDD (510) 637-3242
Director
Deborah W. Randall — 637-3230

Oklahoma Area Office/(Dallas District)

531 Couch Drive
Oklahoma City, Oklahoma 73102
(Hours — 9:00 a.m. — 5:30 p.m. EST)
(Hours — 8:00 a.m. — 4:30 p.m. CST)
(405) 231-4911, TDD (405) 231-5745
Director
Alma Anderson — 231-5843

Philadelphia District Office

1421 Cherry Street, 10th Floor
Philadelphia, Pennsylvania 19102
(Hours — 8:00 a.m. — 4:30 p.m. EST)
(215) 656-7000, TDD (215) 656-7114
Director
Johnny J. Butler — 656-7000
Deputy Director
Marie M. Tomasso — 656-7000
Regional Attorney
Deborah McIver Floyd — 656-7109
Administrative Officer
Doretha B. Johnson — 656-7000
Personnel Management Specialist
Barbara Elan — 656-7008
Management Information Specialist
Catherine Steffler — 656-7024

Phoenix District Office

4520 N. Central Avenue, Suite 300
Phoenix, Arizona 85012-1848
(Hours — 10:00 a.m. — 6:30 p.m. EST)
(Hours — 8:00 a.m. — 4:30 p.m. MST)
(602) 640-5000, TDD (602) 640-2692

Director
 Charles D. Burtner — 640-2496
Deputy Director
 Roscoe Jones — 640-2242
Regional Attorney
 Richard Trujillo — 640-2364
Administrative Officer
 Thomas C. Flores — 640-2390
Personnel Management Specialist
 Betty A. Combs — 640-2425
Management Information Specialist
 Helen E. Charles — 640-2472

Pittsburgh Area Office/(Philadelphia District)

1000 Liberty Avenue, Room 2038-A
Pittsburgh, Pennsylvania 15222
(Hours — 8:00 a.m. - 4:30 p.m. EST)
(412) 644-3444, TDD (412) 644-2720
Director
 Eugene V. Nelson — 644-3444

Raleigh Area Office/(Charlotte District)

1309 Annapolis Drive
Raleigh, North Carolina 27608-2129
(Hours — 8:30 a.m. - 5:00 p.m. EST)
(919) 856-4064, TDD (919) 856-4296
Director
 Richard E. Walz — 856-4085

Richmond Area Office/(Baltimore District)

3600 W. Broad St., Room 229
Richmond, Virginia 23230
(Hours — 8:30 a.m. - 5:00 p.m. EST)
(804) 771-2692, TDD (804) 771-2223
Director
 Gloria L. Underwood — 771-2164

San Antonio District Office

5410 Fredericksburg Rd., Suite 200
San Antonio, Texas 78229-3555
Hours — 9:30 a.m. - 6:00 p.m. EST)
(Hours — 8:30 a.m. - 5:00 p.m. CST)
(210) 229-4810, TDD (210) 229-4858
Director
 Pedro Esquivel — 229-4842
Deputy Director
 James G. Stone — 229-4844
Regional Attorney
 Robert B. Harwin — 229-4843

Administrative Officer
 Sharon Johnson — 229-4828
Personnel Management Specialist
 Vacant — 229-4828
Management Information Specialist
 Ruben A. Martinez — 229-4825

San Diego Area Office/(Los Angeles District)

401 B Street, Suite 1550
San Diego, California 92101
(Hours — 11:00 a.m. - 7:30 p.m. EST)
(Hours — 8:30 a.m. - 5:00 p.m. PST)
(619) 557-7235, TDD (619) 557-7232
Director
 Patrick Matarazzo — 895-7230

San Francisco District Office

901 Market Street, Suite 500
San Francisco, California 94103
(Hours — 11:00 a.m. - 7:30 p.m. EST)
(Hours — 8:00 a.m. - 4:30 p.m. PST)
(415) 744-6500, TDD (415) 744-7392
Director
 Paula Montanez — 744-6505
Deputy Director
 Chester Relyea — 744-7384
Regional Attorney
 John de J. Pemberton Jr. — 744-7378
Administrative Officer
 Philippe Pelletier — 744-7393
Personnel Management Specialist
 Judy Furukawa — 744-7389
Management Information Specialist
 Ted Kalinowski — 744-7355

San Jose Local Office/(San Francisco District)

96 North 3rd Street, Ste. 200
San Jose, California 95112
(Hours — 11:30 a.m. - 7:30 p.m. EST)
(Hours — 8:00 a.m. - 4:30 p.m. PST)
(408) 291-7352, TDD (408) 291-7374
Director
 Linda Kreis — 291-7352

Savannah Local Office/(Atlanta District)

410 Mall Blvd., Ste. G
Savannah, Georgia 31406
(Hours — 8:30 a.m. - 5:00 p.m. EST)
(912) 652-4234, TDD (912) 652-4439

Director
  Gloria J. Barnett — 652-4077

Seattle District Office

Federal Office Building
909 First Avenue, Suite 400
Seattle, Washington 98104-1061
(Hours — 11:30 a.m. - 8:00 p.m. EST)
(Hours —8:30 a.m. - 5:00 p.m. PST)
(206) 220-6883, TDD (206) 220-6883
Director
  Jeanette M. Leino — 220-6870
Deputy Director
  John Montoya — 220-6872
Regional Attorney
  A. Luis Lucero — 220-6878
Administrative Officer
  Diane Farr — 220-6875
Personnel Management Specialist
  Joanne Cantrell — 220-6877
Management Information Specialist
  Tammy Walker — 220-6873

St. Louis District Office

625 N. Euclid Street, 5th Floor
St. Louis, Missouri 63108
(Hours — 9:00 a.m. - 5:30 p.m. EST)
(Hours — 8:00 a.m. - 4:30 p.m. CST)
(314) 425-6585, TDD (314) 425-6547
Director
  Lynn Y. Bruner — 425-6523
Deputy Director
  Richard W. Schuetz — 425-6523

Regional Attorney
  Gretchen Huston — 425-6106
Administrative Officer
  Stephanie M. Strohecker — 425-6570
Personnel Management Specialist
  Vacant — 425-6565
Management Informtion Specialist
  Herman J. Ilges, Jr.— 425-6533

Tampa Area Office/(Miami District)

501 East Polk Street, 10th Floor
Tampa, Florida 33602
(Hours — 8:00 a.m. - 4:30 p.m. EST)
(813) 228-2310, TDD (813) 228-2003
Director
  James D. Packwood Jr. — 228-2280

Washington Field Office

1400 L Street, N.W., Suite 200
Washington, D.C. 20005
(Hours — 8:30 a.m. - 5:00 p.m. EST)
(202) 275-7377, TDD (202) 275-7518
Director
  Susan B. Reilly — 275-6365
Deputy Director
  Tulio L. Diaz — 275-7164
Administrative Officer
  Charlotte Brown — 275-6622
Management Information Specialist
  Alvin Claxton — 275-6900

Appendix J
Department of Defense, Defense Contract Management Command, District Offices

Appendix J

Defense Contract Management Command

Headquarters, Defense Logistics Agency

Address: Cameron Station, Alexandria, VA 22314
Telephone: 703-274-6241

(Listed below are the District Offices under the Defense Contract Management Command. The District Offices conduct compliance reviews, follow-up reviews, pre-award reviews, and compliant investigations. Due to reductions in U.S. Department of Defense contracting, the number of District Offices has been reduced in recent years.)

Defense Contract Management Districts

DCMD - South
805 Walker Street
Marietta, GA 30060
Phone: 404-590-6000

DCMD - West
222 No. Sepulveda
El Segundo, CA 90245-4320
Phone: 310-335-3000

DCMD - Northeast
495 Summer Street
Boston, MA 02210
Phone: 617-451-4335

DCMD - International
2000 Hamilton Street
Dayton, OH 45444-5410
Phone: 513-296-6421

Appendix K

Salary Basis Test for Public Sector Exempt Employees*

*Source: 29 C.F.R. §541.5d

§541.5d Special provisions applicable to public sector employers (Federal, State and local governments)

(a) A Federal, State or local government employee ("public employee") who otherwise meets the requirements of §541.118 shall not be disqualified from exemption under §§541.1, 541.2, or 541.3 of this part on the basis that such employee is paid according to a pay system established by statute, ordinance, regulation or public policy under which the employee accrues personal leave and sick leave and, absent the use of such accrued leave (because the leave has been exhausted or by the employee's choice), requires the public employee's pay to be reduced ("leave without pay") for absences, for personal reasons or because of illness or injury, of less than one work-day.

(b) Deductions from a public employee's pay that are not regular and recurring for absences due to a budget-required furlough shall not disqualify the employee from being paid "on a salary basis" except in the workweek in which such deductions occurred.

Appendix L

Civil Money Penalties Regulations*

*Source: 29 C.F.R. §§578.2–578.4

Appendix L

§578.2 Purpose and scope.

Section 9 of the Fair Labor Standards Amendments of 1989 amended section 16(e) of the Act to subject any person who repeatedly or willfully violates section 6 or section 7 of the Act to a civil money penalty not to exceed $1,000 for each such violation. This part defines terms necessary for administration of the civil money penalty provisions, describes the violations for which a penalty may be imposed, and describes criteria for determining the amount of penalty to be assessed. The procedural requirements for assessment and contest of such penalties are set forth in 29 CFR part 580.

§578.2 Definitions.

(a) *Act* means the Fair Labor Standards Act of 1938, as amended (52 Stat. 1060 (29 U.S.C. 201 et seq.));

(b) *Administrator* means the Administrator of the Wage and Hour Division, Employment Standards Administration, U.S. Department of Labor, and includes any official of the Wage and Hour Division who is authorized by the Administrator to perform any of the functions of the Administrator under this part.

(c) *Person* includes any individual, partnership, corporation, association, business trust, legal representative, or organized group of persons.

§578.3 Violations for which penalty may be assessed.

(a) A penalty of up to $1,000 per violation may be assessed against any person who repeatedly or willfully violates section 6 (minimum wage) or section 7 (overtime) of the Act. The amount of the penalty shall be determined by application of the criteria in §578.4.

(b) *Repeated violations.* An employer's violation of section 6 or section 7 of the Act shall be deemed to be "repeated" for purposes of this section:

(1) Where the employer has previously violated section 6 or 7 of the Act, provided the employer has previously received notice, through a responsible official of the Wage and Hour Division or otherwise authoritatively, that the employer allegedly was in violation of the provisions of the Act; or

(2) Where a court or other tribunal has made a finding that an employer has previously violated section 6 or 7 of the Act, unless an appeal therefrom which has been timely filed is pending before a court or other tribunal with jurisdiction to hear the appeal, or unless the finding has been set aside or reversed by such appellate tribunal.

(c) *Willful violations.* (1) An employer's violation of section 6 or section 7 of the Act shall be deemed to be "willful" for purposes of this section where the employer knew that its conduct was prohibited by the Act or showed reckless disregard for the requirements of the Act. All of the facts and circumstances surrounding the violation shall be taken into account in determining whether a violation was willful.

(2) For purposes of this section, an employer's conduct shall be deemed knowing, among other situations, if the employer received advice from a responsible official of the Wage and Hour Division to the effect that the conduct in question is not lawful.

(3) For purposes of this section, an employer's conduct shall be deemed to be in reckless disregard of the requirements of the Act, among other situations, if the employer shall have inquired further into whether its conduct was in compliance with the Act, and failed to make adequate futher inquiry.

§578.4 Determination of penalty.

(a) In determining the amount of penalty to be assessed for any repeated or willful violation of section 6 or section 7 of the Act, the Administrator shall consider the seriousness of the violations and the size of the employer's business.

(b) Where appropriate, the Administrator may also consider other relevant factors in assessing the penalty, including but not limited to the following:

(1) Whether the employer has made efforts in good faith to comply with the provisions of the Act and this part;

(2) The employer's explanation for the violations, including whether the violations were the result of a bona fide dispute of doubtful legal certainty;

(3) The previous history of violations, including whether the employer is subject to injunction against violations of the Act;

(4) The employer's commitment to future compliance;

(5) The interval between violations;

(6) The number of employees affected; and

(7) Whether there is any pattern to the violations.

Appendix M

Family and Medical Leave Act Poster

Your Rights
Under The
Family and Medical Leave Act of 1993

FMLA requires covered employers to provide up to 12 weeks of unpaid, job-protected leave to "eligible" employees for certain family and medical reasons. Employees are eligible if they have worked for a covered employer for at least one year, and for 1,250 hours over the previous 12 months, and if there are at least 50 employees within 75 miles.

Reasons For Taking Leave:

Unpaid leave must be granted for *any* of the following reasons:

- to care for the employee's child after birth, or placement for adoption or foster care;
- to care for the employee's spouse, son or daughter, or parent, who has a serious health condition; or
- for a serious health condition that makes the employee unable to perform the employee's job.

At the employee's or employer's option, certain kinds of *paid* leave may be substituted for unpaid leave.

Advance Notice and Medical Certification:

The employee may be required to provide advance leave notice and medical certification. Taking of leave may be denied if requirements are not met.

- The employee ordinarily must provide 30 days advance notice when the leave is "foreseeable."
- An employer may require medical certification to support a request for leave because of a serious health condition, and may require second or third opinions (at the employer's expense) and a fitness for duty report to return to work.

Job Benefits and Protection:

- For the duration of FMLA leave, the employer must maintain the employee's health coverage under any "group health plan."

- Upon return from FMLA leave, most employees must be restored to their original or equivalent positions with equivalent pay, benefits, and other employment terms.
- The use of FMLA leave cannot result in the loss of any employment benefit that accrued prior to the start of an employee's leave.

Unlawful Acts By Employers:

FMLA makes it unlawful for any employer to:

- interfere with, restrain, or deny the exercise of any right provided under FMLA;
- discharge or discriminate against any person for opposing any practice made unlawful by FMLA or for involvement in any proceeding under or relating to FMLA.

Enforcement:

- The U.S. Department of Labor is authorized to investigate and resolve complaints of violations.
- An eligible employee may bring a civil action against an employer for violations.

FMLA does not affect any Federal or State law prohibiting discrimination, or supersede any State or local law or collective bargaining agreement which provides greater family or medical leave rights.

For Additional Information:

Contact the nearest office of the Wage and Hour Division, listed in most telephone directories under U.S. Government, Department of Labor.

U.S. Department of Labor
Employment Standards Administration
Wage and Hour Division
Washington, D.C. 20210

WH Publication 1420
June 1993

• U S G P O 353-606

TABLE OF CASES

A

A-AN-E Mfg. Corp., In re, 6 WH Cases 1175 (1946) 95
Aarid Van Lines, In re, 22 WH Cases 1189 (1976) 115
Aaron v. City of Wichita, Kan., 797 F. Supp. 898, 30 WH Cases 1641 (CA 1 1992) 49
Abbott v. Virginia Beach, 29 WH Cases 609 (CA 4 1989) 56
Abernathy & Wood, In re, 29 WH Cases 1258 (WAB 1990) 149
Abshire v. Kern County, Ca., 908 F.2d 483, 29 WH Cases 1417 (CA 9 1990), *cert. denied*, 111 S.Ct. 785, 30 WH Cases 208 (1991) 52
Aetna Ins. Co.; EEOC v., 616 F.2d 719, 24 WH Cases 641 (CA 4 1980) 85
AFSCME v. New Mexico Corrections Dep't, 783 F. Supp. 1320, 30 WH Cases 1506 (DNM 1992) 53
Albrecht; Martin v., 802 F. Supp. 1311, 1 WH Cases2d 74 (WD Pa 1992) 39, 76
Aldrich v. Randolph Cent. School Dist., 963 F.2d 520, 30 WH Cases 1457 (CA 2), *cert. denied*, 1 WH Cases2d 135 (1992) 87
Alex v. California, 30 WH Cases 1353 (ED Cal 1992) 52
Allstate Constr. Co. v. Durkin, 345 U.S. 13, 11 WH Cases 274 (1953) 29
Alvarado Guevara v. Immigration & Naturalization Serv., 902 F.2d 394, 29 WH Cases 1321 (CA 5 1990) 28
American Airlines; Donovan v., 514 F. Supp. 526, 24 WH Cases 1377 (D Tex 1981), *aff'd*, 686 F.2d 267, 25 WH Cases 901 (CA 5 1982) 40
American International Knitters; Martin v., 802 F. Supp. 1311, 1 WH Cases2d 74 (WD Pa 1992) 62
Anaco Reproductions, In re, ASBCA 13799, 70-1 BCA ¶ 8236 (1970) 148
Anclote Manor Found.; Hodgson v., 21 WH Cases 290 (MD Fla 1973) 85
Anderson v. Mt. Clemens Pottery Co., 328 U.S. 680, 6 WH Cases 83 (1946) 6, 58, 65, 67
Anderson & Cristofani, In re, 9 WH Cases 86 (1949), *aff'd*, 9 WH Cases 596 (1950) 92
Applicability of Bargained Wages, In re, 22 WH Cases 831 (1974) 109–110
Armitage v. City of Emporia, 991 F.2d 746, 1 WH Cases2d 312 (CA 10 1993) 42
Associated Builders v. Brennan, 21 WH Cases 1009 (DDC 1974) 32
Atco Constr., Inc., In re, 28 WH Cases 16 (WAB 1986) 127

B

Bailey v. Secretary of Labor, 810 F. Supp. 261, 1 WH Cases2d 361 (D Alaska 1993) 116
Ball v. District of Columbia, 795 F. Supp. 461, 30 WH Cases 1620 (DDC 1992) 58

Ball, Ball & Brosamer v. Martin, 800 F. Supp. 967, 30 WH Cases 1705 (DDC 1992) 128, 137
Beal, In re, 29 WH Cases 367 (US DOL 1988) 117
Beavers v. American Cast Iron Pipe Co., 975 F.2d 792, 1 WH Cases2d 256 (CA 11 1992) 79
Bedell; Martin v., 955 F.2d 1029, 30 WH Cases 1321 (CA 5 1992), *cert. denied*, 1 WH Cases2d 48, *on remand*, 1 WH Cases2d 691 (1993) 25
Belo, A.H., Corp.; Walling v., 316 U.S. 624, 2 WH Cases 39 (1942), *aff'g* 121 F.2d 207, 1 WH Cases 127 (CA 5 1941) 50
Berg v. Newman, 1 WH Cases2d 314 (CA FC 1992) 54, 76
Berry v. Board of Supervisors, LSU, 27 WH Cases 1143 (CA 5 1986) 79
Biggs v. Wilson, 1 WH Cases2d 897 (CA 9 1993) 47
Binghamton Constr. Co.; United States v., 347 U.S. 171, 12 WH Cases 20 (1954) 130, 131
Birdwell v. City of Gadsden, Ala., 970 F.2d 802, 30 WH Cases 1745 (CA 11 1992) 42, 57
Bond v. City of Jackson, 29 WH Cases 1022 (SD Miss 1989) 75
Brandon v. United States, 24 WH Cases 1261 (1981) 59
Brennan v., *see* name of opposing party
Brinkman v. Dep't of Corrections, 1 WH Cases2d 1 (D Kan 1992) 53
Broad Ave. Laundry v. United States, 681 F.2d 746, 25 WH Cases 918 (Ct Clms 1982), *denied attorney's fees*, 693 F.2d 1387, 25 WH Cases 1048 (CA FC 1982) 111, 120
Brock v., *see* name of opposing party
Brookhaven Gen. Hosp.; Hodgson v., 436 F.2d 719, 19 WH Cases 822 (CA 5 1970) 86
Brunner; Marshall v., 668 F.2d 748, 25 WH Cases 313 (CA 3 1982) 29
Building & Constr. Trades v. Donovan, 543 F. Supp. 1282, 25 WH Cases 820 *and* 553 F. Supp. 352, 25 WH Cases 1078 (DDC 1982), *aff'd in part, rev'd in part*, 712 F.2d 611, 26 WH Cases 404 (CA DC), *cert. denied*, 464 U.S. 1069, 26 WH Cases 932 (1983) 130
Building & Constr. Trades Dep't, AFL-CIO v. Labor Dep't (Midway Excavators), 932 F.2d 985, 30 WH Cases 497 (CA DC 1991) 125, 128
Building & Construction Trades Dep't, AFL-CIO v. Martin, 961 F.2d 269, 30 WH Cases 1430 (CA DC), *cert. denied*, 113 S.Ct. 323 (1992) 130
Burch; Walling v., 5 WH Cases 323 (SD Ga 1945) 20
Burnett Constr. Co. v. United States, 18 WH Cases 698 (Ct Clms 1968), *aff'd*, 413 F.2d 563, 19 WH Cases 185 (1969) 132
Burnison v. Memorial Hosp., Inc., 1 WH Cases2d 145 (D Kan 1992) 24
Burris v. Mahaney, 29 WH Cases 760 (MD Tenn 1989) 155
Bushman Constr. Co. v. United States, 164 F. Supp. 239, 13 WH Cases 728 (Ct Clms 1968) 133

C

C. & P. Shoe Corp.; Wirtz v., 336 F.2d 21, 16 WH Cases 624 (CA 5 1964) 32
Calaf v. Gonzalez, 127 F.2d 934, 2 WH Cases 154 (CA 1 1942) 31
Caldwell; Mitchell v., 12 WH Cases 469 (CA 10 1957) 41
Capeletti Bros., Inc.; United States v., 621 F.2d 1309, 24 WH Cases 904 (CA 5 1980) 138
Carrasco dba J.C. Liquid Waste Disposal; Brennan v., 540 F.2d 454, 22 WH Cases 1243 (CA 9 1976) 29
Caryk v. Coupe, 663 F. Supp. 1243, 27 WH Cases 1665 (DDC 1987) 42, 63
Casserly v. Colorado, 1 WH Cases2d 103 (Colo CtApps 1992) 42
Charleston Coca-Cola Bottling Co.; Wirtz v., 237 F. Supp. 857, 16 WH Cases 857 (DSC 1965), *rev'd and remanded*, 356 F.2d 428, 17 WH Cases 230 (CA 4 1966) 24
Cimpi v. Dole, 739 F. Supp. 25, 29 WH Cases 1436 (DDC 1990) 104
Circle C Invs.; Reich v., 1 WH Cases2d 945 (CA 5 1993) 24, 39
Citicorp Indus. Credit v. Brock, 107 S.Ct. 2694, 28 WH Cases 141 (1987) 20
Claridge Hotel & Casino; Brock v., 664 F. Supp. 899, 28 WH Cases 577 (DNJ 1987) 42
Clark v. Unified Servs., 659 F.2d 49, 25 WH Cases 145 (CA 5 1981) 109

Table of Cases

Clay v. City of Winona, 753 F. Supp. 624, 30 WH Cases 201 (ND Miss 1990) 42

Clothing & Textile Workers, Baltimore Regional Joint Bd.; Hodgson v., 462 F.2d 180, 20 WH Cases 697 (CA 4 1972) 87

Coast Van Lines v. Armstrong, 7 WH Cases 969 (CA 9 1948) 31

Cobra Constr. Co. v. United States, 28 WH Cases 1552 (US ClmsCt 1988) 147

Coleman v. Jiffy June Farms, 458 F.2d 1139, 20 WH Cases 321 (CA 5 1971), *reh'g denied*, 458 F.2d 1142, 20 WH Cases 630 (CA 5), *cert. denied*, 409 U.S. 948, 20 WH Cases 937 (1972) 7, 62, 69

Commercial Energies, Inc. v. Cheney, 745 F. Supp. 647 (D Colo 1990) 101

Conagra, Inc.; Martin v., 784 F. Supp. 1394, 30 WH Cases 1307 (SD Iowa 1992) 40

Condo v. Sysco Corp., 1 WH Cases2d 904 (CA 7 1993) 51

Cooper Gen. Contractor, Inc. v. United States, 28 WH Cases 1135 (CA FC 1988) 147, 160

Copper Plumbing & Heating Co. v. Campbell, 290 F.2d 368, 15 WH Cases 34 (CA DC 1961) 150

Coyne Int'l Enters.; Martin v., 966 F.2d 61, 30 WH Cases 1537 (CA 2 1992) 25

D

Dallas Indep. School Dist.; Usery v., 421 F. Supp. 111, 22 WH Cases 1377 (ND Tex 1976) 82

Darby, F.W., Lumber Co.; United States v., 312 U.S. 100, 1 WH Cases 17 (1941) 20

Davis v. Food Lion, 27 WH Cases 1214 (CA 4 1986) 41

Davison Fuel & Dock Co.; United States v., 371 F.2d 705, 17 WH Cases 622 (CA 4 1967) 94

DeArment v. Curtins, Inc., 30 WH Cases 1380 (D Minn 1992) 26

DeArment v. Lehman, 30 WH Cases 1144 (WD Ark 1991) 25

Delaware State College v. Ricks, 449 U.S. 250, 24 FEP Cases 827 (1980) 62

Deluxe Cleaners & Laundry; United States v., 511 F.2d 926, 22 WH Cases 159 (CA 4 1975) 117

Descomp, Inc. v. Sampson, 377 F. Supp. 254, 21 WH Cases 999 (D Del 1974) 108

Dokken, In re, 25 WH Cases 700 (1981) 118

Dole v.; *see* name of opposing party

Donovan v., *see* name of opposing party

Duchon v. Cajon Co., 27 WH Cases 1077 (CA 6 1986) 58

Durham Sandwich Co.; Wirtz v., 367 F.2d 810, 17 WH Cases 474 (CA 4 1966) 58

Dynamic Enters., In re, 22 WH Cases 1163 (1976) 119

E

Eastern Serv. Mgmt. Co., In re, 22 WH Cases 796 (1975) 109

Ebert v. Lamar Truck Plaza, 29 WH Cases 814 (CA 10 1989) 86

Eddleman v. United States Dep't of Labor, 923 F.2d 782, 30 WH Cases 209 (CA 10 1991) 121

EEOC v., *see* name of opposing party

El Paso Natural Gas Co.; Brock v., 826 F.2d 369, 28 WH Cases 629 (CA 5 1987) 42

Electric City Linoleum, Inc., In re, 22 WH Cases 987 (1976) 119

Electrical Workers (IBEW) Local 5 v. United States Dep't of Housing & Urban Dev., 852 F.2d 87, 28 WH Cases 1215 (CA 3 1988) 139

Emerald Maintenance, In re, 20 WH Cases 1174 (1972) *and* 21 WH Cases 10 (1973) 114, 118

Emerald Maintenance Inc. v. United States, 925 F.2d 1425, 30 WH Cases 251 (CA FC 1991) 132

F

Facchiano v. Brock, 28 WH Cases 1529 (CA 3 1988) 141

Facchiano Constr. Co. v. Labor Dep't, 1 WH Cases2d 468 (CA 3), *cert. denied*, 1 WH Cases2d 504 (1993) 141

Fallon v. Illinois, 29 WH Cases 733 (CA 7 1989) 86

Filardo v. Foley Bros., Inc., 297 NY 217, 78 N.E.2d 484, 7 WH Cases 811

(CtApps 1948), *cert. denied*, 336 U.S. 281, 8 WH Cases 576 (1949) 146
Finnan v. Elmhurst Contracting Co., 107 N.Y.S.2d 497, 9 WH Cases 686 (1950) 149
Firefighters Local 2203 v. West Adams County, 877 F.2d 814, 29 WH Cases 542 (CA 10 1989) 55
First State Abstract & Ins. Co.; Wirtz v., 362 F.2d 83, 17 WH Cases 358 (CA 8 1966) 58
First Victoria Nat'l Bank; Hodgson v., 446 F.2d 47, 20 WH Cases 132 (CA 5 1971) 85
Foster v. Parker Transfer Co., 528 F. Supp. 906, 25 WH Cases 848 (WD Pa 1981) 116
Framlau Corp. v. Dembling, 21 WH Cases 1024 (ED Pa 1973) 131
Frank Mossa Trucking, Inc, In re, 27 WH Cases 1428 (US BankrCt Mass 1985) 121
Friedman v. Weiner, 515 F. Supp. 563, 25 WH Cases 38 (D Colo 1981) 82
Friedrich v. U.S. Computer Servs., 974 F.2d 409, 30 WH Cases 1729 (CA 3 1992) 22

G

Garcia v. San Antonio Metropolitan Transit Auth., 469 U.S. 528, 27 WH Cases 65 (1985) 4, 17, 51, 53, 75
Gilbreath v. Cutter Biological, Inc., 931 F.2d 1320, 30 WH Cases 441 (CA 9 1991) 41, 53
Gilioz v. Webb, 99 F.2d 585, 1 WH Cases 210 (CA 5 1938) 130
Glenn Elec. Co. v. Donovan, 755 F.2d 1028, 27 WH Cases 97 (CA 11 1985) 62, 71
Glover dba Safe Bldg. Maintenance Co., In re, 22 WH Cases 702 (1974), *recommendation for relief from penalty*, 22 WH Cases 705 (1975) 118
Great Lakes Indian Fish & Wildlife Comm'n; Martin v., 1 WH Cases2d 58 (WD Wis), *aff'd sub nom.* Reich v., 4 F3d 490, 1 WH Cases2d 929 (CA 7 1992) 21, 56
Griffin & Brand of McAllen, Inc.; Hodgson v., 471 F.2d 235, 20 WH Cases 1051 (CA 5 1973) 39
Griffith Co., In re, 17 WH Cases 49 (1965) 125

Guess v. Montague, 140 F.2d 500, 3 WH Cases 590 (CA 4 1943) 20

H

Hageman v. Park West Gardens, 480 NW2d 223, 30 WH Cases 1198 (ND 1992) 39
Hale v. Arizona, 1 WH Cases2d 602 (CA 9 1993) 41
Harris Mgmt. Co., In re, 791 F.2d 1412, 27 WH Cases 1593 (CA 9 1986) 121
Hawkeye Int'l Trucks, Inc.; Martin v., 30 WH Cases 1346 (SD Iowa 1991) 154
Hay Assocs.; EEOC v., 545 F. Supp. 1064, 25 WH Cases 858 (ED Pa 1982) 85
Henson v. Pulaski County Sheriff Dep't, 6 F.3d 531, 1 WH Cases2d 1057 (CA 8 1993) 42
Hilbert v. District of Columbia, 784 F. Supp. 922, 30 WH Cases 1263, 1382 (DDC 1992) 52
Hill v. J.C. Penney Co., 688 F.2d 370, 25 WH Cases 974 (CA 5 1982) 88
Ho Fat Seto; McLaughlin v., 28 WH Cases 1225 (CA 9 1988) 67
Hodgson v., *see* name of opposing party
Holloway Constr. v. Wage Appeals Bd., 825 F.2d 1072, 28 WH Cases 446 (CA 6 1987) 136
Holt Co. v. Electrical Workers (IBEW) Local 1340, 868 F.2d 671, 29 WH Cases 241 (CA 4 1989) 109
Home Improvement Corp. v. Brennan, 22 WH Cases 295 (ND Ohio 1974) 140
Home of Economy, Inc.; EEOC v., 539 F. Supp. 507, 25 WH Cases 675 (DND 1982), *rev'd*, 712 F.2d 356, 26 WH Cases 481 (CA 8 1983) 80
Hopkins v. Department of Housing & Urban Dev., 929 F.2d 81, 30 WH Cases 379 (CA 2 1991) 139
Hudgins-Dize Co.; United States v., 83 F. Supp. 593, 8 WH Cases 592 (ED Va 1949) 96

I

Inland Serv. Corp. v. United States, 25 WH Cases 1017 (Ct Clms 1982) 149
International Business Invs., Inc. v. United States, 11 ClCt 588, 27 WH Cases 1704 (US ClsCt 1987) 147, 149

Table of Cases

J

Jacksonville Terminal Co.; Walling v., 148 F.2d 768, 5 WH Cases 269 (CA 5 1945) 39

Janik Paving & Constr. v. Brock, 828 F.2d 84, 28 WH Cases 417 (CA 2 1987) 150

Jen-Beck Assocs., In re, 28 WH Cases 1162 (US DOL 1987) 141

Jewell Ridge Coal Corp. v. Mine Workers Local 6167, 325 U.S. 161, 5 WH Cases 301 (1945) 66

K

Kane, John J., Hosp.; Usery v., 544 F.2d 148, 22 WH Cases 1382 (CA 3 1976) 82

Keziah v. W.M. Brown & Son, 29 WH Cases 862 (CA 4 1989) 86

Kirchdorfer v. McLaughlin, 29 WH Cases 426 (WD Ky 1989) 119

Klein v. Rush Presbyterian-St. Luke's Medical Center, 30 WH Cases 1325 (ND Ill 1992), aff'd, 1 WH Cases2d 537 (CA 7 1993) 33

Kos Kam, Inc., In re, 30 WH Cases 370 (WAB 1991) 147

L

Labor Department v.; see name of opposing party

Laborers' Pension Trust Fund v. Safeco Ins. Co. of Am., 29 WH Cases 61 (ED Mich 1988) 160

Laffey v. Northwest Airlines, 567 F.2d 429, 22 WH Cases 1320 (CA DC 1976), cert. denied, 434 U.S. 1086 (1978) 70

Lamon v. City of Shawnee, 972 F.2d 1145, 30 WH Cases 1665 (CA 10 1992) 42

Lauritzen Farms; Brock v., 27 WH Cases 930 (ED Wis 1985) 38

Le Vick v. Skaggs Co., 701 F.2d 777, 26 WH Cases 72 (CA 9 1983) 154

Lease of Space for Outpatient Clinic, Crown Point, Ind., In re, WAB No. 86-33 (1987) 131

Legg v. Rock Prods. Mfg. Corp., 309 F.2d 172, 15 WH Cases 671 (CA 10 1962) 34

Levine v. United States, 1993 WL 278470 (ND Ill 1993) 95

Lewis v. News World Communications, Inc., 28 WH Cases 473 (DDC 1987) 36

Littlefield v. Old Orchard Beach, 780 F. Supp. 64, 30 WH Cases 1206 (D Me 1992) 58

Lyon & Borah, Inc., In re, 8 WH Cases 566 (1949) 95

M

Mabee v. White Plains Publishing Co., 327 U.S. 178, 5 WH Cases 877 (1946) 20

Maguire v. Trans World Airlines, 535 F. Supp. 1283, 25 WH Cases 529 (SD NY 1982) 80, 84

Malcolm Pirnie, Inc.; Martin v., 949 F.2d 611, 30 WH Cases 1057 (CA 2 1991), cert. denied, 113 S.Ct. 298, 30 WH Cases 1784 (1992) 33

Marshall v., see name of opposing party

Martin v.; see name of opposing party

Martinez v. Phillips Petroleum Co., 283 F. Supp. 514, 18 WH Cases 573 (D Idaho 1968), aff'd, 424 F.2d 547, 19 WH Cases 587 (CA 9 1970) 145

McDaniel v. Brown & Root, Inc., 7 WH Cases 978 (ED Okla 1948), aff'd, 172 F.2d 466, 8 WH Cases 487 (CA 10 1949) 146

McDaniel v. University of Chicago, 548 F.2d 689, 23 WH Cases 43 (CA 7), cert. denied, 434 U.S. 1033, 23 WH Cases 556 (1977) 137

McGee Bros. Co.; McLaughlin v., 28 WH Cases 808 (1988) 59

McLaughlin v., see name of opposing party

McLaughlin Storage, Inc., In re, 22 WH Cases 711(1975) 119

Mechmet v. Four Seasons Hotels, 825 F.2d 1173, 28 WH Cases 441 (CA 7 1987) 49

Melos Constr. Corp.; Wirtz v., 408 F.2d 626, 18 WH Cases 794 (CA 2 1969) 23

Military Housing, Ft. Drum, In re (WAB 1985) 131

Miree Constr. Corp., In re, 29 WH Cases 286 (WAB 1989) 132, 135

Miree Constr. Corp. v. Dole, 930 F.2d 1536, 30 WH Cases 502 (CA 11 1991) 109

Mistick & Sons, In re, 30 WH Cases 837 (WAB 1991) 132

Mitchell v., *see* name of opposing party

Molinari v. McNeil Pharmaceutical, 27 WH Cases 1236 (ED Pa 1986) 36

Monk, W.E., & Co.; Martin v., 1 WH Cases2d 36 (SD Ohio 1992) 24

Moreau v. Klevenhagen, 956 F.2d 516, 30 WH Cases 1438 (CA 5 1992), *aff'd*, 113 S.Ct. 1905, 1 WH Cases2d 569 (1993) 49, 56

Mullens v. Howard County, 29 WH Cases 1081 (D Md 1990) 57

Myers & Myers, Inc., In re, 22 WH Cases 961(1975) 118

N

National Electro-Coatings, Inc. v. Brock, 28 WH Cases 1289 (ND Ohio 1988) 104, 144

National League of Cities v. Usery, 426 U.S. 833, 22 WH Cases 1064 (1976) 4, 17, 82

Nealon v. Stone, 958 F.2d 584, 1 WH Cases2d 29 (CA 4 1992) 88

Negri, In re, 9 WH Cases 139 (1949), *aff'd*, 9 WH Cases 578 (1950) 95

New England Coal & Coke Co.; United States v., 318 F.2d 138, 16 WH Cases 11 (CA 1 1963) 95

Nichols v. City of Chicago, 789 F. Supp. 1438, 30 WH Cases 1444 (ND Ill 1992) 42

Norling v. Valley Contracting & Pre-Mix, 773 F. Supp. 186, 30 WH Cases 758 (DND 1991) 138

Norris, Inc., In re, 8 WH Cases 643 (1949) 93

Northwest Airlines v. Transport Workers, 451 U.S. 77, 24 WH Cases 1302 (1981) 87

O

Ohio Turnpike Commission; Martin v., 968 F.2d 606, 30 WH Cases 1601 (CA 6 1992), *cert. denied*, 1 WH Cases2d 296 (1993) 42

Oil Workers Local 2-652 v. EG & G Idaho, Inc., 29 WH Cases 255 (Idaho SupCt 1989) 136

Oji v. PSC Environmental Mgmt., Inc., 771 F. Supp. 232, 30 WH Cases 1054 (ND Ill 1991) 104

Operating Eng'rs Local 3 v. Bohn, 541 F. Supp. 486, 25 WH Cases 740 (D Utah 1982), *aff'd*, 737 F.2d 860, 26 WH Cases 1314 (CA 10 1984) 133

Ortiz v. San Juan Dock Co., 5 WH Cases 662 (DPR 1945) 129

Overstreet v. North Shore Corp., 318 U.S. 125, 2 WH Cases 68 (1943) 19

Owen v. Local 169, 971 F.2d 347 (CA 9 1992) 42

Ozmer; United States v., 8 WH Cases 789 (ND Ga 1949), *aff'd*, 181 F.2d 508, 9 WH Cases 360 (CA 5 1950) 93

P

Painters Local 419 v. Brown, 656 F.2d 564, 25 WH Cases 22 (CA 10 1981) 139

Palardy v. Horner, 29 WH Cases 393 (D Mass 1989) 73

Paniagua v. Galveston, Tex., 1 WH Cases2d 865 (CA 5 1993) 42

Parker Fire Protection Dist.; Martin v., 1 WH Cases2d 505 (CA 10 1993) 40

Parr v. California, 1 WH Cases2d 241 (ED Calif 1992) 47

Patel v. Quality Inn South, 28 WH Cases 1105 (CA 11 1988) 28

Patton-Tulley Transp. Co.; Walling v., 134 F.2d 945, 3 WH Cases 225 (CA 6 1943) 129

Pelham's, In re, 7 WH Cases 966 (1948) 93

Pilgrim Equip. Co.; Usery v., 527 F.2d 1308, 22 WH Cases 783 (CA 5 1976) 38

Poirier & McLane Corp. v. United States, 120 F. Supp. 209, 12 WH Cases 73 (Ct Clms 1954) 132

Portland Terminal Co.; Walling v., 330 U.S. 148, 6 WH Cases 611(1947) 38

Powell v., *see* name of opposing party

Powers Bldg. Maintenance Co.; United States v., 336 F. Supp. 819, 20 WH Cases 434 (WD Okla 1972) 117

Priba Corp.; Martin v., 1 WH Cases2d 137 (ND Tex 1992) 39

Progressive Design & Build Inc., 29 WH Cases 1204 (WAB 1990) 137

Q

Quality Maintenance Co., In re, 20 WH Cases 1010 (1972) *and* 21 WH Cases 303 (1973) 111, 118

Table of Cases

R

Reich v.; *see* name of opposing party
Renfro v. City of Emporia, 948 F.2d 1529, 30 WH Cases 1017 (CA 10 1991) 42
Richland Shoe Co.; McLaughlin v., 799 F.2d 80, 28 WH Cases 1017 (1988) 7, 70
Roman, In re, 22 WH Cases 764 (1975) 111, 112
Romero Community Schools; EEOC v., 976 F.2d 985, 1 WH Cases2d 264 (CA 6 1992) 78
Rutherford Food Corp. v. McComb, 331 U.S. 722, 6 WH Cases 990 (1947) 24

S

Sagner, Inc.; Hodgson v., 326 F. Supp. 371, 20 WH Cases 49 (D Md 1971), *aff'd*, 462 F.2d 180, 20 WH Cases 697 (CA 4 1972) 87
Salinas v. Rodriguez, 963 F.2d 791, 30 WH Cases 1647 (CA 5 1992) 25
Sansone Co. v. California Dep't of Transp., 22 WH Cases 1008 (Cal CtApps 1976) 125
Savannah Bank & Trust Co. of Savannah; Wirtz v., 362 F.2d 857, 17 WH Cases 374 (CA 5 1966) 23
Schultz v., *see* name of opposing party
Service Employees Int'l Union, In re, BSCA Case No. 92-01 (1992) 115
Service Ventures, Inc.; United States v., 899 F.2d 1, 29 WH Cases 1193 (CA FC 1990) 113
Shenandoah Baptist Church; Dole v., 899 F.2d 1389, 29 WH Cases 1209 (CA 4 1990) 26
Sherwood v. Washington Post, 29 WH Cases 399 (CA DC 1989) 36
Skipper v. Superior Dairies, Inc., 512 F.2d 409, 22 WH Cases 272 (CA 5 1975) 58
Sniadach v. Family Finance Corp., 395 U.S. 337, 19 WH Cases 5 (1969) 155
Snell; Dole v., 875 F.2d 802, 29 WH Cases 465 (CA 10 1989) 32
Sorensen v. Holman Erection Co., 1 WH Cases2d 68 (D Or 1992) 138
South Davis Community Hosp.; Brennan v., 22 WH Cases 177 (D Utah 1974), *aff'd*, 538 F.2d 859, 22 WH Cases 1153 (CA 10 1976) 85

Southern Packaging & Storage Co. v. United States, 458 F. Supp. 726, 23 WH Cases 1085 (DSC 1978), *aff'd*, 618 F.2d 1093, 24 WH Cases 701 (CA 4 1980) 108
Southwest Eng'g Corp. v. United States, 21 WH Cases 1069 (Ct Clms 1974) 131
Stafford's Might Maid, Inc.; Department of Labor v., 29 WH Cases 94 (US DOL 1988) 150
Stampco Constr. Co. v. Guffey, 572 NE2d 510, 30 WH Cases 694 (Ind CtApp 1991) 138
Steele v. L.F. Rothschild & Co., 29 WH Cases 259 (CA 2 1988), *dismissing* 29 WH Cases 258 (SDNY 1988) 81
Steuart & Bros. v. Bowles, 322 U.S. 398 (1944) 150

T

Taskpower Int'l, In re, 22 WH Cases 802, *on remand*, 22 WH Cases 807 (1975) 118
Teamsters Local 427 v. Philco-Ford Corp., 661 F.2d 776, 25 WH Cases 185 (CA 9 1981) 116
Tennessee Coal, Iron & RR v. Muscoda Local 123, 321 U.S. 590, 4 WH Cases 293 (1944), *aff'g* 135 F.2d 320, 3 WH Cases 142 (CA 5 1943) 66
Thomas v. Fairfax County, Va., 803 F. Supp. 1142, 1 WH Cases2d 92 (ED Va 1992) 52
Thomas v. Wichita Coca Cola Bottling, 968 F.2d 1022, 30 WH Cases 1606 (CA 10 1992) 25
Tierra Vista, Inc.; Donovan v., 27 WH Cases 1222 (CA 10 1986) 50
Titan IV Mobile Serv. Tower; In re, 30 WH Cases 913 (WAB 1991) 128
Trans World Airlines v. Thurston, 469 U.S. 111, 36 FEP Cases 977 (1985) 70
Travis v. Gary Community Mental Health Center, 921 F.2d 108, 30 WH Cases 122 (CA 7 1990) 62
Trent v. Adria Laboratories, Inc., 25 WH Cases 373 (ND Ga 1982) 85
Trinity Servs., Inc. v. Usery, 428 F. Supp. 318, 22 WH Cases 1452 (DDC 1976), *rev'd*, 593 F.2d 1250, 24 WH Cases 216 (CA DC 1978) 114
Truslow v. Spotsylvania County Sheriff's Dep't, 783 F. Supp. 274 (ED Va 1992) 42

U

United Cal. Discount Corp., 29 WH Cases 1086 (1990)   109
United States v., *see* name of opposing party
Universal Alarm Sys. Inc.; Martin v., 1992 WL 210045 (ED Pa 1992)   24
Universities Research Ass'n v. Coutu, 450 U.S. 754, 24 WH Cases 1273 (1981)   138
U.S. Cartridge Co.; Powell v., 339 U.S. 497, 9 WH Cases 362 (1950)   28, 101
Usery v., *see* name of opposing party

V

Van Elk, In re, 22 WH Cases 708 (1975)   119
Vanskike v. Peters, 974 F.2d 806, 30 WH Cases 1739 (CA 7 1992), *cert. denied*, 1 WH Cases2d 648 (1993)   41
Veader v. Bay State Dredging & Contracting Co., 79 F. Supp. 837, 8 WH Cases 71 (D Mass 1948)   139
Vento, A., Constr., In re, 29 WH Cases 1685 (WAB 1990)   141
Verticare, In re, 29 WH Cases 265 (DOL 1988)   121, 151
Veterans Admin., In re, 28 WH Cases 435 (WAB 1987)   134
Veterans Cleaning Serv., Inc.; Brennan v., 21 WH Cases 218 (CA 5 1973)   47
Victoria Bank & Trust Co.; Brennan v., 493 F.2d 896, 21 WH Cases 798 (CA 5 1974)   86
Vigilantes, Inc. v. Wage & Hour Admin., 968 F.2d 1412, 30 WH Cases 1609 (CA 1 1992)   110, 119

W

Wallace v. Dunn Constr. Co., 968 F.2d 1174, 30 WH Cases 1766 (CA 11 1992)   88
Walling v., *see* name of opposing party
West Coast Hotel Co. v. Parrish, 300 U.S. 379, 1 WH Cases 38 (1937)   3
Westfall v. District of Columbia, 30 WH Cases 921 (DDC 1991)   76
Whelan Sec. Co. v. United States, 7 ClCt 496, 27 WH Cases 124 (US ClsCt 1985)   147
Western Union Tel. Co. v. Lenroot, 323 U.S. 490, 4 WH Cases 951 (1945)   28
White Glove-Building Maintenance, Inc. v. Hodgson, 459 F.2d 179, 20 WH Cases 539 (CA 9 1972)   114
Wilamowsky; Brock v., 833 F.2d 11, 28 WH Cases 608 (CA 2 1987)   49
Williams dba Williams Sand & Gravel Co.; Wirtz v., 369 F.2d 783, 17 WH Cases 526 (CA 5 1966)   32
Wilson v. City of Charlotte, 29 WH Cases 132 (WDNC 1988)   55
Wilson v. City of Charlotte, 964 F.2d 1391, 30 WH Cases 1497 (CA 4 1992)   55
Wirtz v., *see* name of opposing party
Woodside Village, In re, 22 WH Cases 1115 (1976)   140
Wouters v. Martin County, Fla., 793 F. Supp. 310, 30 WH Cases 1552 (SD Fla 1992)   58
Wright v. City of Jackson, 29 WH Cases 1025 (SD Miss 1989)   75

Z

Zachry, H.B., Co.; Mitchell v., 362 U.S. 310, 14 WH Cases 525 (1960)   30
Zachry Co. v. United States, 16 WH Cases 926 (Ct Clms 1965)   125

INDEX

A

Abatement; OSHA   157
Accrual of action   68, 69
Administrative employee   35–36
  directly related test   3, 36
Administrative Procedure Act   130
Affiliated persons   46
After-acquired evidence   88
Age Discrimination in Employment
    Act of 1967 (ADEA)   77,
    159
Airline trainees   40
Aliens   27–28
American Indians; see Native Americans
Americans with Disabilities Act   159
Anti-Kickback Law   153
Appeals; see Board of Appeals
Apprentices   37–38
  appenticeship agreements   37–38
Arbitration
  Davis-Bacon Act   136
  Equal Pay Act   80–81
Area of production   72
Area Redevelopment Act of 1961   159
Armed Services Board of Contract
    Appeals   120
Attorney's fees
  CWHSSA   150–151
  Davis-Bacon Act   133
  FLSA   60, 61
  SCA   119–121

B

Bankruptcy   122
Basic rate of pay; CWHSSA   143–144

Belo plans (see also Fluctuating
    workweek)   45, 50, 143
Blacklist (see Debarment)
Board of Appeals; Armed Svcs.   120
Board of Appeals; SCA   115
Board of Appeals; Wage   115, 130–131,
    135, 141, 147

C

Cause of action
  accrual of   68, 69
Certificate of exemption   44
Child labor   59–60
Child Support Enforcement Act (CSEA)
  in general   12, 155
  notice   12, 155
  penalties   12, 155
  prohibitions   12, 155
  wage withholding   12, 155
Civil money penalties   60–62
Church schools   25–26
  First Amendment   25
Closely related standard   81
Collateral estoppel   141
Commerce clause   17
Common carrier   25
Compensable time   41–43
Competition in Contracting Act   100
Compensatory (comp) time   18, 51,
    53–56
Conciliation; Equal Pay Act
  EEOC duty   80
Consumer Credit Protection Act (CCPA)
  bankruptcy   153–155
  disposable earnings   11, 154
  enforcement   11, 154

269

garnishment 11, 154
in general 11–12, 153–155
penalties 12, 154
prohibitions 11, 154–155
state sovereignty 12, 155
Continuing violation theory 68
Contract Work-Hours and Safety Standards Act (Work-Hours Act; CWHSSA)
   attorney's fees 150–151
   basic rate of pay 143–144
   blacklist 144, 146, 149–150
   conflict with other laws 131, 151
   coverage
      contracts 144–145
      employees 145
   criminal sanctions 146
   debarment 144, 146, 149–150
   dollar-volume standard 151
   in general 10–11, 143–151
   health & safety 145–146
   limitations 148
   liquidated damages 147–149
   open-market contracts 145
   overtime 10–11, 143–144
   penalties 11, 146–151
   prevailing party 150–151
   willful violations 11, 146–150
   withholding of payments 11, 147–148, 160
Copeland Act 153
Criminal penalties; FLSA 60, 62
Criminal penalties; OSHA 157
Criminal sanctions; CWHSSA 146

D

Davis-Bacon Act
   actions against U.S. government 139–140
   arbitration 136
   attorney's fees 133
   conflict with other laws 128–129
   coverage 123–127
   debarment 10, 140–141
   dollar-volume test 123
   employee actions 137–139
   enforcement 135–137
   equitable adjustment 131–132
   fringe benefits 134–135
      mix formula of fringe/wage pay 135
   in general 9–10, 123–141
   helpers 129–130
   initial construction standard 124
   integral part standard 125, 126–127
   limitations 137
   locality 129
   materialmen 123
   prevailing party 133
   prevailing wages 9–10, 129–134
   recordkeeping 139–140
   reimbursement 131–134
   site of work 127–128
   unusual circumstances 150
   willful violations 10, 137, 139, 141
   withholding of payments 10, 136
De minimis rule 59, 70, 119, 147
Debarment
   CWHSSA 146–151
   Davis-Bacon Act 140–141
   Service Contract Act 104, 118–119
Deductions from wages 39–40
Department of Defense Authorization Act of 1986
   affecting Contract Work-Hours Act 10–11, 143
   affecting Walsh-Healey Act 8, 89
Directly essential standard 81
Directly related test (see Administrative employee)
Disposable earnings; CCPA 11, 154
Disputes Clause 148
Dollar-volume test
   CWHSSA 151
   EPA 83–84
   FLSA 5, 18, 19, 21–22
   Service Contract Act 105
   Walsh-Healey Act 93–94
Due care 149
Due process 3, 131, 155

E

Economic realities test 5, 24, 38
Eight-Hour Law 3, 143
Employee; Service Contract Act
   definition 91, 103, 106–107
Employee coverage
   Equal Pay Act 81–87
   FLSA
      engaged in commerce test 26–28
      fringe production employees 29–30, 81
      production for commerce test 15–16, 20, 26, 28
Employee exemptions; FLSA
   administrative employee 35–36
   executive employee 34–35
   in general 30–37
   independent contractors 37–41
   nonemployees 37–41

Index

professional employee 36–37
  directly related standard 35
  long test 36
  primary duty standard 31, 35
  short test 37
  sole charge standard 34
  salary tests 32–37, 51–54
  white-collar exemptions 6, 30–37
Employee exemptions; Walsh-Healey 96–99
Employee protection provisions 159
Employee Retirement Income Security Act of 1974 (ERISA) 159
Employer
  exemptions 24–25
  joint 5
Energy Reorganization Act 159
Enterprise 5, 20–24, 83
Equal Access to Justice Act 119–120, 150–151
Equal Employment Opportunity Commission (EEOC) 16, 77, 80
Equal Pay Act
  comparator 79
  dollar-volume test 83–84
  enterprise 7, 83
  enforcement 80–81
    conciliation 80
  employee coverage 81–82
  employer coverage 82
  establishment 7, 83–84
  exemptions 84–87
  factor other than sex 78, 84–87
  in general 6–7, 16, 77–88
  good-faith defense 77–78
  limitations 87–88
  penalties 87–88
  prejudgment interest 88
  remedies 88
Equivalent combination of fringes & wages; SCA 103
Executive employee 32–34
  sole charge standard 34
Executive Order 12144 77

F

Fair Labor Standards Act (FLSA)
  attorney's fees 60, 61
  child labor 59
  commerce 15
  compensable time 41–43
  congressional policy 15, 18, 26
  coverage
    employees 26–32

    employers 20–26
  dollar-volume test 18, 21–22
  economic realities test 5, 24, 38
  enforcement 60–63
  engaged in production of goods for commerce 15–16, 20, 26, 28
  enterprise 15–16, 20–24
  hot goods 20, 59–60
  in general 2–6, 15–63
  injunctions 60
  Interstate Commerce requirement 19–20
  investigations 61
  limitations (*see* Limitations)
  liquidated damages 63
  minimum wages 43–47
  on-call time 41–42
  overtime 47–50
    compensatory time (*see* Compensatory time)
  penalties 61–62
  posters 59
  primary duty test 31–32
  remedial education 19, 50
  report to Congress 61
  salary-basis test 32–37, 51–54, 158–159
  white-collar exemptions 30–32
Family and Medical Leave Act 1, 2, 13, 27, 34, 157–159
First Amendment 25
Fluctuating workweek (*see also* Belo plans) 45, 48, 50, 143
Freedom of Information Act 138–139
Fringe benefits
  Davis-Bacon Act 134–135
  Service Contract Act
    in general 103, 112–113
    offsets 112–113
Fringe production employees 29–30, 81

G

Garnishment; CCPA 11, 154
General Services Admin. 94–95
Good-faith defense 6, 54, 71–75, 76
  Equal Pay Act 77–78
  Portal Act 6, 54, 71–75, 76
Government employees (*see* State and local government employees)
Great Depression 3, 15

H

Handbook of Blue-Collar Occupational Families and Series 107

Handicapped workers 44
Hazardous occupations 59, 90, 144
Health and safety
　CWHSSA 145–146
　Walsh-Healey Act 90, 101–102
Helpers; Davis-Bacon Act 130
Holiday pay 114
Hot goods 20, 59–60
Hours of work 41–43

I

Immigration Reform & Control Act 27–28
In the picture standard 6, 69–70
Independent contractors 37–41
　test 38
Initial construction standard; Davis-Bacon Act 124
Injunctions; FLSA 60
Integral part standard; Davis-Bacon Act 125, 126–127
Interest
　prejudgment 88
　Service Contract Act 117
Interpretative Bulletin; Wage-Hour Administrator's 72, 73–74
Interstate commerce 19–20
Investigations; FLSA 61
Irregular hours 45, 50, 143

J

Joint employer 5

K

Kickbacks 45, 153

L

Limitations
　accrual of action 68, 69
　CWHSSA 148
　Davis-Bacon Act 68
　FLSA 59, 62, 68
　six-year period 59, 62, 71, 117, 148
　five-year period 71
　Portal Act requirements 62, 67–69
　Service Contract Act 117
　Walsh-Healey 68
Liquidated damages
　CWHSSA 147–149
　EPA 88
　FLSA 60, 63, 69
Locality

Davis-Bacon Act 129
Service Contract Act 108, 110
Long test (*see also* Employee exemptions) 31, 36

M

Market-force theory 85–86
Materialmen; Davis-Bacon Act 123
McNamara-O'Hara Service Contract Act (Service Contract Act)
　attorney's fees 119–122
　bankruptcy 122
　blacklist 9, 104, 118–119
　coverage
　　contracts 104–106
　　employees 91, 103, 106–107
　　exemptions 105–106
　debarment 9, 104, 118–119
　dollar-volume standard 105
　employee; defined 107
　enforcement 115–117
　holiday pay 114
　in general 9, 103–121
　limitations 117
　locality 108, 110
　offsets 114
　overtime 108
　penalties 114–121
　　unusual circumstances 104, 116, 118–119
　prevailing wages 103, 108–109
　principal purpose 104
　recordkeeping 111–112
　service employees 91, 103, 106–107
　severance pay 114
　Standard Metropolitan Statistical Area 108
　statistics 108
　successors 109–110
　underpayments 104, 116–117
　United States; as contracting party 106
　unusual circumstances 103–104, 118–119
　vacation pay 113
　variance proceedings 110–111
　wages 9, 104, 108, 109, 110–112
　　deductions 111–112
　　fringe benefits 103, 112–113
　　equivalent combination 103
　　payments 111–112, 115
　wage determinations 108–109
　willful violation 119
　withholding of payments 103, 117–118

Index 273

Meals, lodgings and other facilities 46
Merchant Marine Act 159
Merit system exemption; Equal Pay Act 78, 84–87
Migrant farmworkers 39
Migrant & Seasonal Agricultural Workers Protection Act (MSAWPA) 159
Miller Act 137, 159, 160
Mineral Land Act 159
Minimum wages
  certificate of exemption 44
  in general 43–47
  handicapped workers 44
  sheltered workshops 44
Mix formula; wage-fringe payments under Davis-Bacon Act 135
Motor Carrier Act 159
Mutual mistake 131–132

N

National Defense Contracts Act of 1958 134
National Foundation on the Arts and Humanities Act 159
National Institute of Occupational Safety and Health (NIOSH) 156
National Recovery Act 89
Native Americans 21, 161
Nonemployees 37–41
  apprentices 37–38
  independent contractors 38–39
  prison inmates 41, 42
  trainees 39–40

O

Occupational Safety and Health Act (OSHA)
  abatement 157
  in general 156–157
  NIOSH 156
  penalties 157
  prohibitions 157
  retaliation 157
  rulemaking 157
Off-the-road employees 29
Office of Personnel Mgmt. 75–76, 80, 107
On-call time 41–42
Open-market agreements 91
Opt-in provision 71
Overtime
  comp time 18, 51, 53–56
  in general 47–50

maximum hours 47
recordkeeping 58–59
regular rate of pay 48–51
remedial education exception 50
Service Contract Act 108
Walsh-Healey Act 90

P

Paramedics 58, 74
Penalties
  CCPA 12, 154
  CWHSSA 11, 146–151
  FLSA 61–62
  OSHA 157
Personal liability; Walsh-Healey 95–96
Personnel Mgmt.; Office of 75–76, 80, 107
Portal-to-Portal Act (Portal Act)
  accrual of action 68–69
  area of production 72
  continuing violation theory 68
  in general 6–7, 65–76
  good-faith belief; defense of 6, 54, 71–75, 76
  Interpretative Bulletin; Wage-Hour Admin. 77–79
  limitations (*see* Limitations)
  liquidated damages (*see* Liquidated damages)
  in the picture standard 6, 69–70
  postliminary activities 43, 63–66
  preliminary activities 43, 63–66
  principal activities 67–68
  representative actions 68, 70
  willful violations 68, 70
Posters; FLSA provisions 59
Postliminary activities 43, 63–66
Prejudgment interest
  Equal Pay Act 88
  Service Contract Act 117
Preliminary activities 43, 63–66
Prevailing party; Davis-Bacon Act 133
Prevailing wages
  Davis-Bacon Act 9–10, 129–134
  Service Contract Act 108–109
  Walsh-Healey Act 8, 90–91
Primary duty standard 31–32
Principal activities 67–68
Principal purpose of contract; Service Contract Act 104
Prison inmates 41, 42
Privacy 139
Production of goods for interstate commerce 15–16, 20–28

Productivity exemption; Equal Pay Act 81–82
Professional employee 35–36
Prohibitions; CCPA 11, 154–155
Public safety, emergency and seasonal personnel 16, 53
Purchase-notice agreement 93

R

Rates of pay
  in general 43–51
  hourly rate 43–44
  mixed rate 45, 48
  piece rate 45, 48
  regular rate 48–51, 89
  tipped employee 43–44
  weekly salary 45
Reasonable inference 67
Reckless disregard 70
Recordkeeping; FLSA
  in general 58–59
  limitations; general 58–59
  limitations; Portal Act 59
  Service Contract Act 117
  Walsh-Healey Act 90
Red circling 85
Regular rate of pay; FLSA 48–51
Rehabilitation Act of 1973 159
Reimbursement; Davis-Bacon Act 131–134
Remedial education 19, 50
Reorganization Act of 1977 77, 80
Reorganization Plan No. 1 of 1978 77
Report to Congress; FLSA 61–62
Representative actions; Portal Act 68, 70
Res judicata 141
Retaliation; OSHA 157
Rule on trifles 59, 70, 119, 147
Rulemaking; OSHA 157

S

Safety standards
  Walsh-Healey Act 90, 101–102
  Work-Hours Act 145–146
Salary tests (*see also* White-collar exemptions) 32–37, 51–54, 158–159
Schools 25–26
Seniority system exemption; Equal Pay Act 84–87
Service Contract Act (*see* McNamara-O'Hara Service Contract Act)
Severance pay 114

Sheltered workshops 44
Short test (*see also* Employee Exemptions) 32, 37
Social Security Act 155
Sole charge standard (*see* Executive employee) 34
Sporadic and substitute employment 16, 50
Standard Metropolitan Statistical Area 108
State and local government employees
  comp time 51, 54–56
  good-faith defense 54
  in general 51–58
  overtime limits 56–57
  paramedics 58
  partial-day absences 52–53
  police and firefighters tour of duty rules 56–58
  public safety, emergency and seasonal employees 53–58
State sovereignty 17, 82, 155
Statistics; Service Contract Act 108
Statute of limitations (*see* Limitations)
Subcontractors; Walsh-Healey 91, 95
Substitute manufacturer 97
Successor; Walsh-Healey 97
Suffer or permit to work standard 38
Supply contract; Walsh-Healey 99
Surface Transportation Assistance Act of 1982 159

T

Tenth Amendment 53–54, 82
Tipped employee 19, 43–44
Title VII, Civil Rights Act of 1964 7, 80
Traditional governmental functions test 17
Trainees 39–40
Tucker Act 147, 159

U

Underpayments; Service Contract Act 104, 116–117
United States
  as defendant in Davis-Bacon Act suits 139–140
United States as contracting party; Service Contract Act 106
Unusual circumstances; Service Contract Act 103–104, 118–119
  CWHSSA 150
U.S. Constitution
  Commerce Clause 17

due process 3, 131, 155
First Amendment 25
state sovereignty 17, 82, 155
Tenth Amendment 53–54, 82

V

Vacation pay 113
Violations, continuing 68
Volunteers 18, 41

W

Wage Appeals Board 115
Wage determinations; Service Contract Act 108–109
Wage rates
  bonuses 45, 48–49
  fluctuating work week 45, 48, 50
  piece rates 45, 48
  see also Rates of pay
Wage withholding; CSEA 12, 155
Wages; Service Contract Act
  deductions 111–112
  determinations 108–109
  payments 111–112, 115
Walsh-Healey Act
  basic rate 89
  blacklist 9, 102
  conflict with other laws 101
  coverage
    contractors 93–94
    contracts 92–93
    employees 97–98
    subcontractors 97
  debarment 102
  dollar-volume standard 93–94
  employees 97–98
  enforcement 100–101
  exemptions 96–99
  in general 8–9, 89–102
  health & safety provisions 90, 101–102
  open-market agreements 91
  overtime 8, 90
  penalties 100
  personal liability 95–96
  prevailing wages 8, 90–91
  purchase-notice agreements 99
  recordkeeping 99–100
  regular dealers 91, 94–95
  successor 97
  supply contracts 99
  urgent and compelling circumstances 100–101
  willful violation 101
Weekly salary; fixed (see also Rates of pay) 45
White-collar exemptions
  Equal Pay Act 82
  FLSA (see Employee exemptions)
Willful violations
  CWHSSA 11, 146–150
  EPA 88
  FLSA 6–7, 60, 62, 69–70
  Walsh-Healey Act 101
Window of correction 33
Withholding of payment; Service Contract Act 103, 117–118
Work-Hours Act (see Contract Work-Hours and Safety Standards Act)
Workweek 45
  fluctuating 45, 48, 50

ABOUT THE AUTHOR

Joseph E. Kalet, a former cryptologist/interpreter for the U.S. Navy, is Assistant Legal Counsel for the Metropolitan Washington Airports Authority. Formerly with The Bureau of National Affairs, Inc., Washington, D.C., Mr. Kalet is an Honors Graduate from the State University of New York at Binghamton, N.Y., and an Honors Graduate from the Foreign Service Institute, Washington, D.C. He received his Juris Doctor from the George Washington University-National Law Center, Washington, D.C.

Mr. Kalet is a frequent speaker on labor law before such organizations as the National Association of Attorneys General and the National Labor Relations Board. He has written for the *American Bar Association Journal*, the *Arbitration Journal*, and other professional publications. He is a member of the National Labor Panel of the American Arbitration Association. He also is a member of the U.S. Supreme Court, District of Columbia, Virginia, and Pennsylvania Bars. Mr. Kalet is also the author of *Age Discrimination in Employment Law*, Second Edition.